CRIMINAL JUSTICE PROCEDURE

CRIMINAL JUSTICE PROCEDURE

8th Edition

STACY C. MOAK
RONALD L. CARLSON

Routledge
Taylor & Francis Group
LONDON AND NEW YORK

First published 2013 by Anderson Publishing

Published 2015 by Routledge
2 Park Square, Milton Park, Abingdon, Oxfordshire OX14 4RN

and by Routledge
605 Third Avenue, New York, NY 10017

Routledge is an imprint of the Taylor and Francis Group, an informa business

First issued in hardback 2015

Library of Congress Cataloging-in-Publication Data
Application submitted

British Library Cataloguing-in-Publication Data
A catalogue record for this book is available from the British Library.

ISBN 978-1-4557-3048-3 (pbk)
ISBN 978-1-138-13187-3 (hbk)

CONTENTS

PREFACE

An inherent conflict in any system of justice is to balance the need for public safety against the rights of individuals. In the United States, our Constitution sets forth those protected rights that limit the powers of the government into our lives. Early in our country's development, the Constitution only protected citizens from unwarranted intrusion by the federal government. Through the process of incorporation, however, most of those rights are now protected from state action as well.

Citizens are entitled to an expectation of privacy in their person, papers, and effects from unwarranted government intrusion. Thus the Fourth Amendment requires that officers have a warrant before searching or seizing citizens. The warrant provides a layer of protection between the citizen and law enforcement. Although exceptions to the warrant requirement exist, which are detailed in this book, those exceptions are limited, and violations of the warrant provision can lead to evidence being excluded from trials.

Once a citizen is arrested by law enforcement, the Fifth Amendment protections from self incrimination come into play and citizens are entitled to have an attorney present to advise them in their custodial interrogations. In this case, the attorney provides an added layer of protection between the citizen and the actions of law enforcement. Cases identifying circumstances in which citizens are entitled to Fifth Amendment protections are detailed in this book.

If a citizen proceeds into the system to the point of a criminal trial, various other protections are afforded that person through the Sixth Amendment. For example, an accused is entitled to an attorney, and the state is required to provide an attorney for one who is indigent. Further, the accused is entitled to a public trial before a jury of his or her peers. In this instance, the jury serves as an added layer of protection between the citizen and the actions of the state.

This book explores constitutionally protected rights enjoyed by citizens in the United States. Cases are presented in each chapter, mostly stemming from the U.S. Supreme Court. The Supreme Court is the law of the land, thus, it applies equally to all jurisdictions within the United States. The cases provide the substance of procedural law. Students should read the cases, delve into the information, and consider both sides of the argument in each case. Criminal Procedure is a topic that must be applied to be understood. The intent of this textbook is to provide students opportunities to apply principles outlined in the chapters through the cases that demonstrate the principles. The goal is for students to then be able to apply the principles in other situations demonstrating the same, or similar, types of conflicts.

The Eighth Edition of this text involved a significant revision, and would not have been possible without the input of several individuals. Research assistance was provided by Alesa Liles who is a PhD student at the University of Arkansas at Little Rock. Additionally, both Jeffery Walker and Craig Hemmens provided important input into the structure and layout of each chapter, as well as review and revision of the case briefs. At the publisher's level, Greg Charlson and Pam Chester provided appreciated editorial oversight.

An understanding of the roles and responsibilities of criminal procedure within the justice system is important for every citizen in the United States. This book is aimed at providing that basic understanding.

Stacy C. Moak,
Professor and Graduate Coordinator
Little Rock, Arkansas
July 2012

ONLINE INSTRUCTOR AND STUDENT RESOURCES

Interactive resources can be accessed for free by registering at www.routledge.com/cw/moak

For the Instructor

- **Test Bank**—Compose, customize, and deliver exams using an online assessment package in a free Windows-based authoring tool that makes it easy to build tests using the unique multiple choice and true-or-false questions created for *Civil Liability in Criminal Justice*. What's more, this authoring tool allows you to export customized exams directly to Blackboard, WebCT, eCollege, Angel, and other leading systems. All test bank files are also conveniently offered in Word format.
- **PowerPoint Lecture Slides**—Reinforce key topics with focused PowerPoint slides, which provide a perfect visual outline with which to augment your lecture. Each individual book chapter has its own dedicated slideshow.
- **Lesson Plans**—Design your course around customized lesson plans. Each individual lesson plan acts as a separate syllabus containing content synopses, key terms, content synopses, directions to supplementary websites, and more open-ended critical thinking questions designed to spur class discussion. These lesson plans also delineate and connect chapter-based learning objectives to specific teaching resources, making it easy to catalogue the resources at your disposal.

For the Student

- **Self-Assessment Question Bank**—Enhance review and study sessions with the help of this online self-quizzing asset. Each question is presented in an interactive format that allows for immediate feedback.
- **Case Studies**—Apply what is on the page to the world beyond with the help of topic-specific case studies, each designed to turn theory into practice and followed by three interactive scenario-based questions that allow for immediate feedback.

SELECTED PROVISIONS OF THE UNITED STATES CONSTITUTION

Amendment I [1791]

Congress shall make no law respecting an establishment of religion, or prohibiting the free exercise thereof; or abridging the freedom of speech, or of the press; or the right of the people peaceably to assemble, and to petition the Government for a redress of grievances.

Amendment II [1791]

A well regulated Militia, being necessary to the security of a free State, the right of the people to keep and bear Arms, shall not be infringed.

Amendment III [1791]

No Soldier shall, in time of peace be quartered in any house, without the consent of the Owner, nor in time of war, but in a manner to be prescribed by law.

Amendment IV [1791]

The right of the people to secure in their persons, houses, papers, and effects, against unreasonable searches and seizures, shall not be violated, and no Warrants shall issue, but upon probable cause, supported by Oath or affirmation, and particularly describing the place to be searched, and the persons or things to be seized.

Amendment V [1791]

No person shall be held to answer for a capital, or otherwise infamous crime, unless on a presentment or indictment of a Grand Jury, except in cases arising in the land or naval forces, or in the Militia, when in actual service in time of War or public danger; nor shall any person be subject for the same offence to be twice put in jeopardy of life or limb; nor shall be compelled in any criminal case to be a witness against himself, nor be deprived of life, liberty, or property, without due process of law; nor shall private property be taken for public use, without just compensation.

Amendment VI [1791]

In all criminal prosecutions, the accused shall enjoy the right to a speedy and public trial, by an impartial jury of the State and district wherein the crime shall have been committed, which district shall have been previously ascertained by law, and to be informed of the nature and cause of the accusation; to be confronted with the witness against him; to have compulsory process for obtaining witnesses in his favor, and to have the Assistance of Counsel for his defence.

Amendment VII [1791]

In Suits at common law, where the value in controversy shall exceed twenty dollars, the right of trial by jury shall be preserved, and no fact tried by jury, shall be otherwise re-examined in any Court of the United States, than according to the rules of the common law.

Amendment VIII [1791]

Excessive bail shall not be required, nor excessive fines imposed, nor cruel and unusual punishments inflicted.

Amendment IX [1791]

The enumeration in the Constitution, of certain rights, shall not be construed to deny or disparage others retained by the people.

Amendment X [1791]

The powers not delegated to the United States by the Constitution, nor prohibited by it to the States, are reserved to the States respectively, or to the people.

Amendment XIII [1865]

Section 1. Neither slavery nor involuntary servitude, except as a punishment for crime whereof the party shall have been duly convicted, shall exist within the United States, or any place subject to their jurisdiction.

Section 2. Congress shall have power to enforce this article by appropriate legislation.

Amendment XIV [1868]

Section 1. All persons born or naturalized in the United States, and subject to the jurisdiction thereof, are citizens of the United States and of the State wherein they reside. No State shall make or enforce any law which shall abridge the privileges or immunities of citizens of the United States; nor shall any State deprive any person of life, liberty, or property, without due process of law; nor deny to any person within its jurisdiction the equal protection of the laws.

Section 5. The Congress shall have power to enforce, by appropriate legislation, the provisions of the article.

CASE CITATION GUIDE

The following list provides an explanation of case citations used in Criminal Justice Procedure, Sixth Edition, for readers who may be unfamiliar with how court decisions are cited.

U.S.	United States Reports. Published by the United States government, this is the official source of United States Supreme Court decisions. It reports only United States Supreme Court decisions.
S. Ct.	Supreme Court Reporter. Published by Thomson/West, this publication reports United States Supreme Court decisions.
L. Ed./L. Ed. 2d	United States Reports, Lawyers' Edition, First Series/Second Series. Published by LexisNexis, this publication reports United States Supreme Court decisions.
F.2d/F.3d	Federal Reports, Second Series/Third Series. Published by Thomson/West, it reports decisions of the Federal Courts of Appeals.
F. Supp.	Federal Supplement. Published by Thomson/West, this reports decisions of the Federal District Courts.

SAMPLE CASE CITATIONS

Gideon v. Wainwright, 372 U.S. 335 (1963). This case is located in volume 372 of the United States Reports, beginning on page 335. It was decided in 1963.

Gideon v. Wainwright, 83 S. Ct. 792 (1963). Gideon v. Wainwright is published in volume 83 of the Supreme Court Reporter, beginning on page 792.

Gideon v. Wainwright, 9 L. Ed. 2d 799 (1963). Gideon v. Wainwright is also published in volume 9 of Supreme Court Reports, Lawyers' Edition, Second Series, beginning on page 799.

Phillips v. Perry, 106 F.3d 1420 (9th Cir. 1997). This case is located in volume 106 of Federal Reports, Third Series, beginning on page 1420. It was decided by the Ninth Circuit Court of Appeals in 1997.

Galen v. County of Los Angeles, 322 F. Supp. 2d 1045 (C.D. Cal. 2004). This case is located in volume 322 of *Federal Supplement*, beginning on page 1045. It was decided in 2004 by the Federal District Court for the Central District of California.

1

AN OVERVIEW OF CRIMINAL JUSTICE IN AMERICA

The Role of Criminal Procedure in the Criminal Justice Process

CHAPTER OUTLINE

KEY TERMS

Adversary theory of justice
Appeal
Arraignment
Arrest
Arrest warrant
Booking
Charge
Closing argument
Common law
Conviction
Cross examination
Custodial interrogation
Custody
Defendant
Diversion
Double jeopardy
Evidence
Exclusionary rule
Federalism
Felony
Grand jury
Habeas corpus
Hearings
Indictment
Information
Investigation
Jury
Jury instructions
Motion
Plea

Post-conviction remedy
Preliminary examination
Probable cause
Prosecution
Reasonable suspicion
Right to counsel
Search warrant
Trial
Warrant

LEARNING OBJECTIVES

- Understand the goals and importance of criminal procedure.
- Understand key concepts related to the study of criminal procedure.
- Identify the steps in the criminal court process.
- Identify the various sources of laws related to criminal procedure.
- Understand how to brief a legal case.

1.1 Introduction

The issues of crime and its control are concerns for Americans today. The public often registers these concerns when voting, and the impact of crime on public consciousness is seen in recurring opinion polls, which rate it at or near the top of "major unresolved problems in America." The criminal justice system and its processes are presented to most Americans via television's police and courtroom dramas. Numerous television shows depict citizen interactions with police and courtroom processes. Although the popularity of these shows seems to be timeless, most citizens will not interact with the criminal justice system during their lifetimes. For those who do encounter the criminal justice system, most will interact with the police through incidents such as routine traffic stops or reporting criminal incidents to the police. Others will encounter police as witnesses to crimes, and some will encounter the system as alleged offenders. The primary function of criminal procedure in these encounters is to balance the protection of society with individual rights of the accused. In all cases, the outcome should be for the guilty to be held accountable and the innocent to be cleared as quickly as possible. This text provides an overview of criminal procedure, primarily police interaction with citizens. To the extent that police interaction extends to the trial process, those areas will also be covered.

1.2 Goals of Criminal Procedure

Criminal procedure contains the body of laws and policies that govern citizen interactions with officials. Several goals of criminal procedure have been identified. First, criminal procedure promotes reliable fact finding that is aimed at discovering the truth. A civilized society requires that the rights of all be recognized in the fact-finding process; for example, police cannot secure a confession by torturing a suspect. Such actions are not permissible, even through the argument that the end justifies the means. In our society, we can only take away the rights of one person to the extent that we are prepared to give up that right ourselves. The system is not designed to protect the rights of the innocent, but to protect the rights of all.

Thus, the first goal of promoting reliable fact finding flows directly into the second goal of protecting and promoting fairness in government/citizen interaction. Criminal procedure is the mechanism employed to limit the power of government over citizens and to strike a balance between individual rights and government actions. Individual rights in criminal cases are generally contained within the Fourth, Fifth, Sixth, Eighth, and Fourteenth amendments to the U.S. Constitution. Citizens are protected from unreasonable searches and seizures and coerced self incrimination, and they are guaranteed public trials before a **jury** of their peers, to name a few individual rights. Although these rights are enumerated in the Amendments to the U.S. Constitution, they originally only protected citizens from actions of the federal government. Many have now been incorporated as protecting citizens against actions from state governments through the Fourteenth Amendment.

Discussions of the powers of state and federal governments lead to the third goal of criminal procedure which is to respect the principles of **federalism**. Federalism is the separation of powers between the state and federal systems of government. The Tenth Amendment to the U.S. Constitution states that all rights not enumerated in the Bill of Rights are reserved to the states. Each state has its own constitution and its own set of criminal laws. States may grant their citizens more rights than those guaranteed by the U.S. Constitution, but they cannot provide fewer rights. The U.S. Supreme Court is considered the supreme law of the land and will resolve conflicts of procedural issues in cases where citizens challenge the constitutionality of a state or federal procedural issue.

The final goal of criminal procedure is finality of the judgment. Neither citizens nor government benefits from having cases tried and retried *ad infinitum*. Accordingly, principles of criminal procedure such as double jeopardy, speedy trial, and statute of limitations help ensure that prosecutions are timely and that results are final.

1.3 Sources of Criminal Procedural Laws

Although many of the rights discussed throughout this book are contained within the Amendments to the U.S. Constitution, state law, statutes, and case laws all contain important provisions that guide criminal procedure. Table 1.1 explains the importance of each of the sources of law.

1.4 Adversary System of Justice

American criminal trials proceed under the **adversary** (or contest) **theory of justice** to arrive at the truth in a given case. One characteristic feature of this system is intensive cross-examination of both defense and prosecution witnesses. In a jury trial, it is for the jury, which observes these witnesses, to weigh the evidence and make the ultimate decision in every case—guilty or not guilty. For this reason, an experienced police officer recognizes that a case is far from over once he or she makes an arrest, no matter how careful the preliminary investigation or how meticulous the officer's seizure of evidence.

1.5 Steps in the Criminal Justice Process

1.5.1 Arrest

The initial contact between a citizen and law enforcement officer is likely to occur during an **arrest** or **investigation.** At this stage, the Fourth Amendment guarantees citizens the right to be free from unreasonable searches and seizures. Some arrests are based upon **arrest warrants** signed by a judge or magistrate. The **warrant** is a written order directing a peace officer (frequently any officer in the state) to take a person into **custody** on a designated **charge.** The warrant is issued in the name of the state, and prior to issuance the magistrate must decide whether the facts known to the police reasonably support

TABLE 1.1 SOURCES OF RIGHTS

The rules governing criminal proceedings in the United States have four basic sources: constitutions, statutes, case law, and court rules.

Constitutions

Federal

The U.S. Constitution contains the most basic and important rights available to accused persons in its first ten amendments, known as the Bill of Rights. The amendments most applicable in criminal justice procedure and the rights they ensure are listed below:

Fourth Amendment
- Right against unreasonable search and seizure and arrest

Fifth Amendment
- Right to a grand jury indictment for capital or other serious crime
- Right against double jeopardy
- Right against self-incrimination
- Prohibition against the taking of life, liberty, or property without due process of law

Sixth Amendment
- Right to a speedy and public trial
- Right to an impartial jury
- Right to be informed of the nature and cause of the accusation
- Right to confront the witness
- Right to summon witnesses
- Right to have assistance of counsel

Eighth Amendment
- Right against excessive bail
- Right against cruel and unusual punishment

Fourteenth Amendment
- Right to due process
- Right to equal protection

State

Each of the 50 states has its own state constitution. These constitutions must comply with the provisions set out in the U.S. Constitution, although they may provide more protection than the federal Constitution allows.

Statutes

Federal and state statutes frequently cover the same rights mentioned in the U.S. Constitution but in more detail. Some rights not constitutionally required, such as the right to a lawyer during probation revocation or the right to a jury trial in juvenile cases, may be given by state law.

Case Law

Many laws are based on the doctrine of *stare decisis*, which literally means "let the decision stand" and refers to the fact that law is built through legal principles that develop as cases are decided in the courts. Thus, precedent is the decision of a court that furnishes authority for an identical or similar case that arises subsequently. The prior decision of a court is binding on that court and the inferior courts (those lower in hierarchical judicial structure) of that particular judicial system. Thus, a decision of the Supreme Court on questions of federal law is binding on all lower federal courts (courts of appeals and district courts). Likewise, the decisions of the highest court of each state are binding on the inferior state courts; however, a decision of the Supreme Court of Illinois is not precedent for a California court. The California court may follow the Illinois precedent voluntarily due to its persuasiveness, but it is not bound to do so. This unwritten law becomes accepted until challenged and changed by subsequent case law. Case law differs from **common law**, which is based on the unwritten laws of England and was transplanted to America through English colonization. Although it served as the basis for laws of the United States, it was adapted to the needs of this country.

Court Rules

The supervisory power of the courts over the administration of criminal justice has resulted in rules of the courts that have been established and have the force and effect of law. These rules may cover details not included in other sources, such as state codes. State and federal rules of criminal procedure provide examples of such court rules, as do the Federal Rules of Evidence.

Source: Adapted from [1]del Carmen, R.V., Criminal Procedure: Law and Practice, 4th ed., Wadsworth, Stamford, CT, 1998, pp. 12-15; [2]Palmer, J.W., *Constitutional Rights of Prisoners*, 5th ed., Anderson, Waltham, MA, 1997, pp.1-5.

a conclusion that the person sought to be arrested committed the crime.

Many arrests are made without a warrant. To make a warrantless **felony** arrest, a law enforcement officer must have probable cause to believe that a crime has been committed and that the **defendant** committed it. Probable cause will be covered in greater detail in the following chapters. It is, however, the threshold issue for determining the application of the Fourth Amendment.

Shortly after the arrest, when the suspect has been transported to the police station, the suspect will be **booked.** At booking, basic information about the suspect is recorded in the arrest book. This information includes the suspect's name, the time of the arrest, and the criminal charge. At this point, the suspect may be fingerprinted and photographed.

Just as an arrest warrant is necessary for an arrest, a **search warrant** is necessary to search for evidence of a crime. Any search conducted without a warrant is presumed to be unreasonable unless it fits within an exception (this principle will be more fully discussed in later chapters, but stems from the Supreme Court case of *Katz v. United States*, 389 U.S. 347 (1976). Like arrests, searches must also be supported by probable cause. The scope and duration of a search differ depending upon the level of certainty an officer has. A more limited search can be based on **reasonable suspicion.**

If a citizen is arrested and questioned by officials, the Fifth Amendment attaches and provides protection from self incrimination. The Supreme Court defined the rights of an accused in a **custodial interrogation** in *Miranda v. Arizona*, 384 U.S. 436 (1966). Determinations of when *Miranda* warnings must be read and whether an accused has waived his or her right to remain silent are issues of concern at this stage of the proceeding.

1.5.2 Prosecution or Diversion

Not all arrested persons are fully prosecuted. A suspect may be released without the filing of a formal charge, perhaps because the police believe there is insufficient evidence to hold him. In addition, a defendant may be released to a **diversion** program. Diversion characteristically involves a discretionary decision on the part of an official that there is a better way to deal with a defendant than to prosecute him. Thus, police or prosecutors may decline to proceed with criminal **prosecution** in the first instance, or they may exercise discretion to terminate an ongoing case if they conclude that prosecution is inappropriate.

Usually the decision to divert is accompanied by an accused person's promise to take certain rehabilitative steps on his or her own behalf. The authorities may discontinue prosecution of a person arrested for public drunkenness, for example, if the accused complies with certain conditions, such as treatment in a detoxification center or participation in a similar program. Juveniles may be diverted from the juvenile justice process by police who conclude that justice is better served by counseling and releasing youths to their parents or to a community agency. In lieu of formal court proceedings, aged or mentally handicapped persons who have committed nonviolent offenses are frequently diverted from criminal prosecution when it is thought that another person or agency is well suited to assume responsibility for future conduct.

Diversion characteristically uses the potential threat of a temporarily suspended criminal process to encourage rehabilitative conduct by the accused. Diversion often takes place after arrest but before a defendant goes to court; however, diversion of offenders into noncriminal programs may take place later in the process, occurring at any stage of the prosecution prior to **conviction.**

1.5.3 First Appearance on the Charge

Once the case moves beyond the questioning phase and the accused is formally charged with a criminal offense, the Sixth Amendment provides trial rights to the defendant. Among those rights is the right to be represented by an attorney at all critical stages of the proceedings.

In a typical case that is proceeding to trial, the arrested person is taken before a magistrate shortly after being arrested. The Federal Rules of Criminal Procedure require any federal officer who makes an arrest with or without an arrest warrant to take the arrested person before the nearest available federal magistrate without unnecessary delay. The magistrate must inform the defendant of the charge against him or her, of the individual's **right to counsel**, and of his or her right to have a **preliminary examination** (Fed. R. Crim. P. 5).

With certain exceptions, the magistrate sets bail and can release the defendant on bail. Statutes and court rules in most states contain provisions similar to those in the Federal Rules. The Eighth Amendment ensures that citizens will be free from excessive bail; thus, if bail is set in a criminal case, that bail must not be excessive. Generally, bail is to be no greater than an amount that will ensure that a defendant will return for trial. Exceptions to this rule exist, and those will be discussed in detail later in the book.

1.5.4 Preliminary Hearing

If the defendant does not waive preliminary examination or hearing, the government must demonstrate **probable cause** to believe that an offense has been committed and that the defendant committed it. Police officers are frequently called as witnesses at preliminary hearings to provide sufficient evidence to bind over the defendant to a court of higher jurisdiction. At the hearing, the magistrate may either find evidence of probable cause and hold the accused to answer in the trial court or dismiss the charge and order the defendant to be released from custody.

1.5.5 Indictment or Information

If the magistrate holds the defendant to answer in trial court, the prosecutor may proceed to the grand jury with the case. There, the **grand jury** can decide whether to issue an **indictment** or to terminate prosecution (at least for the time being) of the defendant. The right to a grand jury is contained within the Fifth Amendment to the U.S. Constitution. Thus, all cases proceeding in federal court must have a grand jury hearing. A grand jury consists of citizens who are empanelled for a period of time to review evidence presented by the prosecution to determine if enough evidence exists in any given case to move forward to prosecution. After reviewing the state's evidence, a grand jury either returns an indictment against the suspect charging him or her with particular criminal actions or fails to indict and the case is dismissed.

Some state courts allow the prosecutor to move a felony case forward without a grand jury indictment. In states that do not require a grand jury, felony prosecutions move forward upon a prosecutor's accusation, which is termed an **information**. This document sets forth in formal legal terms the violation allegedly committed by the accused. In many "information" states, this formal charge must be approved by a trial judge.

1.5.6 Arraignment in the Court of Trial

If an indictment or information is filed against the defendant, he or she is required to appear before a judge of the court that has jurisdiction to hear and dispose of the case. The purpose of this appearance, called an **arraignment**, is to apprise the defendant of the formal charge filed against him or her and to obtain his or her **plea** to this charge. If the defendant pleads not guilty, the case will be set for trial. The Sixth Amendment provides numerous trial rights, including the right to a public trial before a jury of peers, the right to call witnesses, and the right to confront witnesses against the defendant. All of these rights come to bear on the criminal trial process.

1.5.7 Suppression Hearings

When the defendant elects to go to trial on his or her case, special **hearings** are frequently held between the time of the arraignment and the trial to deal with evidentiary matters. The defendant may file motions to suppress evidence or confessions prior to the trial. If incriminating items of physical evidence were seized from the defendant or the environs at the time of arrest, or if a confession was obtained during the custodial interrogation, the police officers who secured such evidence may have to defend their actions in special pretrial hearings. Hearings of this nature are occasioned when the defense lawyer files a **motion** (a legal document asking the judge to take certain action) requesting the court to prevent the government from introducing the seized items into evidence upon trial of the defendant. When unconstitutional methods of seizure have been used, an **exclusionary rule** operates to bar this evidence.[a] The exclusionary rule is covered more fully in subsequent chapters.

1.5.8 Trial

Whether the adversary **trial** of a criminal case will be heard by a jury or a judge frequently depends upon the seriousness of the crime involved. The U.S. Constitution gives every person accused of a serious criminal offense (carrying a punishment in excess of six months) the right to be tried in front of a jury. This right belongs to an accused person whether the trial is in a state or federal court. Of course, even in serious cases, many courts give the defendant the option of waiving a jury trial, and a major case is sometimes tried before a single judge, if the defendant so desires.

Eighty percent or more of all defendants plead guilty in criminal cases. Of those who plead not guilty and then go to trial, the majority are tried before a jury. In a substantial number of criminal trials, however, the accused will waive his or her constitutional right to a jury trial and elect to be tried by the judge alone. Such waivers are possible in most states; however, a small minority of jurisdictions require jury trials in serious criminal cases, notwithstanding the wishes of the defendant.

Whether the case is tried to the judge or a jury, the production of **evidence** on the issues of guilt or innocence frequently leads to vigorous exchanges between the prosecutor and defense attorney. Evidence may be presented through various means, including testimony of the parties and witnesses, records, documents, exhibits, and objects. Scientific evidence issues are hotly contested in modern trials. DNA testing has taken center stage in a number of cases, where a body specimen such as blood

[a]*Mapp v. Ohio*, 367 U.S. 643 (1961)

or semen taken from the crime scene can be matched to the defendant's genetic makeup. Polygraph testimony may form another basis for controversy. Whether "lie detector" test results constitute proper criminal case evidence is often debated, and the Supreme Court entered the fray in 1998 in *United States v. Scheffer* 118S. Ct. 1261 (1998) by excluding polygraph results in a criminal trial, citing doubts about reliability.

Trial rights of the accused include the right to confront and cross-examine witnesses against him. Documents or statements from government witnesses cannot simply be read to the jury by the prosecutor. The author of the document must come to the trial, testify, and be cross-examined. Without this step, the words of the witness will not be heard. In *Crawford v. Washington*, 124S. Ct. 1354 (2004), a witness gave police a statement, but when she did not testify against the defendant at trial the prosecutor played the witness's tape-recorded police statement for the jury. This procedure violated the defendant's right of **cross-examination**.

Closing arguments mark the end of a trial, after which, in jury trials, jurors are instructed in the law via **jury instructions.** They proceed to deliberate, applying the law to the facts, after receiving the judge's instructions. During closing arguments, each attorney attempts to persuade. To keep the persuasion within proper bounds, legal rules have been developed that restrict what the lawyers are permitted to say. These rules are reviewed in subsequent chapters.

Just as the lawyers must exercise care in making their remarks, the judge must observe legal standards when supplying instructions to jurors. In these directives to the jury, the judge will guide them on the elements of the offense or offenses at issue in the trial. Only if these are proved by evidence that establishes guilt beyond a reasonable doubt will the jury convict the accused.

After the instructions, the jury deliberates and reaches a verdict. If the verdict is "guilty," sentencing of the defendant is the next step in the process While sentencing in death penalty cases falls upon the shoulders of a jury, passing sentence in other crimes is the responsibility of the presiding judge. Sentencing is an important part of the justice process that may travel one of several roads: suspended sentence, probation, monetary fine, a term of years in a penitentiary or reformatory, or the death penalty in special cases in capital punishment states.

1.5.9 Hearings after Trial

If a defendant is found guilty, he or she may file a motion requesting the trial judge to set aside the conviction and enter a verdict in his or her favor, or in the alternative to give the defendant a new trial. Jury verdicts are overturned in only a few cases, however. Subsequent to a defendant's conviction and sentencing by the trial judge, a major post-trial hearing is the hearing to revoke probation or parole, in which the police officer might be involved as a witness. In some cases, defendants commit new and separate offenses while free on probation, and the police officer who investigates the new offense may be called upon to testify at a probation revocation hearing. The officer's evidence may be crucial in deciding whether a probationer has violated the terms of his or her conditional freedom.

1.5.10 Appeals and Habeas Corpus

Methods are available under our law whereby convicted persons may seek review of their convictions by judges other than the trial judge who presided over the original trial. The most used of these review methods include appeals and habeas corpus proceedings. Although reliance on these measures is more often unsuccessful than victorious, a large number of prisoners seek new trials through appeals or habeas corpus every year. **Appeals** are taken directly from a conviction in the trial court to an appellate court of the state, and such appeals must be pursued by the defendant within a specified number of days following entry of the judgment convicting him. **Habeas corpus** is called a **post-conviction remedy**, and prisoners in state or federal penitentiaries may attack their convictions several years after the original conviction in habeas corpus proceedings. There is generally no requirement that habeas corpus be pursued within a certain time after the trial, as is the case with an appeal.

1.5.11 Double Jeopardy

The Fifth Amendment contains a **double jeopardy** clause that ensures that defendants may not be tried twice for the same offense. After completing a trial in which a defendant wins an acquittal, he or she cannot be tried again for the same crime. The state is not allowed to make repeated attempts to convict an individual for an alleged offense. In fact, whether acquitted or convicted, the defendant is not tried again unless he succeeds in setting aside his conviction upon motion or appeal. The rule against multiple convictions for the same crime has been reviewed many times by the courts, most recently in a case from Arkansas. On May 24, 2012, the case of *Blueford v. Arkansas*, 566 U.S. ___ (2012) was decided by the

Supreme Court, which held that Blueford could be retried for crimes of capital murder and first-degree murder after the declaration of a mistrial in his first trial. The jury could not reach a verdict on any of the charges. The main issue in the case, however, was that the jury read its opinion aloud in court. The defense argued that the jury clearly reached an opinion that Blueford was not guilty on the counts of capital murder and first degree murder. The Supreme Court disagreed. In a 6-3 decision, the Court held:

> *The jury in this case did not convict Blueford of any offense, but it did not acquit him of any either. When the jury was unable to return a verdict, the trial court properly declared a mistrial and discharged the jury. As a consequence, the Double Jeopardy Clause does not stand in the way of the second trial on the same offenses.*

Affirmation of this decision will allow for the prosecution of Blueford on the counts of capital murder and first-degree murder for a second time. (The full case is reported in the appendix to this chapter.)

In 1996, the Supreme Court examined the issue of what constitutes the same transaction in *Rutledge v. United States*, 116S. Ct. 1241 (1996). Suppose a defendant is charged under two separate state statutes in the same trial and is convicted of both statutory violations. Two convictions result. Close examination, however, reveals that it is exactly the same criminal conduct that is proscribed by both statutes. Supreme Court decisions prohibit this. Where two separate criminal convictions are involved, even if they come under two distinct statutory provisions, double jeopardy bars double convictions unless each statutory provision requires proof of a fact that the other does not. Where the underlying conduct for which defendant is punished is exactly the same under both statutes, one of the convictions must be vacated.

Because of the separate powers of the state and federal governments, a defendant may be tried in state court and in federal court for the same offense without violating double jeopardy, and likewise each state in an independent sovereign. A defendant may be tried in multiple states for the same crime (assuming jurisdiction is appropriate in each state) and held to answer in each one without violating double jeopardy.

1.6 Briefing a Case

Simply memorizing the holding in a particular case is not sufficient to really understand criminal procedure.

Understanding the reasoning behind the ruling and the way that the Court applied legal principles is the essence of understanding this body of law. As such, each chapter in this book contains at least one significant case on the area of law covered in the chapter. Students should read and brief the case to gain a better understanding of the court's reasoning and rationale.

The critical components of a brief include the facts, the issue, the holding, and the rationale. The facts of the case provide the background for understanding what happened. Facts are relevant only as they relate to the issue and the ultimate holding of the case. Your job is to summarize the most important facts. The judicial history may also be included in this section of the brief. You should understand what happened at the trial court, what happened at the appeals court, and what court is issuing the opinion that you are reading.

Next, you need to determine the essential issue in the case. Many times, the court use the words "the central issue before us is...." If they do not use such distinct language, you must determine what issue they are ruling on in this case.

The holding of the case is important to understanding the significance of the case. Many times, students write down the word "reversed" or "upheld" as the holding of the case. Without more, such a statement is insufficient. What was reversed or upheld? The holding should capture the issue and make a statement about what the court determined about the issue. An example of a case holding would be "Juveniles may not be sentenced to life without parole in non-homicide cases." That statement tells you exactly what the court held relevant to the issue.

The final part of a case brief is the rationale. The rationale explains why the court decided the case they way that it did. This will provide justification, rules of law, statutes, history, logic, and possible policy implications of the holding. You must learn to think critically about the reasons offered in support of the court's decision and outline them for yourself. If the opinion contains concurring and dissenting opinions, you should examine those as well. In many controversial decisions, future arguments will be made relying on concurring or dissenting opinions of justices. The case briefs provided in this textbook are abbreviated. The typical Supreme Court case is 30 or more pages. Students are encouraged to look up any case of interest in the case reporters and read the entire case.

1.7 Summary

The study of criminal procedure addresses the most fundamental rights of citizens as they interact with the government. Few areas of law contain such a precarious balance of interests between individual liberties and protection of society. These laws must be followed carefully to ensure that the guilty are held accountable and the innocent are set free as soon as possible. Understanding the reasoning behind the holdings of important cases will foster in students the ability to think critically about issues involved in criminal procedure and determine potential future outcomes in similar cases.

References

[1] Del Carmen RV. Criminal procedure: law and practice. 4th ed. Stamford, CT: Wadsworth; 1998. pp. 12–15.
[2] Palmer JW. Constitutional Rights of Prisoners. 5th ed. Waltham, MA: Anderson; 1997. pp. 1–5.

Further Reading

Blueford v. Arkansas, 566 U.S. ___ (2012).
Crawford v. Washington, 124S. Ct. 1354 (2004).
Federal Rules of Criminal Procedure, Rule 5.
Katz v. United States, 389 U.S. 347 (1976).
Mapp v. Ohio, 367 U.S. 643 (1961).
Miranda v. Arizona, 384 U.S. 436 (1966).
Rutledge v. United States, 116S. Ct. 1241 (1996).
United States v. Scheffer, 118S. Ct. 1261 (1998).

2

THE FOURTH AMENDMENT

CHAPTER OUTLINE

KEY TERMS

Exclusionary rule
Fruits of the poisonous tree
Good faith exception
Independent source
Inevitable discovery
Reasonable expectation of privacy
Warrant

LEARNING OBJECTIVES

- Identify important components of the Fourth Amendment.
- Understand the expectation of privacy, which is protected by the Fourth Amendment.
- Understand the exclusionary rule as consequences for violating the Fourth Amendment.
- Identify specific elements of the warrant requirement of the Fourth Amendment.
- Understand fruits of the poisonous tree doctrine of inadmissible evidence.

The right of the people to be secure in their persons, houses, papers, and effects, against unreasonable searches and seizures, shall not be violated, and no Warrants shall issue, but upon probable cause, supported by Oath or affirmation, and particularly describing the place to be searched, and the persons or things to be seized.

—Fourth Amendment

2.1 Introduction

The Fourth Amendment contains several concepts important to the study of criminal procedure. First is the concept of privacy. Citizens have an expectation of privacy against unwarranted government intrusion into their lives. Case law attempts to specify exactly the circumstances surrounding that expectation of privacy and articulate those areas in which the expectation is considered a reasonable one that society is prepared to recognize. Once such an expectation of privacy is recognized, searches and seizures fall within the protection of the Fourth Amendment. As evident from the language, the freedom from government invasion extends to both searches of persons or places and seizures of persons or places. Accordingly, case law in this area examines both arrests and searches within the overall body of jurisprudence.

The Fourth Amendment further contains a warrant requirement. Any search or seizure conducted without a warrant is presumed to be unreasonable under the Fourth Amendment[a]. Unless the officer involved can prove that one of the limited exceptions to the warrant requirement is present, the evidence will not be admissible in court; thus, understanding the elements of a valid warrant is essential to effective law enforcement duties.

2.2 Background on the Fourth Amendment

The use of unrestricted searches dates back as far as 1335, and such searches have been used historically as a way to control the behavior of certain people, usually of lower socioeconomic status. Examples of behaviors sought to be controlled have included those pertaining to religious rights, the actions of slaves, and other activities of those considered to be of a lower class ([1]Cuddihy and Hardy, 1980). In England, the King would issue a general writ that allowed his guards to search any home for any sign of illegality. A general writ basically allowed

[a]*Katz v. United States*, 389 U.S. 347 (1967).

searching without reference to what the person was alleged to have done or what evidence was to be seized. Officers were allowed to barge into a home and search until they found something that they could use against citizens ([1]Cuddihy and Hardy, 1980; [2]Smith, 2008). Fearing the dreaded unchecked authority of government that they had experienced in England, the framers of the U.S. Constitution sought to restrict government authority to invade a citizen's privacy. Accordingly, they drafted the Fourth Amendment as a part of the Bill of Rights, and it was adopted in 1791. Understanding the specific limitations on the power of government and the rights sought to be protected by the Fourth Amendment is important for the study of criminal procedure.

The Fourth Amendment provides a **warrant** requirement prior to a search or seizure. That requirement goes well beyond any general writ or general warrant in that the warrant must be based on probable cause and must be signed in advance by a neutral and detached magistrate. Accordingly, an independent party, with no interest in the investigation, must determine that a need actually exists for the search or seizure and that evidence of a crime is likely to be found in a particular place prior to the search ever occurring. This requirement limits the ability of law enforcement officers to make independent judgments about probable cause and limits their ability to search or seize without having someone else review the evidence. Although officers have an interest in ferreting out crime, citizens have an equally important interest in not having officers thrust into their lives without proper authority. Thus, when the need for a search outweighs the right of privacy, that decision must be reached by a judicial officer, not by a policeman or government enforcement agent.[b]

Next, the Fourth Amendment requires that a warrant be specific, and those specifics must be outlined in the warrant. Logically, a warrantless search contains no such limitations on the search. The framers of the Bill of Rights were determined that people in the new nation would not be subjected to searches and seizures by officers acting under the unrestricted authority of a general warrant.[c] The particularity requirement of a warrant was intended to prevent so-called "fishing expeditions" on the part of law enforcement officers intent on searching until they find some evidence of some unidentified illegality. Instead, people and items that are the subject of the warrant must be expressly identified and described before officers can invade the personal privacy of citizens.

[b]*Johnson v. United States*, 333 U.S. 10, 13 (1948).
[c]*Stanford v. Texas*, 379 U.S. 476 (1965).

Another concern of the Fourth Amendment is that probable cause to search or seize must exist before the search is conducted. What is discovered as a result of the search cannot be used to justify the search. One of the purposes of the warrant requirement is to prevent hindsight from coloring the evaluation of the reasonableness of a search or seizure.[d] In the case of the Fourth Amendment, the ends do not justify the means. An officer cannot discover illegality first, then use that information as grounds for a warrant. Instead, the belief in the illegality must be established prior to the search or seizure.

Finally, citizens have the right to trust the authority of officers when their personal effects are being searched. A warrant that has been signed by a judge or magistrate specifically spells out what is being searched and what the officer is looking for in the search and what will be seized. The citizen has some assurance that the officer is acting with authority and within appropriate limits; thus, the proposition of justice and fair play between officials and citizens is upheld, or at least supported.

Based on these considerations, the framers of the U.S. Constitution included the Fourth Amendment in the Bill of Rights to specifically limit the power of the government to intrude into the lives of citizens and prevent the use of general warrants or writs. At the time of its adoption, the Fourth Amendment applied only to powers of the federal government; that is, federal authorities could not come into a citizen's home and search without a warrant. The only legal guideline that applied to state actions was the concept of fundamental fairness. The U.S. Supreme Court did not extend Fourth Amendment rights to the states until 1961, when it ruled in *Mapp v. Ohio*, 367 U.S. 643 (1961) (see below).

2.3 Reasonable Expectation of Privacy

The essence of the Fourth Amendment hinges on whether a citizen has a **reasonable expectation of privacy** in the place or over the item to be searched or seized. The Supreme Court determined that the Fourth Amendment protects people, not places; thus, whatever a person seeks to keep private, even in a public place, can be protected by the Fourth Amendment in certain circumstances.[e] The most significant case dealing with the reasonable expectation of privacy is *United States*

[d] *United States v. Martinez-Fuerte*, 428 U.S. 543, 565 (1976).
[e] *Katz v. United States*, 389 U.S. 347 (1967).

v. Katz, 389 U.S. 347 (1967). In that case, the Court determined that a private conversation in a public phone booth was protected.

Even though the Court made the statement that the Fourth Amendment protects people, not places, the expectation of

Katz v. United States, 389 U.S. 347, 88 S. Ct. 508, 19L. Ed. 2d 576 (1967)

Facts Katz was convicted of transmitting wagering information by telephone from Los Angeles to Miami and Boston in violation of a federal statute. The FBI agents who investigated the case attached an electronic listening and recording device to the outside of the public telephone booth so they could record the conversation. Katz argued that the listening device constituted an invasion of privacy and a violation of the Fourth Amendment unreasonable search and seizure.

Issues Two issues were presented in the case.

1. Whether a public telephone booth is a constitutionally protected area so that evidence obtained by attaching an electronic listening recording device to the top of it is obtained in violation of the right to privacy of the user of the booth. YES
2. Whether physical penetration of a constitutionally protected area is necessary before a search and seizure can be said to violate the Fourth Amendment. NO

Supreme Court Decision The Fourth Amendment protects people, not places. What a person knowingly exposes to the public, even in his own home or office, is not a subject of Fourth Amendment protection. But, what he seeks to preserve as private, even in an area accessible to the public, may be constitutionally protected.

Reasons When a person enters a telephone booth, shuts the door, and pays the toll for a call, the person is entitled to assume that the words he utters into the mouthpiece will not be broadcast to the world. The Fourth Amendment not only governs the seizure of tangible items, but extends as well to the recording of oral statements, overheard without any technical trespass under local property law. Thus, the reach of the Fourth Amendment cannot turn upon the presence or absence of a physical intrusion into any given enclosure. The government's activities in electronically listening to and recording the petitioner's words violated the privacy upon which he justifiably relied while using the telephone booth and constituted a search and seizure within the meaning of the Fourth Amendment. The fact that the electronic device employed to achieve that end did not happen to penetrate the wall of the booth has no constitutional significance.

Case Significance Even though the search in this case was conducted reasonably, the officers did not get a warrant. The Fourth Amendment requires adherence to judicial process, and searches conducted outside of the judicial process, without prior approval by judge or magistrate, are per se unreasonable under the Fourth Amendment. Because the actions of the government in this case fell outside of the judicial process, the evidence must be excluded and the conviction overturned.

privacy continues, to some extent, to be tied to the place. For example, searches and seizures in the home receive the greatest protection. The home is still considered to be a person's "castle," and limited government intrusion is tolerated in our society. The farther away from the home a search or seizure occurs, the more likely it will be considered reasonable; for example, the curtlidge of the home is generally still protected space, but open fields are not (see Chapter 6). Likewise, public places such as parks, streets, parking lots, and even public restrooms have less protection. General criteria in determining the reasonable expectation of privacy includes how far the place is from the home, the efforts a person has used to protect the place from public view, and the purpose of the area (see Chapter 6). Understanding the expectation of privacy, how far that expectation extends, and the extent to which society is prepared to recognize the expectation as reasonable is the starting point for analysis in any search and seizure case. Once an expectation of privacy has been identified, a warrant should be secured unless one of the limited exceptions outlined in this book can be identified.

2.4 Warrant Requirement

The Fourth Amendment contains the warrant provision, which provides a layer of protection between citizens and government prior to any search or seizure being conducted. A warrant refers to a writ from a judge, permitting law enforcement personnel to take some action, such as make an arrest, search a location, or seize some piece of property. Accordingly, officers must present their facts and circumstances to a neutral and detached magistrate before conducting a search or seizure, so that the magistrate can make an independent determination of probable cause. Once the warrant is signed, the officer is free to execute the warrant within specifications contained within the warrant, and as proscribed by state law.

The first requirement of a valid warrant application involves the articulation of probable cause. To determine probable cause, a degree of certainty that goes beyond suspicion must be present. The facts and circumstances, taken together, must cause a reasonable person to believe that a crime has been committed and that a particular person committed the crime. For a search, the facts and circumstances, taken together, must cause a reasonable person to believe that evidence of a crime is present in a particular place.

The warrant requirement contains the additional burden of specificity. Officers seeking a warrant must describe, with particularity, the person or thing to be searched and the person or thing to be seized. Stating "a house on Oak Street" would not be specific, but stating "the yellow house located at 121 Oak Street" would be more specific. As much detail as is known to the officer at the time the warrant is sought should be included in the warrant application.

2.5 The Fourth Amendment and Arrests

The Fourth Amendment covers both searches and seizures; thus, laws of arrest are covered within the purview of the Amendment. Arrests fall into two categories: (1) those made with arrest warrants, and (2) those made without arrest warrants. Although many arrests are made under the authority of warrants, the majority are warrantless arrests. Specifics regarding both types of arrests are provided in Chapter 3.

2.6 The Fourth Amendment and Searches

Like arrests, searches must be conducted with a warrant or upon probable cause. The requirements of a valid search warrant are the same as a valid arrest warrant. Furthermore, any search conducted without a warrant is considered to be unreasonable unless it fits within one of the limited exceptions to the warrant requirement. The circumstances that give rise to exceptions to the warrant requirement have developed a considerable amount of case law. Exceptions include search incident to a lawful arrest, plain view searches, open fields, vehicle exceptions, border and airport searches, and other exigent circumstances. Each of the exceptions to the warrant requirement is covered in subsequent chapters in this book.

2.7 Exclusionary Rule

The penalty for improperly conducting a search or seizure is that the evidence obtained will be excluded from the trial through a legal construct known as the **exclusionary rule**. The exclusionary rule is not contained within the wording of the Fourth Amendment. Instead, it is a Court-issued sanction intended specifically to deter police misconduct. The case of

Mapp v. Ohio, 367 U.S. 643 (1961) demonstrates the rationale for, and the application of, the exclusionary rule. Through the early and mid-1900s, the exclusionary rule barred illegally seized evidence from federal trials. Then, in 1961, the case of *Mapp v. Ohio* applied the exclusionary rule to state courts, and as a result federal supervision of state unreasonable search and seizure cases increased markedly.

After the *Mapp* decision, state law enforcement had to comply with the same standards as did federal law enforcement. Prior to this holding, Fourth Amendment protections applied only to actions by the federal government in that evidence unlawfully obtained by state officials could be used in trial proceedings in state courts. *Mapp* changed the practices of local and state law enforcement to provide Fourth Amendment protections by providing exclusion of evidence as a sanction for conducting illegal searches and seizures.

Mapp V. Ohio, 367 U.S. 643 (1961)

Facts Three Cleveland police officers went to Mapp's home based on information that she was hiding a person wanted in connection with a bombing. The officers knocked on the door and demanded entrance. Mapp refused to let them in without a warrant. Eventually the officers broke the door down to enter the home. Mapp asked to see the search warrant, and the officers showed her a piece of paper. Mapp grabbed the paper and hid it in her bosom. The officers struggled with her and put her in handcuffs. They then retrieved the paper, which was actually not a search warrant. When the officers searched her house looking for the fugitive, they found a trunk in the basement that contained pornography. The materials were admitted into evidence at trial and Mapp was convicted of possession of obscene materials.

Issue Was the evidence from the search admissible in state court since it was obtained in violation of the Fourth Amendment protection from unreasonable searches and seizures? NO

Supreme Court Decision The exclusionary rule that applies in federal cases also applies in state criminal proceedings.

Reason Because the Fourth Amendment's right of privacy applies to state actions through the due process clause of the Fourth Amendment, the sanction of exclusion also applies to state cases. The rule is in place to sanction law enforcement who violate the protections of the Fourth Amendment. If the sanction were not in place, the assurance against unreasonable searches and seizures would really not have any meaning because no penalty would be attached to it. Law enforcement would have no incentive to abide by the rule and citizens would have no recourse for violations of privacy by the police.

Case Significance *Mapp* is significant because it applied the same standard of exclusion to unlawfully obtained evidence in state courts that applied in federal courts. Thus, Fourth Amendment protections were provided to citizens against state invasions of privacy.

2.7.1 Exceptions to the Exclusionary Rule—Good Faith Exception (*Leon*)

As with most rules in criminal procedure, exceptions have been developed to the exclusionary rule through interpretation of the exact meaning and rationale for the rule. The Court, in *United States v. Leon*, 468 U.S. 897 (1984), carved out a **good faith exception** to the exclusionary rule. The basic essence of the Court's rationale was that the exclusionary rule was designed to deter police misconduct. In the *Leon* case, the police persuaded the Court that no intentional misconduct had occurred.

United States v. Leon, 468 U.S. 897 (1984)

Facts A confidential informant of unproven reliability told an officer that two persons known to him were selling large quantities of cocaine and methaqualone from their residences. The information also indicated that he had witnessed a sale of methaqualone about five months earlier and had observed a shoebox containing a large amount of cash. On the basis of this information, the police launched an investigation. After extensive investigation, the officers sought a search warrant, which was reviewed by three deputy district attorneys and issued by a state court judge. The warrant authorized a search of both the homes and automobiles of the suspects. The search produced large quantities of drugs. The court granted the motions to suppress that were filed by the defendants because it found that the affidavit that supported the warrant was insufficient to establish probable cause. The warrant, however, was valid on its face, and the officers had relied on the signed warrant when they conducted the search. They argued that a good faith exception should apply when the officers relied on the magistrate's issuance of the warrant; thus, the officers argued that the evidence should not be thrown out.

Issue Is evidence obtained as the result of a search conducted pursuant to a warrant that was issued by a neutral and detached magistrate admissible in court if the warrant is ultimately found invalid through no fault of the police officer? YES.

Supreme Court Decision When officers reasonably rely on a search warrant that is signed by a neutral and detached magistrate, but the warrant is later determined to be invalid through no fault of the officers involved in the case, a "good faith" exception to the exclusionary rule allows the use of evidence.

Reason "In the ordinary case, an officer cannot be expected to question the magistrate's probable cause determination or his judgment that the form of the warrant is technically sufficient. '[O]nce the warrant issues, there is literally nothing more the policeman can do in seeking to comply with the law.' Penalizing the officer for the magistrate's error, rather than his own, cannot logically contribute to the deterrence of Fourth Amendment violations."

Case Significance This case, together with *Massachusetts v. Sheppard*, 468 U.S. 981 (1984), which was decided on the same day, are arguably the most important cases decided on the exclusionary rule since *Mapp v. Ohio*, 367 U.S. 643 (1961). They represent a significant, although narrow, exception to that rule. In these two cases, the Court said that there were objectively reasonable grounds for the officers' mistaken belief that the warrants authorized the searches. The officers took every step that could reasonably have been taken to ensure the warrants were valid. The *Leon* and *Sheppard* cases differ in one substantial way. In *Sheppard*, the issue was improper use of a search warrant form (it was one used in another district to search for controlled substances), which the judge said he would change where necessary but mistakenly failed to do so. In *Leon*, the issue was the use of a questionable informant and stale information (failing to constitute probable cause), which the judge mistakenly approved. The cases are similar, however, in that the mistakes were made by the judges, not the police. The Court said that the evidence in both cases was admissible because the judge, not the police, erred and the exclusionary rule is designed to control the conduct of the police, not the conduct of judges.

In this case, the Court determined that to exclude the evidence would not serve the purpose of the rule which was designed to deter police misconduct. Although the underlying warrant was found to be deficient after the fact, the officers had relied on the warrant to conduct what they believed to be a valid search; thus, the Court allowed the evidence into the trial. The specific ruling was that police may reasonably rely on a search warrant issued by a neutral magistrate and that appears to be proper, even though a lack of probable cause may be established in a later proceeding. Although the good faith of the officer in relying on a search warrant that is later determined to be invalid allows the evidence to be used in a federal case, a number of states will not allow the evidence to be used at trial.

2.8 Fruits of the Poisonous Tree

The **fruits of the poisonous tree** metaphor is a branch off of the exclusionary rule. The exclusionary rule is based on the principle that if evidence is obtained illegally then it is excluded from the trial. Fruits include any additional evidence that is obtained from the results of the initial bad search. Examine the case of *Wong Sun v. United States*, 371 U.S. 471 (1963) to better understand this concept.

This case is somewhat complicated and has many issues involved. The essence of the case, however, is that once the police start a chain of events based on an illegal search or seizure, any additional evidence that is traced directly or indirectly to that illegality is excluded from evidence at trial. The "fruit" of the illegal search in this case was the statement from Toy that implicated Johnny Yee. Basically, all evidence after the unlawful

Wong Sun v. United States, 371 U.S. 471 (1963)

Facts Federal narcotics agents arrested Hom Way and found heroin in his possession. In an attempt to minimize the charges against himself, Hom Way told the agents that he had bought the drugs from "Blackie Toy," who owned a laundry called "Oye's Laundry." Based on that statement, agent Wong went to the laundry and convinced Toy to open the door by telling him that he needed dry cleaning services. Wong then announced that he was a federal agent but Toy slammed the door shut and retreated. The agents broke open the door and chased Toy into his bedroom, where they arrested him. A search of the premises uncovered no drugs, and nothing linked Toy to "Blackie Toy." After his arrest, the police interrogated him about selling narcotics and he stated that he had not sold any drugs, but that he knew a person named Johnny Yee who had. He told the officers where Johnny lived, and described the bedroom where the heroin was kept and where he had smoked some of the heroin the night before. Based on this information, the agents went to the home of Johnny Yee and found him in possession of an ounce of heroin. Yee was arrested, and when he was interrogated he stated that he had purchased the heroin from Toy and another individual named "Sea Dog." Federal agents again questioned Toy and found out that "Sea Dog" was the street name of a person named Wong Sun. Toy then took the agents to a multifamily dwelling where Wong Sun lived. Agent Wong identified himself as a federal agent, and Wong Sun's wife led him to the back of the house where Wong Sun was asleep. Wong Sun was arrested by the agents. A search incident to the arrest did not produce any narcotics. Each of the offenders was arraigned and released on his own recognizance. A few days later, Toy, Yee, and Wong Sun were interrogated again and written statements were made. Neither Toy nor Wong Sun signed their statements, but Wong Sun admitted to the accuracy of his statement. At the trial, the government's evidence consisted of: (1) the statements made by Toy at the time of his arrest, (2) the heroin taken from Yee, (3) Toy's pretrial statement, and (4) Wong Sun's pretrial statement. Wong Sun and Toy were convicted on narcotics charges.

Issues Several issues related to the exclusionary rule were decided in this case:

1. Were the statements made by Toy after an unlawful arrest admissible? NO
2. Were the narcotics taken from Yee after an unlawful arrest admissible? NO
3. Was Wong Sun's statement admissible? YES

Supreme Court Decision Statements or evidence obtained indirectly as a result of an unlawful arrest or search are not admissible in court because they are "tainted fruit of the poisonous tree." A suspect's intervening act of free will, however, breaks the chain of illegality, purges the evidence of the taint, and makes the evidence admissible.

Reason The exclusionary rule has traditionally barred from trial physical, tangible materials obtained either during or as a direct result of an unlawful invasion. ". . .Thus, verbal evidence which derives so immediately from an unlawful entry and an unauthorized arrest as the officers' action in the present case is no less the 'fruit' of official illegality than the more common tangible fruits of the unwarranted intrusion. . . .We turn now to the case of. . .Wong Sun. We have no occasion to disagree with the finding of the Court of Appeals that his arrest, also, was without probable cause or reasonable grounds. For Wong Sun's unsigned confession was not the fruit of that arrest, and was therefore properly admitted at trial. On the evidence that Wong Sun had been released on his own recognizance after a lawful arraignment, and had returned voluntarily several days later to make the statement, we hold that the connection between the arrest and the statement had 'become so attenuated as to dissipate the taint.'"

Case Significance This case addresses the "tainted fruit of the poisonous tree" aspect of the exclusionary rule. The exclusionary rule provides that evidence obtained in violation of the Fourth Amendment prohibition against unreasonable searches and seizures is not admissible in a court of law. The rule goes beyond that, however, and also says that any other evidence obtained directly or indirectly as a result of the illegal behavior is not admissible, either. Hence, once an illegal act on the part of law enforcement has been proved, any evidence obtained either directly or indirectly from that act cannot be admitted in court. The subsequent evidence is tainted by the original illegality.

This case goes one step further, however, and carves out an exception to the exclusionary rule. That exception is that the original taint can be overcome by the independent actions of a defendant that purge the initial taint. An example is this case, in which the statement of Wong Sun, which initially was the product of unlawful behavior by the agents, was nonetheless admitted because of subsequent events. After Wong Sun was released on his own recognizance and after lawful arraignment, he returned several days later, of his own free will, and made a statement that was then admitted by the trial court. The Court said that the voluntary return by Wong Sun purged the evidence of the initial taint and therefore made the statement admissible.

act of breaking down Toy's door and arresting him in his bedroom was fruits. The only thing that saved some of the evidence from being excluded was the independent act of Wong Sun several days later.

The basic idea behind the fruits of the poisonous tree doctrine is that the government should not be in a better position after it breaks the law than it was before. The rule, however, is not without exceptions. One such exception is that of *attenuation*, which was discussed above in the Wong Sun case. Because Wong Sun returned voluntarily and gave statements, the acts of the officers in illegally obtaining evidence had become so attenuated that the taint was no longer important.

Another instance in which evidence can be admitted that would otherwise be excluded is that of discovery by an **independent source**. An example of an independent source is found in the case of *Murray v. United States*, 478 U.S. 533 (1988), in which federal agents illegally entered a warehouse and saw marijuana in plain view. They left the warehouse, kept it under surveillance, and applied for a search warrant. In their warrant application, they did not use any of the evidence they had seen illegally to support probable cause. At trial, the evidence was admitted based on the independent source rule. The Supreme Court determined that the government should not be placed in a worse position that it would otherwise be in as long as the evidence was genuinely gathered independent of the earlier unlawful police conduct.

If the evidence would have been discovered anyway, even without the illegal action on the part of law enforcement, it may be admitted at trial. This is called the **inevitable discovery** doctrine. In *Nix v. Williams*, 467 U.S. 431 (1984), Robert Williams was suspected of murdering a 10-year-old girl after he had abducted her. During an illegal police interrogation, Williams led police officers to the place where he hid the body. At the same time, a separate search party was combing the same area near where the victim's clothing was found. The search party took a break from the search only 2 miles from where Williams had led the officers, and the search was planned to continue into the area where the body was found. Two searches were occurring simultaneously in the same area for the same body. One search was lawful, and the other search was the fruit of an illegal interrogation. The Supreme Court determined that the body would have been discovered anyway by the legal search party. The Court stated that, "exclusion of evidence that would inevitably have been discovered would. . .put the government in a worse position, because the police would have obtained that evidence if no misconduct had taken place." Thus, the evidence was admitted at trial.

2.9 USA Patriot Act

After the terrorist attacks of September 11, 2001, several pieces of federal legislation were passed with the intent of facilitating the ferreting out of potential future terrorist acts against the United States. One such act was the USA Patriot Act. The USA Patriot Act tips the balance in favor of government power and offers less protection for private citizens when acts of terrorism are the subject of the investigation. The Act allows the government to access stored "wire and electronic communication," such as voice mail and e-mail. Second, the power applies to any criminal investigation, not just to the serious crimes. When federal agents are investigating terrorism suspects, there may be physical entry into private premises without the owner's permission or knowledge. Often the occupant of the residence is absent when entry occurs, and the process is conducted in secret. Notations in diaries or data in other documents may be inspected and photographed by the authorities. To ensure the stealth of the enterprise, no copy of the warrant or receipt is left behind.

The USA Patriot Act also allows enhanced wiretap and electronic surveillance. The most controversial provision of the Act, however, is the sneak-and-peek search warrant provision. Sneak-and-peek searches are a variation of the no-knock entries discussed later in Chapter 3. Sneak-and-peek search warrants allow officers to enter private places without the owner or occupant consenting or knowing about it. The USA Patriot Act represents the first time sneak-and-peak warrants became part of a statute that authorizes judges to issue such warrants when (1) they have reasonable cause to believe that providing immediate notification of the execution of the warrant may have an adverse effect, including endangering life, flight from prosecution, destruction of evidence, intimidating potential witnesses, or otherwise seriously jeopardizing the investigation; (2) the warrant prohibits seizure of any tangible goods unless it is reasonably necessary to do so; and (3) the warrant provides for the giving of such notice within a reasonable time of its execution and this time can be extended for good cause.

Civil libertarians responded that the U.S. government must not violate standards of decency in the name of preserving a decent society and suggested that the framers of the U.S. Constitution would have abhorred sneak-and-peek searches. Another observation was that allowing warrants to be stealthily executed marks a radical departure from accepted search warrant procedure and that this practice poses a dangerous threat to the security of American homes. The debate about whether national security justifies this sort of deviation from accepted, conventional search warrant norms will likely continue for years.

2.10 Summary

Chapter 2 contains basic information pertaining to the Fourth Amendment. Subsequent chapters will examine searches and seizures in more detail as well as many of the exceptions to the requirements of a warrant. The purpose of this chapter, however, is to give students an overview of the many facets of the Fourth Amendment.

At its very core, the Fourth Amendment sets forth limitations of government actions involving citizens. The extent to which citizens enjoy an expectation of privacy in their person, places, and effects depends upon the extent to which society is willing to recognize that expectation as reasonable. Generally, the home and areas close to the home are protected. Although the Court stated that the Fourth Amendment protects persons and not places, analysis of each case continues to consider the proximity of the place to a person's home in determining what level of privacy is reasonable in it.

Additionally, the Fourth Amendment provides for a warrant requirement that must be followed before searches and seizures meet the presumption of reasonableness. Such a requirement was designed to give citizens some confidence when interacting with the government that the actions are legal, based on independent judgment, and supported by probable cause. Thus, police officers are not allowed to search around until they find something that allows them to arrest citizens.

This chapter also outlined some of the limitations of prosecution by the government when actors do not follow proper procedure. For example, the exclusionary rule and the fruits of the poisonous tree doctrines call for the exclusion of evidence that has been unlawfully obtained by law enforcement.

Finally, the USA Patriot Act is addressed to give students a working knowledge of the Act and some of the expansions of government authority under it. The Act was largely a response to the 9/11 terrorist attack on the United States. The extent to which it will be upheld over time remains to be seen, as is the extent to which it will lead to the discovery of accurate information in the war on terrorism.

References

[1] Cuddihy W, Hardy CB. A man's house was not his castle: origins of the Fourth Amendment to the United States Constitution. *The William and Mary Quarterly* 1980;37(3):371–400.

[2] Smith BP. The Fourth Amendment, 1789–1868: a strange history. *Ohio State Journal of Criminal Law* 2008;5:663–78.

Further Reading

Johnson v. United States, 333 U.S. 10 (1948).

Katz v. United States, 389 U.S. 347 (1967).

Legal Information Institute. (2010). *Fruit of the Poisonous Tree,* <http://www.law.cornell.edu/wex/fruit_of_the_poisonous_tree>.

Mapp v. Ohio, 67 U.S. 635 (1961).

Massachusetts v. Sheppard, 468 U.S. 981 (1984).

Murray v. United States, 487 U.S. 533 (1988).

Nix v. Williams, 467 U.S. 431 (1984).

Stanford v. Texas, 379 U.S. 476 (1965).

United States v. Leon, 468 U.S. 897 (1984).

United States v. Martinez-Fuerte, 428 U.S. 543 (1976).

USA Patriot Act, U.S. H.R. 3162, Public Law 107-56 (2001).

Wong Sun v. United States, 371 U.S. 471 (1963).

3

ARRESTS

CHAPTER OUTLINE

KEY TERMS

Arrest	In the officer's presence
Warrant	Reasonable grounds
Probable cause	Use of force

LEARNING OBJECTIVES

- Understand what constitutes an arrest.
- Identify when an arrest can be made without a warrant.
- Understand the requirements of obtaining an arrest warrant.
- Understand the appropriate use of force in making an arrest.

3.1 Introduction

The law of arrests and seizures of persons are governed by the Fourth Amendment to the U.S. Constitution. The requirements of valid arrests are covered generally in Chapter 2; however, this chapter addresses the specifics of valid arrests in more detail. Arrests, like searches, include both those made with **warrants** and those made without warrants. In both instances, **probable cause** must be established. The primary difference is that, in arrests with a warrant, probable cause has been determined before the arrest by a judge or magistrate. An arrest warrant must be supported by oath or affidavit, which details the probable cause upon which it was issued, and it must particularly describe the person to be arrested. In arrests without a warrant, the police make the determination of probable cause and have to be able to articulate it at a later point to justify the arrest. If the arrest is deemed to be unlawful, a person's constitutional rights are violated and the police can be held accountable legally.

An **arrest** is defined as the taking of a person into custody against his or her will for the purpose of criminal prosecution or interrogation.[a] A seizure of a person only occurs if the person actually submits to the show of authority by the police and his or her movement is restrained.[b] Thus, if police command a person to stop, but that person continues to flee, no arrest has been made.

Arrests are different from other types of stops made by the police. Arrests are longer in duration and allow the police more breadth in subsequent actions. For example, on the basis of a lawful arrest, an officer can conduct a full search of the person and the area within that person's immediate control. For other stops, officers can only conduct a brief, pat-down search that is investigatory in nature and intended for officer safety. Additionally, arrests usually involve a change in location from the point of contact to a subsequent place. Other stops are usually conducted at the point of contact and no change of location occurs.

3.2 General Elements of Arrests

An arrest has four elements: (1) arrest authority, (2) intention to arrest, (3) seizure and detention, and (4) understanding by the person arrested. The seizure referred to in the requirements for arrests can be actual or constructive. In the case of actual seizure, the police touch defendants in some way, usually by placing their hands on them to physically stop them. Actual seizure is not required, however, and constructive seizure can be accomplished through words only if the defendant submits to the show of authority. Thus, when a police officer says, "Stop, you are under arrest," if the person stops and surrenders to the officer, an arrest has been made without the officer touching the person in any way. Although the intent to arrest exists solely in the mind of the police officer, it can be inferred from the

[a]*Dunaway v. New York*, 442 U.S. 200 (1979).
[b]*California v. Hodari D.*, 499 U.S. 621 (1991).

facts and circumstances surrounding the encounter with the defendant. For example, if an officer places handcuffs on a suspect or takes the suspect to the police station in a police car, intent to arrest the person is evident even if the officer never says, "You are under arrest." Furthermore, the authority to arrest is inherent in every police officer. Some jurisdictions make a distinction between officers who are on-duty or off-duty at the time of arrest, but generally, officers are authorized to act when the necessary probable cause exists to necessitate intervention. The test to determine whether a person has been arrested is whether a reasonable person would conclude that the police had restrained the person's liberty so that he or she is no longer free to leave.

Michigan v. Chesternut, 486 U.S. 567 (1988)

Facts Chesternut began to run after observing the approach of a police car. Officers followed him to "see where he was going." As the officers drove alongside Chesternut, they observed him pull a number of packets from his pocket and throw them away. The officers stopped and seized the packets, concluding that they might be contraband. Chesternut was then arrested. A subsequent search revealed more drugs. Chesternut was charged with felony narcotics possession.

Issue Did the officer's investigatory pursuit of Chesternut to "see where he was going" constitute a seizure of him under the Fourth Amendment? NO.

Supreme Court Decision The appropriate test to determine whether a person has been seized is whether a reasonable person, viewing the police conduct and surrounding circumstances, would conclude that he or she is not free to leave. There is no seizure per se in police investigatory pursuits because the person still has freedom of movement.

Reason "(a) No bright-line rule applicable to all investigatory pursuits can be fashioned. Rather, the appropriate test is whether a reasonable man, viewing the particular police conduct as a whole and within the setting of all the surrounding circumstances, would have concluded that the police had in some way restrained his liberty so that he was not free to leave. (b) Under this test, respondent [Chesternut] was not 'seized' before he discarded the drug packets....The record does not reflect that the police activated a siren or flashers; commanded respondent to halt or displayed any weapons; or operated the car aggressively to block his course or to control his direction or speed. Thus, the police conduct was not so intimidating that respondent could reasonably have believed that he was not free to disregard the police presence and go about his business. The police, therefore, were not required to have a particularized and objective basis for suspecting him of criminal activity, in order to pursue him."

Case Significance This case provides guidelines for determining when a person has been seized within the Fourth Amendment. The question is important because seizure by the police sets in motion constitutional guarantees, particularly the requirements of probable cause and, whenever possible, a warrant. Absent seizure, the police do not have to abide by constitutional guarantees. Although the Court did not make a definitive rule for determining when a seizure has occurred, it set forth the following guideline: "whether a reasonable man, viewing the particular police conduct as a whole and within the setting of all the surrounding circumstances, would have concluded that the police had in some way restrained his liberty so that he was not free to leave." The standard is not whether the police intended to make a seizure, but whether the suspect would have concluded (as a reasonable person would have) that the police had in some way restrained his or her liberty so that he or she was not free to leave.

The ultimate question in this area of law is the perception of the person regarding whether he or she believes a seizure or arrest has been made. In considering the issue, the trier of fact must consider all surrounding circumstances, including such things as use of siren or flashers, commands to halt, and so forth. If the behavior of the police is passive rather than active, chances are that there is no seizure. Likewise, if the officer intends to make an arrest, but the suspect never surrenders to the show of authority, then no seizure occurs.

California v. Hodari D., 499 U.S. 621 (1991)

Facts Two police officers were patrolling a high-crime area in Oakland, California, late one evening. They saw four or five youths huddled around a small red car parked at the curb. When the youths saw the police car approaching, they fled. One officer, who was wearing a jacket with the word "Police" embossed on its front, left the car to give chase. The officer did not follow one of the youths, who turned out to be Hodari, directly; instead, the officer took another route that brought them face to face on a parallel street. Hodari was looking behind as he ran and did not turn to see the officer until they were upon each other, whereupon Hodari tossed away a small rock. The officer tackled Hodari and recovered the rock, which turned out to be crack cocaine. This was used as evidence against Hodari in a subsequent juvenile proceeding.

Issue Had Hodari been "seized" within the meaning of the Fourth Amendment at the time he dropped the crack cocaine? NO.

Supreme Court Decision No "seizure of a person" occurs under the Fourth Amendment when a law enforcement officer seeks to arrest a suspect through a show of authority but applies no physical force and the suspect does not willingly submit. "Seizure" under the Fourth Amendment occurs only when there is either use of physical force or submission by the suspect to the authority of the officer.

Reason "To say that an arrest is effected by the slightest application of physical force, despite the arrestee's escape, is not to say that for Fourth Amendment purposes there is a *continuing* arrest during the period of fugitivity. If, for example, [Officer] Pertoso had laid his hands upon Hodari to arrest him, but Hodari had broken away and had *then* cast away the cocaine, it would hardly be realistic to say that disclosure had been made during the course of an arrest. . . .The present case, however, is even one step further removed. It does not involve the application of any physical force; Hodari was untouched by Officer Pertoso at the time he discarded the cocaine. His defense relies instead upon the proposition that a seizure occurs 'when the officer, by means of physical force or show of authority, has in some way restrained the liberty of a citizen.' Hodari contends that Pertoso's pursuit qualified as a 'show of authority' calling upon Hodari to halt. The narrow question before us is whether, with respect to a show of authority as with respect to application of physical force, a seizure occurs even though the subject does not yield. We hold that it does not.. . .The language of the Fourth Amendment, of course, cannot sustain respondent's contention. The word 'seizure' readily bears the meaning of a laying on of hands or application of physical force to restrain movement, even when it is ultimately unsuccessful.. . .It does not remotely apply, however, to the prospect of a policeman yelling 'Stop, in the name of the law!' at a fleeing form that continues to flee. That is no seizure. Nor can the result respondent wishes to achieve be produced indirectly, as it were, by suggesting that Pertoso's uncomplied-with show of authority was a common law arrest, and then appealing to the principle that all common-law arrests are seizures. An arrest requires *either* physical force. . .*or,* where that is absent, *submission* to the assertion of authority."

Case Significance Four elements must be present for a seizure to take place: intention to seize, authority to seize, seizure and detention, and the understanding of the individual that he or she is being seized. This case clarifies one of these elements—seizure and detention. The issue here was whether, at the time Hodari threw away the crack cocaine, he had been seized. Had he been seized before throwing away the crack cocaine, the evidence would have been excluded because at that time there was no probable cause for his seizure. On the other hand, if he had not been seized, the evidence would be admissible because what Hodari did would constitute abandonment.

The Court held that, at the time Hodari dropped the drugs, he had not been "seized" within the meaning of the Fourth Amendment. This is because for "seizure" to be present under the Fourth Amendment, there must be "either the application of physical force, however slight, or, where that is absent, submission to an officer's 'show of authority' to restrain the subject's liberty." There are generally two types of seizures: actual and constructive. Actual seizure is accomplished by taking the person into custody with the use of hands or firearms (denoting **use of force** without touching the individual) or by merely touching the individual without the use of force. Constructive seizure is accomplished without any physical touching, grabbing, holding, or the use of force. It occurs when the individual peacefully submits to the officer's will and control. The facts show that Hodari was untouched by the officer before he dropped the cocaine, hence no physical force had been applied. The officer had told Hodari to "halt," but Hodari did not comply; therefore, he was not seized until he was tackled. There was no actual or constructive seizure; hence, one of the elements of a seizure under the Fourth Amendment was missing. Because no illegal seizure had taken place at the time the crack cocaine was tossed away, the evidence recovered by the police was admissible in court.

If the suspect never surrenders to the show of police authority, no seizure has occurred. This becomes important in police work because people do not always surrender to the show of authority. Police are often required to chase suspects and physically seize them for an arrest to occur. What happens between the initial contact and the final seizure can be varied.

In *Galas v. McKee,* 801F.2d 200 (6th Cir., 1986), for example, police attempted to arrest the suspect, but he fled. While running from police, the suspect ran onto a freeway, was struck by a car, and was killed. The court ruled that the suspect was not "seized" by the police at the time he was killed.

3.3 Arrests in Homes

As a general rule, officers may make an arrest for a felony on the basis of probable cause without having an arrest warrant. An exception to that general rule, however, is entering into a home to make an arrest. The Court has held that officers may not enter into the home of a suspect, even for a felony offense, unless they have first obtained an arrest warrant.

Payton v. New York, 445 U.S. 573 (1980)

Facts On January 14, 1970, after two days of intensive investigation, New York detectives had assembled evidence sufficient to establish probable cause to believe that Theodore Payton had murdered the manager of a gas station two days earlier. At about 7:30 p.m. on January 15, six officers went to Payton's apartment in the Bronx, intending to arrest him. They had not obtained a warrant. Although light and music were coming from the apartment, there was no response to their knock on the metal door. They summoned emergency assistance and about 30 minutes later used crowbars to break open the door and enter the apartment. No one was there. In plain view, however, was a .30-caliber shell casing that was seized and later admitted into evidence at Payton's murder trial.

In due course, Payton surrendered to the police, was indicted for murder, and moved to suppress the evidence taken from his apartment. The trial judge held that the warrantless and forcible entry was authorized by the New York Code of Criminal Procedure and that the evidence in plain view was properly seized. He found that exigent circumstances justified the officers' failure to announce their purpose before entering the apartment as required by the statute. He had no occasion, however, to decide whether those circumstances also would have justified the failure to obtain a warrant, because he concluded that the warrantless entry was adequately supported by the statute without regard to the circumstanced. The appellate Division, First Department, summarily affirmed.

Issue Are police required to have an arrest warrant before they enter into a home to make a routine felony arrest? YES

Supreme Court Decision The Fourth Amendment protects the individual's privacy most clearly in the home. Protection of privacy in the home finds its roots in the specific language of the Fourth Amendment: "The right of the people to be secure in their...houses...shall not be violated." That language unequivocally established the proposition that "at the very core of the Fourth Amendment stands the right of a man to retreat into his own home and there be free from unreasonable governmental intrusion." In terms that apply equally to seizures of property and to seizures of persons, the Fourth Amendment has drawn a firm line at the entrance to the house. Thus, that threshold may not be breached without a warrant absent exigent circumstances. "Thus, for Fourth Amendment purposes, an arrest warrant founded on probable cause implicitly carries with it the limited authority to enter a dwelling in which the suspect lives when there is reason to believe the suspect is within." Because police did not obtain an arrest warrant in this case, the judgment is reversed.

Case Significance Unless the officers are in hot pursuit of a fleeing felon, officers may not enter into a home to make an arrest, even for a felony offense, unless they have first obtained an arrest warrant.

The questions concerning whether police may enter into the home to arrest a felon appear straightforward. Once armed with the arrest warrant, the officer is charged with the responsibility to locate the person named in the warrant. If the suspect can be located at his or her own residence, the arrest warrant is generally sufficient to complete the arrest. If, however, the suspect is not found in his or her own home, the officer may also need to get a search warrant[c] (see Chapter 4). That case established the principle that the arrest of a suspect in another person's home requires a search warrant for entry into the home (an arrest warrant is not sufficient), except: (1) if exigent circumstances are present, or (2) if consent is given by the owner of the house.

The Supreme Court has ruled that officers can only enter into the home of a third party to make an arrest, without a search warrant, if the suspect is a fleeing felon. But, what if some other circumstance arises that makes the situation an emergency circumstance, but not for a felony offense? Take, for example, the *Welsh v. Wisconsin* 466 U.S. 470 (1984) case, in which the emergency circumstance was that the suspect's blood alcohol level needed to prove that he was driving while intoxicated would go down if police could not enter into his home for an arrest. In that case, at around 9:00 on a rainy night, the suspect drove his car off the road into a field. Witnesses called the police, but before the police could arrive the driver of the car got out and walked home. After the police arrived at the scene, they determined the identity of the driver and went to his home without a warrant. The police went into the home when the suspect's stepdaughter opened the door and found the suspect upstairs in his bed. They arrested him for driving under the influence and took him to the police station. The charge was a misdemeanor in that state. The Court ruled that this case did not involve hot pursuit

[c]*Steagald v. United States,* 451 U.S. 204 (1981).

of a fleeing felon because no immediate or continuous pursuit of the driver from the scene of a crime had occurred. Because the driver walked to his house, he was no longer a threat to public safety. Because the underlying criminal offense was classified as a misdemeanor by the state, the Court would not authorize the warrantless entry into a home to make an arrest simply to obtain evidence. Thus, the arrest was held to be unlawful.

These two cases taken together guide the laws of arrests. Police should always obtain an arrest warrant if they have to enter into a person's home to make an arrest. The only exception to the rule is if they are pursuing a fleeing felon. The underlying offense, however, that is the subject of the pursuit, must be a felony. Any emergency that might arise because of the need for evidence of a crime that is not a felony does not appear to satisfy the requirement.

3.4 Arrests without a Warrant

Arrests without a warrant, like searches without a warrant, may be made only in limited circumstances. Authority to arrest without a warrant varies depending upon whether the offense is a felony or a misdemeanor. A felony offense is one for which the penalty could be at least one year in prison. A misdemeanor offense is anything less than that. The determination of whether an offense is a felony or a misdemeanor comes from state legislatures and is set forth in state criminal law statutes. Officers are generally authorized to arrest for felony offenses on the basis of probable cause. In misdemeanor situations, however, probable cause is not enough to make an arrest. For misdemeanor offenses, however, some part of the offense must be committed in the presence of the officer, and an arrest must take place immediately following the offense for the arrest without a warrant to be valid.

If a felony offense is committed or attempted in an officer's presence, the officer may arrest without a warrant. Whether something happens **in the officer's presence** is not as straightforward as it may seem at first glance. The term "in the officer's presence" has been given a liberal reading, and an offense may be committed a considerable distance from an officer and still be "within his or her presence" if the officer is able to see what happened. Some courts hold that an offense takes place in the officer's presence if one of the officer's senses can detect the offense. If an officer outside a residence hears the screams of a woman inside being beaten, the assault is committed in the officer's presence. The smell of illegal whiskey being brewed has been held to authorize police entry into a building to make a warrantless arrest of the violators.

Officers may also arrest a suspect without a warrant on the basis of probable cause. The officer must be able to articulate the probable cause that existed at the point of the arrest to determine the legality of that arrest. The Court has held that probable cause exists where "the facts and circumstances within [the arresting officers'] knowledge and of which they had reasonably trustworthy information [are] sufficient in themselves to warrant a man of reasonable caution to believe that" an offense has been or is being committed.[d] This belief lies along a continuum that begins with a hunch, then progresses to reasonable suspicion, and then becomes probable cause.

Probable cause is a commonsense rule. It involves a careful balance between the societal interest in crime control and individual interests in being free from intrusive government action. Officers are required to make decisions about probable cause in the blink of an eye, and that decision is reviewed by many people who have much more time to analyze it. Probable cause is an objective standard. The belief has to be supported by facts. According to the cases in this area of law, probable cause deals with probabilities that are not technical. They are factual and practical considerations on which a reasonable and prudent person would act.[e] Thus, to determine whether an officer acted reasonable in any given situation, all of the facts and circumstances must be taken together.

Direct information that the officer can see, hear, feel, taste, and smell can offer grounds for probable cause. Direct information does not automatically provide the probable cause but does provide support in the totality of the circumstances that are considered. Some direct evidence that can be used to support probable cause determinations include direct knowledge of such things as attempting to destroy evidence, resisting officers, giving evasive answers, and providing contradictory explanations of events, as well as fingerprints, blood samples, DNA information, and physical descriptions of assailants. All of these types of evidence can provide the basis for probable cause.

In some instances, informants' tips are combined with officers' observations to provide probable cause for an arrest without a warrant. Consider the case of *Draper v. United States*, 358 U.S. 307 (1959).

[d]*Carroll v. United States*, 267 U.S. 132, 162 (1925).
[e]*Brinegar v. United States*, 338 U.S. 160, 175 (1949).

Draper v. United States, 358 U.S. 307 (1959)

Facts An informant told an experienced narcotics agent that Draper had gone to Chicago to bring three ounces of heroin back to Denver. The agent had a previous relationship with the informant and the informant had been reliable. The information from the informant was specific in that the trip was to occur on the morning of either September 8 or 9, and the informant provided a physical description of Draper, including the clothes he would be wearing and mention of the fact that he habitually walked fast. Based on this information, police officers set up surveillance of all trains coming from Chicago. On the morning of September 8, surveillance showed no one matching the description. On the morning of September 9, however, a person matching the exact description provided by the informant got off the train from Chicago and began to walk quickly toward the exit. Officers arrested the suspect. Officers conducted a search incident to the arrest and found heroin and a syringe. Before the trial took place, the informant died and was therefore unavailable to testify. Draper was convicted of knowingly concealing and transporting drugs.

Issue Can information provided by an informant that is subsequently corroborated by an officer provide probable cause for an arrest without a warrant? YES

Supreme Court Decision "The Narcotics Control Act of 1956 provides, in pertinent part: 'The Commissioner. . .and agents, of the Bureau of Narcotics. . .may. . .(2) make arrests without warrant for violations of any law of the United States relating to narcotics drugs. . .where the violation is committed in the presence of the person making the arrest or where such person has **reasonable grounds** to believe that the person to be arrested has committed or is committing such violation.' The crucial question for us then is whether knowledge of the related facts and circumstances gave March 'probable cause' within the meaning of the Fourth Amendment, and 'reasonable grounds' within the meaning of said Section 7607, to believe that the appellant had committed or was committing a violation of the narcotics laws. If he did, the arrest, though without a warrant, was lawful and the subsequent seizure of the heroin from the person of the appellant was validly made incident to a lawful arrest, and therefore the motion to suppress was properly overruled and the existence of the heroin on the person of the appellant was properly considered by the court in its determination of the appellant's guilt."

The petitioner contended that the information given by the informant to the agent was hearsay, and because hearsay is not legally competent evidence in a criminal trial it could not be considered to establish probable cause. The second contention was that, even if hearsay could be used to establish probable cause, the information in this case was insufficient. The court considered both arguments and found on the first one that the criterion for determining probable cause is different from that required to determine guilt beyond a reasonable doubt, and these two principles should not be confused. They also determined that the information provided by the informant was sufficient to show probable cause and reasonable grounds to believe that the petitioner had violated or was violating the narcotics laws and to justify his arrest without a warrant.

Reason The information may have been hearsay, but it was coming from one employed for that purpose whose information had always been found to be accurate and reliable. Further, in pursuing the information at the train station, the officer observed a man step off a train who had the exact physical attributes described by the informant. The man was also wearing the same clothing described by the informant and was carrying the tan zipper bag mentioned by the informant; also, he walked quickly toward the exit. Through his observations, the agent was able to personally verify every bit of the information given him by the informant, except whether or not the petitioner had heroin in the bag. With every other bit of the information being personally verified, the experienced agent had probable cause and reasonable grounds to believe that the heroin was also present. Thus, the arrest was legal.

Case Significance The officer's personal observations combined with the detailed information from the informant created probable cause that the suspect was transporting narcotics at the time he was arrested. Thus, the arrest was lawful without an arrest warrant.

3.5 Stops Differ from Arrests

While arrests of prsons can only be made with probable cause, officers are able to stop citizens with less than probable cause under certain conditions. Generally, an officer in the performance of his or her duties has a right to contact people who may be witnesses or suspects and to ask them questions. The officer may ask them questions on the street and may call upon them at their homes for such purposes. Simply asking a person to voluntarily answer questions without detention of the person normally does not constitute an arrest. In these cases, the person being questioned is not a suspect, is not detained in any way, and is voluntarily communicating with law enforcement. Differences often exist, however, in the perception of these. For example, a person may believe he or she is not free to leave (is detained) or is being required to talk to the police. This becomes a matter to be sorted out by the courts.

Situations may arise that involve interaction between citizens and police that fall somewhere in between mere contact and arrests, however. Those situations differ from arrests in three important ways: (1) the degree of certainty required to make the stop, (2) the duration of the stop, and (3) the scope of the search that follows the stop. Stops can be made to investigate situations. These stops can be made on the basis of reasonable suspicion instead of probable cause. The stop is for the limited purpose of investigating a possible criminal event.

For a stop to be valid, it must be based on reasonable suspicion. The scope of the stop must be limited to a short duration at the scene of the stop. The stop must be limited in duration to no longer than necessary to get enough information either to make an arrest or to let the suspect go. It also has to take place at the location of the stop.

Court cases following *Terry* have involved whether citizens have to cooperate with law enforcement when they are asked brief investigative questions. The Supreme Court dealt with

Terry v. Ohio, 392 U.S. 1 (1968)

Facts Officer McFadden testified that while he was patrolling in plainclothes in downtown Cleveland at approximately 2:30 in the afternoon two men caught his attention. They were standing on the corner near the shops. The officer could not testify to what exactly made him notice the men, but stated that he had been a policeman for 39 years and a detective for 35 and that he had been assigned to patrol this vicinity of downtown for 30 years. He explained that he had developed routine habits of observation over the years from watching people closely. When he looked at these men, they would not make eye contact with him. Based on his intuition, he began to watch the men closely.

The men took turns walking up and down the street peering into the store windows, first one and then the other. Each time, they would rejoin each other at the corner and confer. They repeated this activity five or six times. Eventually, a third man joined them. Based on his observations and experience, Officer McFadden suspected that the men were "casing a job, a stick-up" and that he considered it his duty to investigate further. He added that he feared they might have a gun.

Officer McFadden approached the men, identified himself as a police officer, and asked for their names. The men mumbled something in response to his question. Officer McFadden grabbed one of the men, Terry, spun him around, and patted down the outside of his clothing. In the left breast pocket of Terry's overcoat, Officer McFadden felt a pistol. He patted down the other men and retrieved a gun from one of them as well. All three men were arrested.

Issue Was the stop and frisk of these men valid under the Fourth Amendment? YES

Supreme Court Decision The police have the authority to detain a person for questioning even without probable cause to believe that the person has committed or is committing a crime. Such an investigatory stop does not constitute an arrest and is permissible when prompted by both the observation of unusual conduct leading to a reasonable suspicion that criminal activity may be afoot and the ability to point to specific and articulable facts to justify the suspicion. Subsequently, an officer may frisk a person if the officer reasonably suspects that he or she is in danger.

Reason "[T]he police should be allowed to 'stop' a person and detain him briefly for questioning upon suspicion that he may be connected with criminal activity. Upon suspicion that the person may be armed, the police should have the power to 'frisk' him for weapons. If the 'stop' and the 'frisk' give rise to probable cause to believe that the suspect has committed a crime, then the police should be empowered to make a formal 'arrest' and a full incident 'search' of the person. This scheme is justified in part by the notion that a 'stop' and a 'frisk' amount to a mere 'minor inconvenience and petty indignity,' which can properly be imposed upon the citizen in the interest of effective law enforcement on the basis of a police officer's suspicion." [Footnotes omitted.]

Case Significance The Terry case made clear that the stop and frisk practice is valid. Prior to Terry, the police practice of stopping and frisking was questionable because the level of certainty employed by the police was less than the probable cause that is necessary in arrest and search cases. The Court held that the practice of stop and frisk is constitutionally permissible despite the lack of probable cause for either full arrest or full search, and despite the fact that a brief detention not amounting to full arrest is a "seizure," requiring some degree of protection under the Fourth Amendment. Thus, for investigatory purposes, and based on reasonable suspicion, police can briefly detain citizens without violating their Fourth Amendment rights.

these issues in a recent decision. In that case, the police asked a man to identify himself because they considered the circumstances suspicious. "After continued refusals to comply with the officer's request for identification, the man began to taunt the officer by placing his hands behind his back and telling the officer to arrest him and take him to jail. This routine kept up for several minutes; the officer asked for identification 11 times and was refused each time. After warning the man that he would be arrested if he continued to refuse to comply, the officer placed him under arrest."[f]

The case occurred in Nevada, which had a statute that required citizens to identify themselves when requested to by law enforcement, or be subjected to arrest. More than 20 states have such a law. The defendant in the Nevada case was convicted of a misdemeanor, and the Supreme Court affirmed the conviction. The Court remarked upon the validity of "stop and identify" statutes: "Although it is well established that an officer may ask a suspect to identify himself in the course of a *Terry* stop, it has been an open question whether the suspect can be arrested and prosecuted for refusal to answer.... A state law requiring a suspect to disclose his name in the course of a valid *Terry* stop is consistent with Fourth Amendment prohibitions against unreasonable searches and seizures."[g] Accordingly, in a number of states, citizens who refuse to give their names to police can be arrested, even if they have done nothing else wrong.

3.6 Use of Force in Making Arrests

At times, officers may be in a situation where use of force is necessary to complete an arrest of a suspect. The primary issue for consideration in such incidents is how much force is reasonable in a given situation. Use of force falls into two broad categories: deadly force and non-deadly force. Throughout most of our history, states allowed officers to follow the common-law rule that allowed officers to use deadly force when necessary to stop a fleeing felon. By the 1960 s, however, many departments had developed departmental policies that restricted officers' use of deadly force. Most of those rules related to whether the suspect was considered dangerous and not putting innocent people in danger. In 1985, the Supreme Court defined the rules of deadly force in making arrests that are required under the Fourth Amendment for a lawful use of force.[h]

[f] *Hiibel v. Sixth Judicial District Court of Nevada*, 542 U.S. 177 (2004).
[g] *Hiibel v. Sixth Judicial District Court of Nevada*, 542 U.S. 177 (2004).
[h] *Tennessee v. Garner*, 471 U.S. 1 (1985).

Tennessee v. Garner, 471 U.S. 1 (1985)

Facts At about 10:45 p.m. on October 3, 1974, Memphis police officers responded to a call regarding a prowler. Upon arriving at the scene, they were told by a neighbor that she had heard glass breaking in the house next door and believed that someone was inside the house. One of the officers went next door to investigate while the other called to report that they were on the scene. The investigating officer heard the back door slam and saw someone run across the yard. The fleeing suspect, Garner, stopped at a 6-foot-high chain-link fence at the edge of the yard. With the aid of a flashlight, the officer could see Garner's face and hands, revealing that he was a young male, approximately 17 to 18 years old, who was unarmed. Garner began to climb over the fence to escape. The officer shot him and killed him to prevent him from escaping. Ten dollars and a purse taken from the house were found on his body.

Tennessee law at the time allowed the officer in this case to use deadly force to prevent escape. The statute provides that, "If, after notice of the intention to arrest the defendant, he either flees or forcibly resists, the officer may use all the necessary means to affect the arrest."[i] The department policy was slightly more restrictive than the statute, but still allowed the use of deadly force in cases of burglary.

Garner's father brought an action in the Federal District Court for the Western District of Tennessee, seeking damages under 42 U.S.C. Section 1983 for asserted violations of Garner's constitutional rights. The complaint alleged that the shooting violated the Fourth, Fifth, Sixth, Eighth, and Fourteenth Amendments of the U.S. Constitution. After a 3-day bench trial, the District Court entered judgment in favor of the defendants, concluding that the officer's actions were authorized by the Tennessee statute, which in turn was constitutional. Garner had "recklessly and heedlessly attempted to vault over the fence to escape, thereby assuming the risk of being fired upon."

Supreme Court Decision "Whenever an officer restrains the freedom of a person to walk away, he has seized that person.. . .[T]here can be no question that apprehension by the use of deadly force is a seizure subject to the reasonableness requirement of the Fourth Amendment. A police officer may arrest a person if he has probable cause to believe that person committed a crime. Petitioners and appellant argue that if this requirement is satisfied the Fourth Amendment has nothing to say about how that seizure is made. The submission ignores the many cases in which this Court, by balancing the extent of the intrusion against the need for it, has examined the reasonableness of the manner in which a search or seizure is conducted.. . .

"The use of deadly force to prevent the escape of all felony suspects, whatever the circumstances, is constitutionally unreasonable. It is not better that all felony suspects die than that they escape. Where the suspect poses no immediate threat to the officer and no threat to others, the harm resulting from failing to apprehend him does not justify the use of deadly force to do so. It is no doubt unfortunate when a suspect who is in sight escapes, but the fact the police arrive a little late or are a little slower afoot does not always justify killing the suspect. A police officer may not seize an unarmed nondangerous suspect by shooting him dead. The Tennessee statute is unconstitutional insofar as it authorizes the use of deadly force against such fleeing suspects.. . .

[i]Tennessee Code Annotated, Section 40–7–108 (1982).

"Officer Hymon could not reasonably have believed that Garner—young, slight, and unarmed—posed any threat. Indeed, Hymon never attempted to justify his actions on any basis other than the need to prevent escape.. . ..[T]he fact that Garner was a suspected burglar could not, without regard to the other circumstances, automatically justify the use of deadly force. Hymon did not have probable cause to believe that Garner whom he correctly believed to be unarmed, posed any physical danger to himself or others."

Case Significance The old common-law rule of shooting the fleeing felon is expressly overruled in this case. Police officers cannot shoot a suspect to make an arrest. The use of deadly force to stop a felon would only be considered reasonable in cases of necessity to protect public safety.

Although police officers are authorized to use force to arrest a suspect, they can only use the amount of force necessary to complete the arrest, and that consideration is based on the perceived dangerousness of the suspect. Thus, if a suspect is unarmed and not committing a violent crime, then officers are not authorized to use deadly force to prevent the suspect from fleeing.

3.7 Summary

The basic foundation of this chapter deals with the Fourth Amendment and the details of arrest. According to the Fourth Amendment, arrests of persons must be accompanied with an arrest warrant unless the arrest fits within one of the two limited exceptions. Arrests may be made without warrants for felonies committed in the officer's presence in public places. Arrests may also be made without warrants on the basis of probable cause.

Furthermore, if the arrest is to take place in a home, the officer must have a valid arrest warrant. The Court has determined that the expectation of privacy in a home is of sufficient importance that obtaining a warrant to enter into the home is necessary to fundamental fairness.

Finally, even if officers have justification to make an arrest, that arrest must be made in a reasonable manner. Officers may use force to effect an arrest, but only such force as is necessary to make the arrest. The old common law rule of shooting the fleeing felon has fallen by the way side and now deadly force is only justified in cases in which the fleeing felon poses an immediate threat to the officer or other citizens.

Further Reading

Brinegar v. United States, 338 U.S. 160 (1949).
California v. Hodari D., 499 U.S. 621 (1991).
Carroll v. United States, 267 U.S. 132 (1925).
Draper v. United States, 358 U.S. 307 (1959).
Dunaway v. New York, 442 U.S. 200 (1979).
Galas v. McKee, 801 F.2d 200 (CA6, 1986).
Hiibel v. Sixth Judicial District Court of Nevada, 542 U.S. 177 (2004).
Michigan v. Chesternut, 486 U.S. 567 (1988).
Minnesota v. Olson, 495 U.S. 91 (1989).
Payton v. New York, 445 U.S. 573 (1980).
Steagald v. United States,451 U.S. 204 (1981).
Tennessee v. Garner, 471 U.S. 1 (1985).
Terry v. Ohio, 392 U.S. 1 (1968).
Welsh v. Wisconsin, 466 U.S. 470 (184).

4

SEARCHES: GENERAL

CHAPTER OUTLINE

KEY TERMS

Due process
Exigent circumstances
Knock-and-announce
Neutral and detached magistrate
Particularity
Probable cause
Searches
Warrant

LEARNING OBJECTIVES

- Understand what constitutes a search.
- Understand the circumstances that require a search warrant.
- Understand the requirements of obtaining a search warrant.
- Understand requirements of executing a search warrant.

4.1 Introduction

The Fourth Amendment includes both searches and seizures of both persons and things. The preceding chapters have explored issues related to seizures, primarily of persons (arrests). This chapter and subsequent chapters examine issues related to searches. A search is defined as the exploration or examination of an individual's house, premises, or person to discover things or items that may be used by the government for evidence in a criminal prosecution. As discussed earlier, the rules governing searches are dependent upon the reasonable expectation of privacy a person has in the place or item that is the subject of the search.[a] Because the Court has determined that the Fourth Amendment protects persons and not places, protections of privacy can apply anywhere, even in a public place (as in a parking lot or a telephone booth, on a person's computer, or a person's Internet account). As a general rule, the Fourth Amendment requires that searches (and seizures) must be authorized by a **warrant** issued by a judge or magistrate. Just as with arrests, any search conducted without a warrant is presumed to be unreasonable unless it fits within one of the narrow exceptions. This chapter examines the rationale behind the search warrant requirement, the process of conducting a search, and a detailed explanation of probable cause necessary to support a search. The exceptions to the warrant requirement are covered in subsequent chapters.

4.2 Search Warrant Requirement

As stated previously, to comply with the Fourth Amendment protections, **searches** must be accompanied by a search warrant except for limited exceptions defined later in this book. For a search warrant to be issued, it must meet four criteria: (1) the search must be based on **probable cause**, (2) it must be supported by an oath or affirmation, (3) it must be signed by a **neutral and detached magistrate**, and (4) it must particularly describe the place to be searched and the thing to be seized. Several of those provisions are discussed in more detail below.

4.3 Neutral and Detached Magistrate Requirement

One of the primary rationales for requiring a warrant is that of independent determination of probable cause by one who is not connected to the investigation process. Inherent in that consideration is that the probable cause must be determined prior to the search. Thus, the concept of a neutral and detached magistrate is at the heart of the warrant requirement and at the heart of protecting citizens against unwarranted government intrusion.

In the search warrant context, the issue of a neutral and detached magistrate brings up two primary issues. First, to be

[a]*Katz v. United States*, 389 U.S. 347 (1967).

considered neutral and detached, the magistrate must not have any interest in the outcome of the case. Second, the magistrate must be able to arrive at an independent judgment that probable cause exists and that the item to be seized is located in the place to be searched. As to the first, if the magistrate is associated with the investigation in any way, that magistrate can no longer be considered neutral. See the case of *Coolidge v. New Hampshire* below.

In addition to the neutrality requirement, the magistrate must be able to make an independent determination of probable cause and not be a rubber stamp for police officer's assertions that probable cause exists. A classic set of facts in which the information supplied by the police was ruled insufficient for

Coolidge v. New Hampshire, 403 U.S. 443 (1971)

Facts A 14-year-old girl left her home in response to a man's request for a babysitter. Thirteen days later, her body was found by the side of a major highway. On January 28, the police questioned Coolidge in his home concerning the ownership of guns and asked if he would take a lie detector test with regard to his whereabouts on the night of the girl's disappearance. He produced three guns voluntarily and agreed to the lie detector test. The following Sunday, Coolidge was called to the police station to take the lie detector test and for further questioning.

While he was being questioned, two officers (not those who had questioned him earlier) went to his house and questioned his wife. During the course of the questioning, she voluntarily produced four of Coolidge's guns and the clothes he was believed to have been wearing on the night of the girl's disappearance. After a meeting involving the officers working on the case and the Attorney General, the Attorney General signed an arrest warrant for Coolidge and search warrants for his house and car. Pursuant to those warrants, Coolidge was arrested and his cars impounded. The car was searched two days later and twice after that. Evidence presented over Coolidge's objection included gunpowder residue, microscopic particles taken from the car and from the clothes provided by Coolidge's wife, and a .22-caliber rifle also provided by her. Coolidge was charged and convicted of murder.

Issues Three issues were presented in the case.

1. Was the warrant authorizing the search of Coolidge's house and car valid? NO
2. If the warrant was not valid, could the seizure of the evidence in Coolidge's house and car be justified as an exception to the warrant requirement? NO
3. Were the guns and clothes given to the officers by Coolidge's wife prior to issuance of the warrant admissible as evidence? YES

Supreme Court Decisions

1. The warrant issued by the state's chief investigator and prosecutor (the state attorney general) was not issued by a neutral and detached magistrate; hence, the warrant was invalid.
2. The evidence seized from Coolidge's house (vacuum sweepings of the clothes taken from the house) and from the car (particles of gunpowder) could not be admissible as exceptions to the warrant requirement.

3. The guns and clothes given by Coolidge's wife to the police were given voluntarily; hence, they were admissible.

Reasons

1. "When the right of privacy must reasonably yield to the right of search is, as a rule, to be decided by a judicial officer, not by a policeman or government enforcement agency." A warrant must, therefore, be issued by a neutral and detached magistrate.
2. "Since the police knew of the presence of the automobile and planned all along to seize it, there was no 'exigent circumstance' to justify their failure to obtain a warrant." Such warrantless seizures could not be justified under any of the exceptions to the warrant requirement.
3. "[T]he policemen were surely acting normally and properly when they asked her [Coolidge's wife], as they had asked those questioned earlier in the investigation, including Coolidge himself, about any guns there might be in the house. The question concerning the clothes Coolidge had been wearing the night of the disappearance was logical and in no way coercive. Indeed, one might doubt the competence of the officers involved had they not asked exactly the questions they did ask. And surely when Mrs. Coolidge of her own accord produced the guns and clothes for inspection, rather than simply describing them, it was not incumbent on the police to stop her or avert their eyes."

Case Significance The Coolidge case is best known for the principle that a warrant is valid only if issued by a neutral and detached magistrate. If the person issuing the warrant has any interest in the outcome of the case (such as the state attorney general who was also the state's chief investigator and prosecutor in the case), the warrant is invalid. The evidence (guns and clothes) given by Coolidge's wife in this case was admissible because it was given not as the result of improper conduct on the part of the police but because she wanted to help clear her husband of the crime.

the magistrate to reach an independent determination about probable cause was presented in *Aguilar v. Texas*, 373 U.S. 108 (1964). There, a justice of the peace had issued a search warrant on the basis of an application submitted by police officers which read in relevant part, "Affiants have received reliable information from a credible person and do believe that heroin, marijuana, barbiturates, and other narcotics and narcotic paraphernalia are being kept at the above described premises for the purpose of sale and use contrary to the provisions of the law."

The Supreme Court ruled that the search warrant in *Aguilar* had been issued improperly. Rather than making an independent assessment of the facts necessary to supply probable cause, the justice of the peace had served "merely as a rubber stamp for the police." In the case, the Court identified two crucial components of probable cause decisions that depend on informants' tips. The first relates to the informant's basis of knowledge, the underlying circumstances from which the informant concluded that the narcotics were where he claimed they were. The second concerns the informant's veracity, credibility, or reliability, the underlying circumstances from which the officer concluded that the informant was credible or his information reliable.

4.4 Particularity Requirement

The Fourth Amendment also contains a **particularity** requirement stating that warrants must "particularly describe the place to be searched, and the persons or things to be seized." The Fourth Amendment prohibits searches from turning into unregulated fishing expeditions conducted at the whim of the executing officers by requiring that magistrates detail in the warrant the things to be seized. In *Andresen v. Maryland*, 427 U.S. 463 (1976), a judge issued a warrant authorizing the police to search the defendant's law office for a long list of itemized documents; however, the warrant concluded by stating that the officers were directed to seize the enumerated documents, "together with other fruits, instrumentalities and evidence of a crime at this [time] unknown." The defendant contended that this clause converted the search warrant to a general warrant in violation of the Fourth Amendment. The Court rejected this argument, holding that the "fruits, instrumentalities, and evidence of a crime" that were referred to in the warrant only related to the seizure of evidence relative to the specific crime named in the warrant, that of false pretenses. This case takes into consideration that officers cannot possibly list every item that might be discovered that is relevant to a criminal event. The list, however, must be as specific as possible and related only to items of the particular crime in question.

In addition to describing the things to be seized, a warrant must particularly describe the place to be searched. Questions arise when a warrant authorizes the police to search the premises of a particular address but the location is actually an apartment complex or has more than one person living in the unit. In *Maryland v. Garrison*, 480 U.S. 79 (1987), Baltimore police officers obtained a warrant to search the premises of Lawrence McWebb for marijuana and related paraphernalia; the premises were described as the third-floor apartment at 2036 Park Avenue. They obtained the warrant under the belief that there was only one apartment on the premises. When they got there, however, they discovered that the third floor was divided into two apartments, one occupied by McWebb and the other by a different person. Before the officers were aware that they had entered the apartment occupied by the other person, they discovered drugs and ultimately convicted the resident of that apartment of a crime. The search and seizure were deemed to be valid in this case because there was no way for the officers to have known that more than one apartment was on the third floor of the building. Their description of the dwelling must be judged on the information available to them at the time. In this case, the officers relied on the building's floor plan and had no way of knowing before entering the dwelling that it had been altered. Thus, the warrant was valid, as was the search they conducted pursuant to the warrant. The general rule regarding the requirements for a particular description of a place to be searched is that it "is enough if the description is such that the officer with a search warrant can, with reasonable effort, ascertain and identify the place intended."[b]

4.5 Manner of Conducting a Search

Whether or not officers have a search warrant, an otherwise valid search will be deemed invalid if officers do not conduct the search in a reasonable manner. Several cases in this section identify circumstances in which the search was invalid because of violations of fundamental fairness. In some instances, officers had a search warrant, and in other instances they had probable cause to search. In all of the cases, however, the manner of conducting the search was at issue.

One of the earlier cases in this area defined the manner of conducting a search as one that cannot "shock the conscience" of society. In the case of *Rochin v. California*, 342 U.S. 165 (1952), discussed below, officers pumped a suspect's stomach against his will to retrieve evidence of narcotics violations. Because of the intrusive nature of the procedure, the Court determined that officers had gone too far in trying to seize evidence and that their actions were unlawful.

Based on *Rochin*, police officers must act reasonably when extracting evidence of a crime. They cannot take intrusive actions that are so contrary to societal concepts of fairness that they violate our concepts of due process.

In cases involving a search warrant, the Court has also mandated that certain restraints be placed on the manner of

[b]*Steele v. United States*, 267 U.S. 498 (1925).

Rochin v. California, 342 U.S. 165 (1952)

Facts Having some information that Rochin was selling narcotics, three deputy sheriffs of the County of Los Angeles, on the morning of July 1, 1949, made for the two-story dwelling house in which Rochin lived with his mother, common-law wife, brothers, and sisters. Finding the outside door open, they entered and then forced open the door to Rochin's room on the second floor. Inside, they found the petitioner sitting partly dressed on the side of his bed, upon which his wife was lying. On the night stand beside the bed the deputies spied two capsules. When they asked Rochin what they were, Rochin seized the capsules and put them in his mouth. A struggle ensued, and in the course of it the three officers jumped on him and attempted to extract the capsules. They were not able to overcome his resistance with their force. Rochin was handcuffed and taken to the hospital. At the direction of the officers, a doctor forced an emetic solution through a tube into Rochin's stomach against his will and pumped his stomach. When he vomited, officers recovered the two capsules which proved to contain morphine. Rochin was convicted and sentenced to prison, and the two capsules from his stomach were the primary evidence against him.

Issue Was the **due process** clause of the Fourth Amendment violated when the officers pumped the stomach of the defendant against his will? YES

Supreme Court Decision "Due process of law is a summarized constitutional guarantee of respect for those personal immunities which. . .are so rooted in the traditions and conscience of our people as to be ranked as fundamental or are implicit in the concept of ordered liberty.. . .The proceedings by which this conviction was obtained do more than offend some fastidious squeamishness or private sentimentalism about combating crime too energetically. This is conduct that shocks the conscience. Illegally breaking into the privacy of Rochin, the struggle to open his mouth and remove what was there, the forcible extraction of his stomach contents—this course of proceedings by agents of government to obtain evidence is bound to offend even hardened sensibilities. They are methods too close to the rack and the screw to permit of constitutional differentiation."

Case Significance This case is significant because it indicates further limits on the ability of law enforcement to extract evidence from an individual under the due process clause. Thus, even if officers have probable cause to conduct a search, that search must be conducted within the boundaries of due process of law.

executing the warrant. For example, search warrants can become "stale." A warrant signed in January authorizing the search of a dwelling for illegal drugs may be outdated if the police delay searching until April. Even if probable cause existed to believe that illegal drugs were in the named place when the warrant was issued, there may be no basis to assume that the drugs remain there several months later. The Fourth Amendment does not contain specific inflexible time limitations, but statutes in many jurisdictions fix a specific time within which a search warrant must be executed (usually 30 to 60 days from the date it is issued). In any event, the reasonableness provision of the Fourth Amendment will apply.

Many statutes also require that search warrants be executed during daytime hours unless the issuing judge or magistrate specifically approves of a nighttime search. The requirement of daytime searches takes into consideration other people living in the place to be searched who might not be involved in the criminal activity; particularly, children or elderly people may be living in a home authorized to be searched by a warrant. If officers have a specific reason for needing to conduct the search at night, they have to articulate that reason in the warrant application. In *Gooding v. United States*, 416 U.S. 430, 458 (1974), the Court ruled that a federal statute governing searches for controlled substances "requires no special showing for a nighttime search, other than a showing that the contraband is likely to be on the property of the person to be searched at that time."

In addition to the time-of-day restriction, police officers are required to knock on the door and announce that they are about to conduct a search in most cases. The **knock-and-announce** issue has generated several decisions from the Supreme Court.

This case upheld the common law requirement of knocking and announcing before entering a home; however, it left the reasonableness determination up to the lower courts, who must determine circumstances that qualify as exigent where announcement need not be made. In a subsequent case, the Court held that the Fourth Amendment does not allow a blanket exception to the knock-and-announce requirement in felony drug investigations.

Wilson v. Arkansas, 514 U.S. 927 (1995)

Facts Wilson conducted several narcotics transactions with an informant over a period of several months. Based on these transactions, police officers obtained an arrest warrant for Wilson and a search warrant for her home. At Wilson's residence, officers identified themselves and stated that they had a warrant as they entered the home through an unlocked door. Officers seized various drugs, a gun, and ammunition inside Wilson's home. They found Wilson in the bathroom flushing marijuana down the toilet. At trial, Wilson moved to suppress the evidence on the argument that the officers did not properly knock and announce their intentions before entering her home.

Issue Does the Fourth Amendment reasonableness requirement require officers to knock and announce before entering a home? YES, absent **exigent circumstances**

Supreme Court Decision The reasonableness requirement of the Fourth Amendment requires officers to knock and announce before entering a dwelling unless there are exigent circumstances.

Reason "An examination of the common law of search and seizure leaves no doubt that the reasonableness of a search of a dwelling may depend in part on whether law enforcement officers announce their presence and authority prior to entering." (This common law rule of knock and announce dates back to at least 1603 with the decision in *Semayne's Case*, 77 Eng. Rep. 194, which held: "But before he breaks it, he ought to signify the cause of his coming, and to make request to open doors.") "Our own cases have acknowledged that the common law principle of announcement is embedded in Anglo-American law, but we have never squarely held that this principle is an element of the reasonableness inquiry under the Fourth Amendment. We now so hold." [Citations omitted.]

Case Significance This case holds that, absent exigent circumstances, officers are required to "knock and announce" to meet the reasonableness requirements of the Fourth Amendment. The announcement requirement is based on common law practice that was woven quickly into the fabric of early American law. The Court stressed, however, that the "Fourth Amendment's flexible requirement of reasonableness should not be read to mandate a rigid rule of announcement that ignores countervailing law enforcement interest." The Court considers "countervailing law enforcement interest" as justifying entries without announcement. Such interest, said the Court, includes threats of physical harm to police, pursuit of recently escaped arrestees, and when there is reason to believe that evidence would likely be destroyed if advance notice was given. The Court refrained from presenting a "comprehensive catalog of the relevant countervailing factors," saying instead that, "For now, we leave to the lower courts the task of determining the circumstances under which unannounced entry is reasonable under the Fourth Amendment." The rule may be summarized as follows: Any time officers enter into the home of a suspect, they are required to announce their presence in advance unless they can articulate exigent circumstances. Whether an unannounced entry is reasonable is left to the discretion of lower courts.

Several additional issues arise in executing search warrants for drug violations in which the opportunity to destroy evidence is great and the potential for violence is high. For example, if the police violate the no-knock rule, can the evidence still be offered at the trial? In a recent fairly recent case, the Court determined that the evidence could be used.[c] Further consideration involved the question of how much time must elapse between the knock and announce and the entry by law enforcement. In *United States v. Banks*, 540 U.S. 31 (2003), the Court held that after knocking and announcing their presence and intention to search, 15 to 20 seconds is sufficient time for officers to wait before forcing entry into a home to execute a search warrant for drugs.

4.6 Arrest Warrant Does Not Equal a Search Warrant

A final note of caution about search warrants in general is that an arrest warrant and a search warrant are two different

[c]*Hudson v. Michigan*, 547 U.S. 586 (2006).

Richards v. Wisconsin, 520 U.S. 385 (1997)

Facts Richards was believed to be one of several individuals selling drugs from a hotel room. Based on this belief, police officers obtained a search warrant for the hotel room. Officers requested a no-knock entry, which was explicitly denied by the magistrate. One officer knocked on Richard's door and identified himself as a maintenance worker. When Richards opened the door, he saw one of the uniformed officers and slammed the door. At that point, officers identified themselves and began to break down the door. When they got inside, officers caught Richards trying to escape through a window. A search of the room revealed cash and cocaine hidden in plastic bags above the bathroom ceiling tiles. The no-knock entry was later justified by the officer based on the rule, in place before Wilson, that "police officers are never required to knock and announce when executing a search warrant in a felony drug investigation because of the special circumstances of today's drug culture."

Issue Does the Fourth Amendment allow a blanket exception to the knock-and-announce requirement for felony drug investigations? NO

Supreme Court Decision The Fourth Amendment does not allow a blanket exception to the knock-and-announce requirement in felony drug investigations. The fact that felony drug investigations may frequently involve threats of physical violence or destruction of evidence (either or both of which may justify not having to knock and announce) does not automatically exempt it from the review of a court to determine the reasonableness of the police decision not to knock and announce in a particular case.

Reason "[T]he fact that felony drug investigations may frequently present circumstances warranting a no-knock entry cannot remove from the neutral scrutiny of a reviewing court the reasonableness of the police decision not to knock and announce in a particular case. Instead, in each case, it is the duty of a court confronted with the question to determine whether the facts and circumstances of the particular entry justified dispensing with the knock-and-announce requirement. . . .In order to justify a 'no-knock' entry, the police must have a reasonable suspicion that knocking and announcing their presence, under the particular circumstances, would be dangerous or futile, or that it would inhibit the effective investigation of the crime by, for example, allowing the destruction of evidence."

Case Significance This case clarifies an issue that was not clearly addressed in the case of *Wilson v. Arkansas*, 514 U.S. 927 (1995). Wilson held that the knock-and-announce rule is required by the Fourth Amendment but that there were numerous exceptions to it; such exceptions are to be determined by lower courts. The police in this case sought a blanket exception from this requirement in felony drug investigations, saying that these cases frequently involved threats of physical violence or possible destruction of evidence. The Court rejected this based on two grounds. First, it said that there will be situations in which "the asserted governmental safety may not outweigh the individual privacy interests" involved in a particular case. Second, "the blanket exception would threaten to swallow the rule." In other words, if a blanket exception were allowed in felony drug investigations, it might lead to other exceptions (such as in bank robbery cases) that might then completely negate the rule.

items. While the police must have an arrest warrant to enter the home of a suspect to effect an arrest (see Chapter 3), they must have a search warrant to enter the home of a third party to effect an arrest.

On the basis of this case, officers must obtain both an arrest warrant and a search warrant if they are going to arrest an individual who is in the home of another person. The only exceptions to that would be if they are in pursuit of a fleeing felon who darts into the home of another person, of if the owner of the property gives expressed consent to officers to enter and conduct a search for the person named in the arrest warrant.

Steagald v. United States, 451 U.S. 204 (1981)

Facts Acting on an arrest warrant issued for a person named Lyons, Drug Enforcement Administration agents entered the home of Steagald to search for Lyons. The entry was made without a search warrant. While searching the home of Steagald, the agents found cocaine and other incriminating evidence but did not find Lyons. Steagald was arrested and convicted on federal drug charges.

Issue May an officer search for the subject of an arrest warrant in the home of a third party, absent exigent circumstances, without a search warrant? NO

Supreme Court Decision An arrest warrant is valid for entry into a suspect's place of residence. It does not authorize entry into another person's residence. If the suspect is in another person's home, a search warrant is needed to gain entry into that home, unless the homeowner gives consent for the search or some emergency circumstance is articulated that justifies a warrantless search.

Reason "Two distinct interests were implicated by the search in this case—Lyons' interest in being free from an unreasonable seizure and petitioner's [Steagald's] interest in being free from an unreasonable search of his home. Because the arrest warrant for Lyons addressed only the former interest, the search of petitioner's home was no more reasonable from petitioner's perspective than it would have been if conducted in the absence of any warrant." The search therefore violated the Fourth Amendment.

Case Significance Having an arrest warrant does not authorize the police to enter a third person's home without a search warrant. Such an entry violates the Fourth Amendment rights of the third person, who may not be involved in the crime. This rule, however, is subject to two exceptions: "exigent circumstances" and consent of the third person. Under exigent circumstances, the police do not have to obtain a search warrant if circumstances are such that to obtain one would jeopardize the arrest; for example, if the police can establish that obtaining a warrant would allow the suspect to leave the premises and avoid arrest, a warrantless arrest would be justified. Another example would be cases of hot pursuit. If a suspect being pursued by the police enters a third person's home, the police may enter the home without a warrant to capture the suspect. Consent of the third person makes the warrantless search valid as long as the consent is intelligent and voluntarily given.

4.7 Summary

This chapter examines some of the basic requirements of search warrants, including the meaning of a neutral and detached magistrate and the particularity requirement. In addition, it examines the manner in which searches should be conducted for them to be considered valid. Two very basic rules govern searches generally:

1. No fishing expeditions are allowed.
2. Do not look for an elephant in a breadbox.

Warrants must be particular as to both the place to be searched and the person or item to be seized. Officers cannot get a general warrant and search until they find something illegal. That would be the equivalent to a fishing expedition and such is not allowed. Furthermore, officers can only search in areas where the item could reasonable be found. Thus, even with a warrant, if officers are looking for a stolen car, they cannot search the living room, basement, and attic of a home. If, however, they are searching for a stolen diamond ring, then the searches of all of those areas may be reasonable because a diamond ring could reasonably be located in any of those areas.

Finally, even with probable cause or a search warrant, the manner in which the search is conducted must be reasonable and comply with due process. Officers cannot pump the stomach of a suspect to possibly retrieve evidence of narcotics violations over the objection of the suspect. Additionally, warrants must be executed in the day and officers must announce their presence unless some exigent circumstances exists to eliminate that requirement. The greatest protection of privacy from intrusive government invasion continues to be the home. Any time officers are entering a home to conduct a search or to look for a person named in an arrest warrant, special caution must be made to protect the legitimate privacy interest of the occupants.

Further Reading

Andresen *v. Maryland*, 427 U.S. 463 (1976).
Aguilar *v. Texas*, 373 U.S. 108 (1964).
Coolidge *v. New Hampshire*, 403 U.S. 443 (1971).
Gooding *v. United States*, 416 U.S. 430 (1974).
Hudson *v. Michigan*, 547 U.S. 586 (2006).
Katz *v. United States*, 389 U.S. 347 (1967).

Maryland *v. Garrison,* 480 U.S. 79 (1987).
Semayne's *Case,* 77 Eng. Rep. 194 (K.B. 1604).
Steele *v. United States,* 267 U.S. 498 (1925).
Richards *v. Wisconsin,* 520 U.S. 385 (1997).
Rochin *v. California,* 342 U.S. 165 (1952).
Steagald *v. United States,* 451 U.S. 204 (1981).
United *States v. Banks,* 540 U.S. 31 (2003).
Wilson *v. Arkansas,* 514 U.S. 927 (1995).

5

EXCEPTIONS TO THE WARRANT REQUIREMENT: AUTOMOBILE SEARCHES

CHAPTER OUTLINE

KEY TERMS

Automobile	Inventory search
Consent to a search	Investigatory stop
Containers	Probable cause
Dog sniff	Roadbocks and checkpoints

LEARNING OBJECTIVES

- Identify the expectation of privacy involved in a vehicle.
- Determine when the search of a vehicle is based on probable cause.
- Determine the scope of the probable cause of a search of a vehicle.
- Identify an investigatory stop and search of a vehicle.
- Determine the proper scope of a search incident to a lawful arrest involving a vehicle.
- Identify a properly conducted inventory search.

5.1 Introduction

The Fourth Amendment imposes two general requirements for searches and seizures to be valid: a search warrant and probable cause. Searches involving an automobile fall under one of the exceptions to the warrant requirement for two reasons. First, people have a diminished expectation of privacy in their automobiles. Vehicles are already subject to governmental regulations and licensing requirements and may be stopped and inspected for a variety of reasons. Additionally, and possibly more importantly, automobiles are highly moveable and can be driven away at any time. This makes obtaining a search warrant often impractical. Thus, the primary consideration in determining whether a vehicle search is lawful is whether probable cause exists to make the search.

Beyond probable cause, two other considerations come to bear in this area of law. These are the purpose of the initial stop and what qualifies as a vehicle. The initial stop of a vehicle must be based on either reasonable suspicion or probable cause. At the lowest end of the spectrum, officers only need reasonable suspicion (less than probable cause) of unlawful activity to stop a vehicle. This does not mean that police can stop an automobile randomly without any justification. In *Delaware v. Prouse*, 440 U.S. 648 (1979), the Court determined that a stop is unreasonable under the Fourth Amendment when police officers randomly stopped a car for no apparent reason. They were not conducting spot checks or license checks, and no initial probable cause or reasonable suspicion existed. Even though they retrieved marijuana that they found in plain view once the stop was made, the initial stop was unlawful; thus, the evidence was excluded. Once a vehicle is stopped, however, the search is governed by a different rule. A search must be based on **probable cause** or valid consent of the occupants of the vehicle. Cases in this area of law revolve around what constitutes probable cause for the stop and what constitutes probable cause for the subsequent search. Cases also address who can **consent to a search** of a vehicle, the extent of the search to **containers** within the vehicle, and whether people in the vehicle can be searched as part of the vehicle search. The general rule for the search of automobiles is that police may search where probable cause exists to believe that the item they are searching for could reasonably be concealed (including containers and the trunk of the car). Furthermore, a special consideration in vehicle cases involves inventories of vehicle contents after the vehicle has been taken into custody by law enforcement.

Other considerations for this area of law revolve around the definition of an **automobile** for Fourth Amendment purposes. The general rule is that if the item is easily movable, it is considered an automobile. This includes houseboats, motorcycles, and motor homes that are found on the roadway. Therefore, warrantless searches are valid once probable cause is established.[a]

5.2 Search Based on Probable Cause

One of the first cases to establish rules related to automobile searches was *Carroll v. United States*, 267 U.S. 132 (1925), in which the Supreme Court held that the search of an automobile without a warrant is valid as long as probable cause is present. The case was significant because it marked the first case that identified automobiles as unique for search and seizure considerations.

Carroll v. United States, 267 U.S. 132 (1925)

Facts On September 29, 1921, federal prohibition agents Cronenwelt and Scully were in an apartment in Grand Rapids, Michigan. Three men came to that apartment: a man named Kruska and the two defendants, Carroll and Kiro. Cronenwelt was introduced to them and made a request to buy three cases of whisky. The price was fixed at $130 a case. The men said they had to go to the east end of Grand Rapids to get the liquor and they would be back within an hour to complete the sale. In a short time, however, Kruska returned and stated that they could not get the liquor until the next day. They did not return the next day to deliver the liquor. At a later point, the same officers were patrolling the road between Detroit and Grand Rapids looking for violations of the Prohibition Act. They spotted Carroll and Kiro in the same car they had been in the night of the liquor transaction. A couple of days later, they observed the car again on the same thoroughfare. The officers followed the defendants to a point 16 miles east of Grand Rapids where they stopped them and searched the car. No liquor was visible in the front seat of the automobile. Next the officers opened the rumble seat and looked under the cushions, again finding no liquor. One of the officers then struck the "lazyback" of the seat and tore open the seat cushion. They found 68 bottles of whisky and gin behind the upholstering. Carroll was arrested and convicted of transporting intoxicating liquor.

Issue May officers search an automobile without a search warrant but with probable cause that it contains illegal contraband? YES

Supreme Court Decision The risk of the vehicle being moved from the jurisdiction, or the evidence being destroyed or carried off, justifies a warrantless search as long as the search is based on probable cause to believe that the vehicle contains contraband.

[a]*California v. Carney,* 471 U.S. 386 (1985).

Reason "[T]he guaranty of freedom from unreasonable searches and seizures by the Fourth Amendment has been construed, practically since the beginning of the government, as recognizing a necessary difference between a search of a store, dwelling house, or other structure in respect of which a proper official warrant readily may be obtained and a search of a ship, motor boat, wagon, or automobile for contraband goods, where it is not practicable to secure a warrant, because the vehicle can be quickly moved out of the locality or jurisdiction in which the warrant must be sought."

Case Significance This case, decided in 1925, created the "automobile exception" to the warrant requirement by ruling that warrantless searches of motor vehicles are valid as long as there is probable cause to believe that seizable items are contained in the vehicle. The justification for this exception is the mobile nature of the automobile.

Subsequent cases have continued to expand the automobile exception. Even when the automobile is under the exclusive custody and control of the police, it may still be searched under the rationale of inherent mobility. In *Chambers v. Maroney*, 399 U.S. 42 (1970), the Supreme Court held that police could search a vehicle, and all of the contents within it, even after the vehicle had been relocated to the police station. The Court determined that a car may be searched without a warrant as long as probable cause is present. The search made at the police station, some time after the arrest, was justified because the officers had probable cause to arrest the occupants of the car and, therefore, had probable cause to search the car for guns and stolen money. This case is significant because it does away with the previous requirement that the police must obtain a warrant to search a vehicle with probable cause if there was time to obtain a warrant. What the former rule said was that, once the police take control of the vehicle, the danger of it being driven away by the suspect is gone because the vehicle is now under police control. A warrant must first be obtained if the vehicle is to be searched further. *Chambers* (1970) does away with that rule, saying instead that if the police had probable cause to search the vehicle when it was first stopped, then it can be searched without a warrant even if there is time to obtain a warrant.

5.3 Search of Containers

Cases concerning stops and searches of vehicles include the discussion of what to do with containers found within the vehicle. Once the automobile has been justifiably stopped, and a reasonable search is being conducted, how far that search extends to items found within the vehicle has been a subject of debate, as well as whether compartments including the glove box and the trunk may be searched. The Court has determined that, regardless of the efforts of a person to conceal his or her possessions in a car, a warrantless search of containers, packages, and other items within the car may be upheld if the officers can establish that probable cause exists to search the automobile for contraband.

Conflicts in these cases turn on the specific facts. In one case, a footlocker was being taken off of a train and placed into an automobile. In that case, the Court determined that the police needed to get a warrant to search the footlocker because they could take control over it independently from the automobile. The probable cause that the officers had only extended to the footlocker; thus, officers should have obtained a search warrant. The Court said that, "Unlike an automobile, whose primary function is transportation, luggage is intended as a repository of personal effects." A footlocker, by virtue of it being a repository of personal effects, enjoys greater protection and its owner has greater expectations of privacy.[b] Continuing this line of thought, the Court determined in *United States v. Ross*, 456 U.S. 789 (1982), that the warrantless search of an automobile includes a search of closed containers found inside the car when there is probable cause to search the vehicle.

Based on these two cases, officers could only search containers in vehicles if they had separate probable cause to search both the vehicle and the container. If they had probable cause to search the container but not the vehicle, they had to get a warrant.

In *California v. Acevedo*, 500 U.S. 565 (1991), however, the Court continued to expand police power to search containers in vehicles, holding that the search of a closed container was lawful even if probable cause did not exist to search the entire vehicle.

California v. Acevedo, 500 U.S. 565 (1991)

Facts A Santa Ana, California, police officer received a telephone call from a federal drug enforcement agent in Hawaii who had intercepted a package containing marijuana that was supposed to be delivered to the Federal Express office in Santa Ana and that was addressed to J.R. Daza. The agent arranged to have the package sent to

[b] *United States v. Chadwick*, 433 U.S. 1 (1977).

the police officer, who verified the contents as marijuana and took it to the Federal Express office for a controlled delivery. A man claiming to be Daza picked up the package and took it to an apartment.

A short time later, Daza left the apartment and dropped the Federal Express box and the paper that had contained the marijuana into a trash bin. At that point, one police officer left to get a search warrant. A short time later, other officers observed a different man leave the apartment carrying a knapsack, which appeared to be half full. The officers stopped the man as he was driving off, searched the knapsack, and found one and one-half pounds of marijuana.

Later, Acevedo arrived at the apartment, stayed about 10 minutes, and left carrying a brown paper bag. The brown paper bag was the same size as the marijuana packages they had seen earlier. Acevedo put the bag into the trunk of his car. As he drove away, the police stopped his car, opened the trunk, opened the bag, and found marijuana. The Court held it was reasonable to search the container without a warrant because they had probable cause to believe the bag contained marijuana. The Court recognized Acevedo's expectation of privacy in the brown bag but concluded that the risk the car might drive off and the marijuana disappear trumped the expectation of privacy.

Issue Does the Fourth Amendment require the police to obtain a warrant to open a closed container in a vehicle if they lack probable cause to search the car but have probable cause to believe that the container itself holds contraband? NO

Supreme Court Decision Probable cause to believe that a container in a car holds contraband or seizable evidence justifies a warrantless search of that container even in the absence of probable cause to search the vehicle.

Reason "We therefore interpret *Carroll* [*v. United States*, 267 U.S. 132 (1925)] as providing one rule to govern all automobile searches. The police may search an automobile and the containers within it where they have probable cause to believe contraband or evidence is contained."

Case Significance This case provides a more definite rule for law enforcement to follow related to containers in vehicles. If police have probable cause to believe that a container within a vehicle is being used to conceal or transport contraband, they can search that container even if they do not have probable cause to search the vehicle.

In *Acevedo*, the Court returned to earlier considerations. In *Carroll v. United States*, 267 U.S. 132 (1925), the Court held that a warrantless search of an automobile based upon probable cause to believe that the vehicle contained evidence of crime, and in the light of the vehicle's likely disappearance, did not violate the warrant requirement of the Fourth Amendment. Acevedo expands the scope of that warrantless search to a container found within the vehicle, as long as there is probable cause to believe that the container has contraband within it, even if no probable cause exists to search the entire car. The question for law enforcement is the scope of the probable cause. Once a container is placed in an automobile to be driven away, probable cause still only extends to that container, not the entire car. Police would not be able to justify the search of an entire car that contained the item because they had no reason to believe that the contraband was placed anywhere in the vehicle except in that container. If, however, probable cause is present to search for a particular item of contraband, and police do not know where within the vehicle that contraband may be located, they may search the entire car and open the trunk and any packages or luggage found therein that could reasonably contain the items for which they have probable cause to search.

5.4 Vehicle Search Incident to Lawful Arrest

Another area in which cases have developed related to automobile searches is a search incident to a lawful arrest. In these instances, the stop of a vehicle led to the arrest of the driver and/or passengers within the vehicle. Once the passengers have been arrested, to what extent the police may search the car and to what areas of the car a warrantless search may extend are issues to be determined. Further, whether the search takes place at the initial point of arrest or whether the vehicle is transported to the police station or impound yard has been addressed in case law. In *New York v. Belton*, 453 U.S. 454 (1981), the Court determined that the police may search the passenger compartment of a car and of the contents if it is incident to a lawful arrest. The case identified the permissible scope of a search inside on automobile after a valid arrest of the occupant.

New York v. Belton, 453 U.S. 454 (1981)

Facts Belton was a passenger in an automobile that was stopped by the police. When the police checked the driver's licenses and registration, none of the occupants of the vehicle actually owned the vehicle or was related to the owner. During the stop, the officer smelled burning marijuana and saw an envelope marked "Supergold" on the floor of the automobile. Based on these items in plain view, the officer arrested the occupants of the vehicle. Subsequent to the arrest, the officer picked up the envelope and found marijuana. He then searched the passenger compartment of the automobile and, on the backseat, found a jacket belonging to Belton. He unzipped one of the pockets of the jacket and found cocaine. Belton was arrested for and convicted of possession of a controlled substance.

Issue Is the warrantless seizure of evidence in the passenger compartment of a car, after a lawful arrest, valid? YES

Supreme Court Decision A search incident to a lawful arrest allows the officers to search the occupants of the vehicle and the passenger compartment without a warrant. The search may include containers found within the passenger compartment. The term "container" denotes any object capable of holding another object. It includes closed or open glove compartments, consoles, or other receptacles located anywhere within the passenger compartment, as well as luggage, boxes, bags, clothing, and similar items.

Reason "[I]n *United States v. Robinson*, 414 U.S. 218, the Court hewed to a straightforward rule, easily applied, and predictably enforced: '[I]n the case of a lawful custodial arrest a full search of the person is not only an exception to the warrant requirement of the Fourth Amendment, but is also a "reasonable" search under that Amendment.. . .Accordingly, we hold that when a policeman has made a lawful custodial arrest of the occupant of an automobile, he may, as a contemporaneous incident of that arrest, search the passenger compartment of that automobile.. . .It follows from this conclusion that the police may also examine the contents of any containers found within the passenger compartment, for if the passenger compartment is within the reach of the arrestee, so also will containers in it be within his reach."

Case Significance This case defined the extent of allowable searches inside the automobile after a lawful arrest. Prior to this, there was confusion about whether the police could search parts of the automobile outside the driver's "wingspan." The Court expanded the area of allowable search to the entire passenger compartment, including the backseat; it also authorized the opening of containers found in the passenger compartment that might contain the object sought. In this case, Belton's jacket could contain prohibited drugs; its search was therefore valid. This case also authorizes the police to search the interior of the car even if the occupant has been removed from the car or no longer constitutes a danger to the police (such as when the occupant has been handcuffed). Note, however, that the Belton case did not decide whether the trunk could also be searched. This case was decided later in *United States v. Ross*, 456 U.S. 798 (1982).

Belton dealt with the arrest of the occupants of a car for a felony possession of a controlled substance. In *Knowles v. Iowa*, 525 U.S. 113 (1998), the Court determined that traffic offenses were not the same as felony offenses. Officers may not search a vehicle incident to the issuance of a traffic citation, absent consent or probable cause. The Court, however, continued to expand the scope of permissible warrantless searches of vehicles in *Thornton v. United States*, 541 U.S. 615 (2004), holding that officers may search the passenger compartment after a lawful arrest, even if the suspect was not in the vehicle at the time of arrest.

5.5 Investigatory Stops/Reasonable Suspicion

Up to this point, the cases involving the automobile exception to the warrant requirement have been based on warrantless searches based on probable cause. Circumstance can arise, however, in which an officer only has reasonable suspicion that a crime has been or is about to be committed. Just like the stop and frisk allowed in *Terry v. Ohio*, the Court has recognized the stop of a vehicle for investigatory purposes. In those cases, the stop is based on reasonable suspicion instead of probable cause. The standard used to determine whether reasonable suspicion exists is that of the totality of the circumstances. The totality of the circumstances must yield a particularized suspicion that contains two elements that must be present before the stop can occur. First, the assessment of the situation must be based on an analysis of all of the circumstances. Second, "the whole picture must yield a particularized suspicion" that the individual being stopped is engaged in criminal activity.[c]

The decision to stop must be made with justification. This means that the police cannot arbitrarily stop anyone for investigative purposes. There must be a particularized and objective basis for suspecting that the person stopped has engaged in or will engage in criminal activity. Such suspicion must be based on "the whole picture," as observed by the police. In deciding to make an **investigatory stop**, the experience and training of the law enforcement officer may be taken into account. What may look like innocent activity to an untrained person may look otherwise to a trained officer. Such observation gives an officer a legitimate basis for suspicion that can then justify an investigatory stop.

In addition to an investigatory stop, officers may also conduct a brief inspection of the vehicle for weapons, equivalent to the concept of a "pat-down" under *Terry v. Ohio*, 392 U.S. 1 (1968). The Court addressed this "protective sweep" of a vehicle in *Michigan v. Long*, 463 U.S. 1032 (1983).

Michigan v. Long, 463 U.S. 1032 (1983)

Facts Officers observed an automobile traveling erratically and at a high rate of speed. When the automobile swerved into a ditch, the officers stopped to investigate. They were met at the rear of the car by Long, who "appeared to be under the influence of something" and did not respond to a request to produce his license. Upon a second request, Long did produce his license. After a second request to see his registration, Long began walking toward the open door of the vehicle. The officers followed him and noticed a large hunting knife on the floorboard

[c]*United States v. Cortez*, 449 U.S. 411 (1981).

of the vehicle. They then stopped Long and frisked him. No other weapons were found. One of the officers shined his flashlight into the car and discovered marijuana. Long was then arrested. The officers then opened the unlocked trunk and discovered approximately 75 pounds of marijuana. Long was charged with and convicted of possession of marijuana.

Issue May officers conduct a protective search, similar to the pat-down search authorized in *Terry v. Ohio*, 392 U.S. 1 (1968), of the passenger compartment of a lawfully stopped vehicle to look for possible weapons? YES

Supreme Court Decision The search of an automobile, after a valid stop and limited to the areas in which a weapon may be placed or hidden, is permissible if the officer has a reasonable belief that the suspect is dangerous and might gain immediate control of a weapon.

Reason "[A]rticles inside the relatively narrow compass of the passenger compartment of an automobile are in fact generally, even if not inevitably, within the area into which an arrestee might reach in order to grab a weapon. . . .If there is reasonable belief that the suspect is dangerous and might gain control of weapons, the officer is justified by self-protection to make search of the interior of the automobile. . . .If, while conducting a legitimate *Terry* search of the interior of the automobile, the officer should, as here, discover contraband other than weapons, he clearly cannot be required to ignore the contraband. . . ."

Case Significance This case gives the police authority to conduct a limited search (similar to a pat-down search of a person) of the passenger compartment of a car if the officers have reasonable belief that they may be in danger. In this case, the officer saw a hunting knife on the floorboard of the driver's side of the car, hence justifying the search of the passenger compartment. Such a search, however, must be limited to the areas in which a weapon may be placed or hidden. If, while conducting such a search, contraband or other illegal items are discovered, they can be seized and may be admitted as evidence into court. The Court added that the fact that the suspect is under the officers' control during the investigatory stop does not render unreasonable their belief that the suspect could injure them. This implies that, as long as the officers have probable cause to believe that they are in danger, the search may continue even after the suspect has been placed under control, such as when the suspect has been handcuffed.

The basic rule for investigatory stops of automobiles is that they must be based on reasonable suspicion that gives rise to the need to investigate. They must be limited in scope and duration. Investigatory searches of automobiles have to comply with the limitations set forth in *Terry v. Ohio*, 392 U.S. 1 (1968).

5.6 Inventory Searches

After a valid stop and search of a vehicle and the arrest of the occupants, the vehicle is often impounded by the police. At the point where police take control of the vehicle, the concept of an **inventory search** arises. Inventory searches can be made of both the person and the person's possessions, and they do not require a warrant.

Colorado v. Bertine, 479 U.S. 367 (1987)

Facts Bertine was arrested for driving under the influence of alcohol. After he was taken into custody, and prior to the arrival of a tow truck to impound the van, another officer inventoried the van in accordance with departmental procedures. During the inventory search, the officer opened a backpack in which he found various containers containing controlled substances, drug paraphernalia, and money. Bertine was charged with and convicted of driving under the influence of alcohol, unlawful possession of cocaine with intent to distribute, and unlawful possession of methaqualone.

Issue Is evidence seized by opening a closed container without a warrant during an inventory search incident to a lawful arrest admissible? YES

Supreme Court Decision Inventory searches without a warrant of the person and possessions of arrested individuals are permissible under the Fourth Amendment:

1. To protect an owner's property while it is under police control
2. To ensure against claims of lost, stolen, or vandalized property
3. To protect the police from danger

Evidence found in the course of the inventory search, even if found by opening a closed backpack, is admissible.

Reason "The policies behind the warrant requirement, and the related concept of probable cause, are not implicated in an inventory search, which serves the strong governmental interests in protecting an owner's property while it is in police custody, insuring against claims of lost, stolen or vandalized property, and guarding the police from danger. There was no showing here that the police, who were following standardized caretaking procedures, acted in bad faith or for the sole purpose of investigation. Police, before inventorying a container, are not required to weigh the strength of the individual's privacy interest in the container against the possibility that the container might serve as a repository for dangerous or valuable items."

Case Significance This case allows inventory searches without a warrant even in situations in which containers must be opened. This is significant because prior to this decision it was not clear whether the police, in the course of an inventory search, could open a closed container. The current rule is to allow this type of inventory, as long as the police follow standardized caretaking procedures and they do not act in bad faith or for the sole purposes of an investigation. It is questionable whether the opening of a closed container in the absence of departmental rules authorizing the police to do so is valid. This case synthesized *South Dakota v. Opperman*, 428 U. S. 364 (1976) (inventory search of an impounded vehicle), and *Illinois v. Lafayette*, 462 U.S. 640 (1983) (inventory search of individual possessions while person is in custody).

These searches must be conducted pursuant to the departmental policy. That policy must be followed for the search of closed containers to be valid;[d] otherwise, officers must get a search warrant to open a closed container.

[d]*Florida v. Wells*, 495 U.S. 1 (1989).

5.7 Vehicle Searches by Police Dogs

Often at driver's license checkpoints or other types of checkpoints, police dogs will be on the scene. These specially trained dogs assist law enforcement in examining vehicles in a fast and efficient manner because the dog's sense of smell is so acute. The issue has been debated as to whether these dogs are conducting a search within the Fourth Amendment. Consider the following case.

Illinois v. Caballes, 543 U.S. 405 (2005)

Facts An officer stopped Caballes for speeding and radioed the dispatcher. When the dispatch communication was transmitted, another officer drove to the scene with his drug detection dog. While the first officer wrote Caballes a warning ticket, the K-9 officer walked his dog around Caballes' car. The dog alerted on the trunk. Based on that alert, the officers searched the trunk and found marijuana. Caballes sought suppression of the evidence, arguing that, because there was no suspicion of him being involved in drug activity, use of the dog violated the Fourth Amendment.

Issue Does the Fourth Amendment require reasonable, articulable suspicion to justify using a drug detection dog to sniff a vehicle during a legitimate traffic stop? NO

Supreme Court Decision "A **dog sniff** conducted during a concededly lawful traffic stop that reveals no information other than the location of a substance that no individual has any right to possess does not violate the Fourth Amendment."

Reason "In our view, conducting a dog sniff would not change the character of a traffic stop that is lawful at its inception and otherwise executed in a reasonable manner, unless the dog sniff itself infringed respondent's constitutionally protected interest in privacy. Our cases hold that it did not. . . .We have held that any interest in possessing contraband cannot be deemed 'legitimate,' and thus, governmental conduct that only reveals the possession of contraband 'compromises no legitimate privacy interest'. . . .Accordingly, the use of a well-trained narcotics-detection dog—one that 'does not expose non-contraband items that otherwise would remain hidden from public view,' *Place*, 462 U.S. at 707—during a lawful traffic stop, generally does not implicate legitimate privacy interest. In this case, the dog sniff was performed on the exterior of respondent's car while he was lawfully seized for a traffic violation. Any intrusion on respondent's privacy expectations does not rise to the level of a constitutionally cognizable infringement."

Case Significance This case ruled that the use by the police of dogs to sniff cars during a lawful stop is valid. The defendant here was validly stopped for speeding but not for drug possession. Caballes argued that the use of the dog to sniff for drugs in the absence of any "specific and articulable facts to suggest drug activity" extended the routine traffic stop and converted it into a drug investigation. The Court disagreed and held the seizure valid, saying, "In our view, conducting a dog sniff would not change the character of a traffic stop that is lawful at its inception and otherwise executed in a reasonable manner. . .." The Court added that no privacy interest was violated because "the dog sniff was performed on the exterior of respondent's car while he was lawfully seized for a traffic violation. Any intrusion on respondent's privacy expectation does not rise to the level of a constitutionally cognizable infringement."

The argument in Caballes was that the dog sniff was conducted without any suspicion at all. Generally to conduct a search, even an investigatory search, the officer must be able to articulate some fact or circumstance that gives rise to reasonable suspicion or probable cause. Neither of those standards was met in this case. The Court determined that a dog does not conduct a search within the meaning of the Fourth Amendment and that the dog did not intrude on any expectations of privacy. The stop of the vehicle was reasonable at its inception and nothing that occurred after the initial stop caused any violation of the defendants' rights.

5.8 Consent Searches

Many times, when people pass through a license check point or other type of traffic stops, officers ask for permission to search the vehicle. Citizens often think that they must submit to the search or they will be considered guilty for refusing. The truth is, however, that citizens are not required by law to consent to a search of their vehicles. Once they give consent to search, that consent applies to all containers in the vehicle unless they limit their consent.[e] The same two requirements for consent to be valid apply to vehicle searches as to other types of searches. The consent must be freely and voluntarily given, and the person giving consent must have authority over the item to be able to consent (see Chapter 6). The person can also withdraw consent at any time. Consider the case of *Schneckloth v. Bustamonte*, 412 U.S.218 (1973).

Schneckloth v. Bustamonte, 412 U.S. 218 (1973)

Facts An officer on routine patrol stopped an automobile containing Bustamonte and five others after observing that a headlight and the license plate light were burned out. When the driver could not produce a driver's license,

[e] *Florida v. Jimeno*, 499 U.S. 934 (1991).

the officer asked if any of the others had any type of identification. Only one, Joe Alcala, was able to produce a driver's license. He explained that the vehicle belonged to his brother. The men were ordered out of the car, and the officer asked Alcala if he could search the car. Alcala replied, "Sure, go ahead." Prior to the search, no one had been threatened with arrest or given the impression they were suspected of any wrongdoing. Alcala assisted in the search by opening the trunk and glove compartment. During the search, the officer found three checks under the left rear seat that had been stolen from a car wash. Using the checks as evidence, Bustamonte was convicted of possession of a check with intent to defraud.

Issue Is knowledge by a suspect of the right to refuse consent required for consent to a search to be valid? NO

Supreme Court Decision Voluntariness of consent to search is to be determined from the totality of the circumstances, of which consent is one element. Knowledge of the right to refuse consent is not a prerequisite for voluntary consent.

Reason "Our decision today is a narrow one. We hold only that when the subject of a search is not in custody and the State attempts to justify a search on the basis of his consent, the Fourth and Fourteenth Amendments require that it demonstrate that the consent was in fact voluntarily given and not the result of duress or coercion, expressed or implied. Voluntariness is a question of fact to be determined from all the circumstances, and while the subject's knowledge of a right to refuse is a factor to be taken into account, the prosecution is not required to demonstrate such knowledge as a prerequisite to establishing voluntary consent."

Case Significance In *Miranda v. Arizona*, 384 U.S. 436 (1966), the Court said that the suspect must be made aware of the right to remain silent during questioning if responses to questions are later to be admissible in court. Schneckloth says that there is no such requirement in consent search cases. The suspect does not have to be advised that he or she has the right to refuse consent for the search to be valid. All that is required is that the consent be voluntary. The Court also observed that, "Voluntariness is a question of fact to be determined from all the circumstances, and while the subject's knowledge of a right to refuse is a factor to be taken into account, the prosecution is not required to demonstrate such knowledge as a prerequisite to establishing voluntary consent." The police must prove that consent is voluntary; however, unlike *Miranda*, where the police must say "you have the right to remain silent," the police in consent searches do not have to say "you have the right to refuse consent."

Based on this case, officers are not required to inform citizens that they can refuse the search for the consent to be considered valid. Accordingly, most citizens do not know that they can refuse, and they fear that refusal will result in the articulation of probable cause. Consent searches of automobiles, however, are consistent with consent searches in other circumstances: Consent must be freely and intelligently given.

5.9 Roadblocks and Checkpoints

Governmental **roadblocks and checkpoints** are set up for a variety of legitimate government interests, such as vehicle safety checks, driver's license checks, weigh stations, game warden road checks, sobriety checkpoints, and border stops. Roadblocks to apprehend fleeing felons and to prevent illegal aliens from entering the country are all legal. The extent to which states can set up roadblocks to apprehend drunk drivers has created some level of controversy. This issue was addressed in *Michigan v. Sitz*, 496 U.S. 444 (1990).

Michigan v. Sitz, 496 U.S. 444 (1990)

Facts The Michigan Department of State Police and its director established a sobriety checkpoint pilot program in early 1986. Checkpoints were set up at selected sites along state roads. All vehicles passing through the checkpoint would be stopped and their drivers briefly examined for signs of intoxication. If a driver was suspected of being intoxicated, the vehicle would be directed to a location out of the traffic flow for further investigation.

In the initial execution of the checkpoint program, a checkpoint was set up for an hour and a half. During that time, 126 vehicles passed through it and the average delay for each vehicle was 25 seconds. Two drivers were detained for field sobriety testing, and one was arrested for being under the influence of alcohol. A third drivor was pulled over for driving through the checkpoint without stopping and was arrested for drunk driving.

Issue Does the suspicionless stop of a motorists at a sobriety checkpoint constitute an unreasonable seizure under the Fourth Amendment? NO

Reason The Supreme Court balanced the state's interest in preventing accidents caused by drunk drivers, the effectiveness of checkpoints in achieving that goal, and the level of intrusion on individual privacy caused by the checkpoints. The initial stop of a motorist passing through a checkpoint is seizure within the meaning of the Fourth Amendment. The problem of drunk driving is great and the intrusion on a person of passing through a checkpoint is minimal. Further, some evidence indicated that the checkpoints were effective in removing drunk drivers from the roadways. The Court determined that the balance of the state's interest in preventing drunken driving incidents weighed in favor of the state program. Thus, the program did not violate the Fourth Amendment.

Case Significance This case upheld the concept of roadblocks for legitimate government interests. The intrusion on motorists must be minimal, and at least some evidence must be presented of both the problem to be addressed and the likelihood of the checkpoint addressing the problem for them to be upheld.

The general rule on roadblocks is that they must promote a legitimate government interest which is not designed for general detection of crime.[f] Furthermore, they must not "generate fear and surprise" in motorists. The "fear and surprise" to be considered are not the natural fear over the prospect of being stopped for one who has been drinking, but rather the fear and surprise

[f] *Indianapolis v. Edmond*, 531 U.S. 32 (2000).

of law-abiding motorists due to the nature of the stop. As long as the stop is short in time, positioned in a place where alternative routes may allow motorists to avoid it, and does not involve any unreasonable intrusion into the privacy of the motorists, the checkpoint is likely to be upheld. Checkpoints must also follow specific guidelines that treat every motorist the same.

5.10 Summary

At the beginning of this chapter, automobile searches and seizures were identified as an exception to the Fourth Amendment warrant requirement. The exception is based on two primary issues: (1) the reduced expectation of privacy in a vehicle that is placed upon a public road and governed by governmental rules and regulations, and (2) the inherent mobility of the vehicle and its contents. As cases have demonstrated, however, many additional issues have come before the courts. Courts have been called upon to determine the extent to which containers within the vehicle can be searched, whether the scope of the search includes the glove compartment and trunk space, and whether people within the vehicle can be searched. In each case, the automobile exception continues to be considered as a guiding principle. Because the automobile is easily movable, it, the contents inside of it, and the people riding in it may easily leave the scene and evidence may be destroyed. Thus, in most cases, warrantless searches will be upheld.

The primary consideration in conducting a warrantless search of a vehicle revolves around probable cause. If the officers know what they are searching for, they may search in any place within the vehicle where that thing could be located. This includes dismantling the vehicle on the side of the road to find secret compartments. If, however, the officer's probable cause is limited to a particular container placed within the vehicle, then the search should be limited to that container. If the occupants of the vehicle are arrested, a warrantless search of the entire passenger compartment of the vehicle, and all of its containers, is permissible. If the search is not conducted at the point of arrest, departmental policy that allows inventory searches will guide the warrantless search.

Further Reading

California v. Acevedo, 500 U.S. 565 (1991).
California v. Carney, 471 U.S. 386 (1985).
Carroll v. United States, 267 U.S. 132 (1925).

Chambers v. Maroney, 399 U.S. 42 (1970).
Colorado v. Bertine, 479 U.S. 367 (1987).
Delaware v. Prouse, 440 U.S. 648 (1979).
Florida v. Jimeno, 499 U.S. 934 (1991).
Florida v. Wells, 495 U.S. 1 (1989).
Illinois v. Caballes, 543 U.S. 405 (2005).
Illinois v. Lafayette, 462 U.S. 640 (1983).
Knowles v. Iowa, 525 U.S. 113 (1998).
Michigan v. Long, 463 U.S. 1032 (1983).
Michigan v. Sitz, 496 U.S. 444 (1990).
New York v. Belton, 453 U.S. 454 (1981).
Schneckloth v. Bustamonte, 412 U.S. 218 (1973).
South Dakota v. Opperman, 428 U.S. 364 (1976).
Terry v. Ohio, 392 U.S. 1 (1968).
Thornton v. United States, 541 U.S. 615 (2004).
United States v. Chadwick, 431 U.S. 1 (1977).
United States v. Cortez, 449 U.S. 411 (1981).
United States v. Place, 462 U.S. 696 (1983).
United States v. Robinson, 414 U.S. 218 (1973).
United States v. Ross, 456 U.S. 798 (1982).

6

EXCEPTIONS TO THE WARRANT REQUIREMENT: PLAIN VIEW, OPEN FIELDS, ABANDONED PROPERTY, AND CONSENT SEARCHES

CHAPTER OUTLINE

KEY TERMS

Abandoned property
Apparent authority
Authority to consent
Curtilage
Open fields
Plain view doctrine
Reasonable expectation of privacy
Voluntary and intelligent consent

LEARNING OBJECTIVES

- Identify requirements for the plain view doctrine.
- Understand issues related to open fields.
- Identify requirements for property to be considered abandoned.
- Understand requirements of valid consent.

6.1 Introduction

The Fourth Amendment's protection against unreasonable searches and seizures extends only to items in which a person has a **reasonable expectation of privacy** (see Chapter 2). The Court has determined that various situations give rise to circumstances where that expectation of privacy has been eliminated either by the actions of the citizen or by the circumstances surrounding the location of the item. For example, as you move farther away from the home and the curtilage of the home, the expectation of privacy diminishes. At some point, the owner of the property no longer has an expectation of privacy in that property. Another example is when the owner of property consents to a search by law enforcement. At that point, any expectation of privacy is eliminated. Once the expectation of privacy no longer covers the person or property, officers can search without a search warrant. This chapter examines instances in which warrantless searches do not violate the Fourth Amendment.

6.2 Plain View

An item that is exposed to others cannot support a legitimate expectation of privacy; thus, items in plain view, technically, cannot be searched within the meaning of the Fourth Amendment. The **plain view doctrine** allows officers to make a warrantless seizure of items exposed to their view. Cases covered within this area of law identify limits on the authority of law enforcement to be in a position to come across contraband or other incriminating evidence. These limitations are in place to prevent officers from engaging in general exploratory searches prior to seizing an item that they see. The plain view doctrine states that items within the sight of an officer who is legally in a place may be seized without a warrant as long as such items are readily identifiable as contraband. Several specific criteria must be met for the search to be permissible:

1. Officers must be lawfully on the premises where the view is made.
2. Officers must be able to see the item in question.
3. Items must be readily identifiable as contraband without being moved or manipulated.

The first of these requirements means that an officer must be at the place lawfully. Officers can legally be in a position to recognize evidence in many ways. One example would be that officers are responding to a call and enter a business, they see contraband through an open window, or they come across it during an investigation. Another example is presented in *Washington v. Chrisman*, 455 U.S. 1 (1982), where an officer noticed a university student who appeared underage but was carrying alcohol across campus. In an effort to determine the student's age, the officer followed the student to his dorm room so the student could produce his identification badge. The officer waited at the doorway, and through the open door saw marijuana seeds and a pipe lying on the desk. The officer entered the room and seized the evidence. The student and his roommate were arrested. The Supreme Court ruled that the officer had legally gone to the doorway of the room, and since the evidence initially found was in plain view he did not need a warrant to enter the room and retrieve the contraband. In this case, the officer was lawfully on the premises from which the view was made.

The next requirement is that the officer must be able to see the item in question without "searching" for it. This means that the officer cannot conduct a search outside the scope of the intended purpose of his or her presence on the property. In the example above of *Washington v. Chrisman*, the officer would not have been justified in entering the dorm room and conducting a warrantless search to retrieve the student's identification badge. However, when the door was opened and the officer could see the drug items through the door, the subsequent actions were justified. Although officers are required to be able to see the contraband with their own eyes, courts have upheld the use of items, generally available to the public, that allow officers to enhance their senses. For example, officers can use binoculars or telescopes as well as helicopters and planes to see evidence in plain view. In *California v. Ciraolo*, 476 U.S. 207 (1986), for example, officers flew a helicopter over the backyard of a defendant and noticed a patch of marijuana growing in the back yard. The owner was arrested for drug charges because the marijuana was in plain view and no warrant was required.

California v. Ciraolo, 476 U.S. 207 (1986)

Facts After receiving an anonymous telephone tip that Ciraolo was growing marijuana in his backyard, police went to his residence to investigate. Realizing that the area in question could not be viewed from ground level, officers used a private plane and flew over the home at a low altitude. Officers trained in the detection of marijuana readily identified marijuana plants growing in Ciraolo's yard. Based on that information and an aerial photograph of the area, officers were able to get a search warrant for the premises. A search was made pursuant to the warrant and numerous marijuana plants were seized. Ciraolo was charged and convicted of growing of marijuana.

Issue May officers make an aerial observation of an area within the curtilage of a home without a search warrant? YES

Supreme Court Decision The constitutional protection against unreasonable searches and seizures is not violated by the naked-eye aerial observation of a suspect's backyard, which is a part of the curtilage, by the police.

Reason "That the area is within the curtilage does not itself bar all police observation. The Fourth Amendment protection of the home has never been extended to require law enforcement officers to shield their eyes when passing by a home on public thoroughfares. Nor does the mere fact that an individual has taken measures to restrict some views of his activities preclude an officer's observations from a public vantage point where he has a right to be and which renders the activities clearly visible."

Case Significance The term **curtilage** refers to the grounds and buildings immediately surrounding a dwelling. Ordinarily, the curtilage is not considered an open field and hence is protected against unreasonable searches and seizures. This means that searching a curtilage requires a warrant. In this case, however, the Court said that there was no need for a warrant because the naked-eye aerial observation of a suspect's backyard is not a "search" within the meaning of the Fourth Amendment. The Court held that even an area within the curtilage does not in itself prohibit all police observation. This case, therefore, expands police power to observe the curtilage without a warrant through aerial observation.

In the case above, officers flew a helicopter over the property but used their own sense of sight to discern the marijuana growing in the back yard. The Court, however, reached a different conclusion when high-tech equipment was used to enhance the officers' vision. In *Kyllo v. U.S.*, 533 U.S. 27 (2001), for instance, thermal imaging technology was used to view contraband not otherwise visible to the naked eye. Thermal imaging devices detect, measure, and record infrared radiation not visible to the naked eye. The imagers convert radiation into images based on the amount of heat. In *Kyllo*, the Court determined that the use of thermal imaging to see into a person's home violated the Fourth Amendment. The opinion stated that, "Where, as here, the Government uses a device that is not in general public use to explore details of a private home that would previously have been unknowable without physical intrusion, the surveillance is a Fourth Amendment 'search' and is presumptively unreasonable without a warrant."

The final element of the analysis is that the items must be readily identifiable as contraband. According to this principle, officers may not move the items in question or manipulate them in any way to determine whether they are, in fact, contraband. Consider the case of *Arizona v. Hicks*, 480 U.S. 321 (1987).

Arizona v. Hicks, 480 U.S. 321 (1987)

Facts A bullet fired through the floor of Hicks' apartment, injuring a man below, prompted the police to enter Hicks' apartment to search for the shooter, weapons, and other victims. The police discovered three weapons and a stocking cap mask. An officer noticed several pieces of stereo equipment that seemed to be out of place in the apartment. Based on this suspicion, he read and recorded the serial numbers of the equipment. He had to move the pieces around to see the serial numbers. A call to police headquarters verified that one of the pieces of equipment was stolen. A subsequent check of the serial numbers of the other pieces of equipment revealed that they were also stolen. On the basis of that information, the officer got a search warrant and the other equipment was seized. Hicks was charged and convicted of robbery.

Issue Were these items "readily identifiable" as contraband so as to be considered a plain view search that did not require a search warrant? NO

Supreme Court Decision Probable cause to believe that items being searched are, in fact, contraband or evidence of criminal activity is required for the items to be covered under the plain view doctrine. The items may not be moved or manipulated in an effort to determine whether they are contraband without securing a search warrant first.

Reason The officer's "moving of the equipment, however, did constitute a 'search' separate and apart from the search for the shooter, victims, and weapons that was the lawful objective of his entry into the apartment. Merely inspecting those parts of the turntable that came into view during the latter search would not have constituted an independent search, because it would have produced no additional invasion of respondent's privacy interest.. . .But taking action, unrelated to the objectives of the authorized intrusion, which exposed to view concealed portions of the apartment or its contents, did produce a new invasion of respondent's privacy unjustified by the exigent circumstance that validated the entry."

Case Significance The plain view doctrine states that items within the sight of an officer who is legally in the place from which the view is made, and who had no prior knowledge that the items were present, may properly be seized without a warrant as long as the items are immediately recognizable as contraband. This case holds that, even after the officer has seen an object in plain view, any movement or manipulation of the item constitutes an independent search of the item that is outside of plain view and requires either probable cause or a warrant. Therefore, if, at the moment the object is picked up, the officer did not have probable cause to believe it was contraband, but only "reasonable suspicion" (as was the case here), the seizure is illegal.

These cases, taken together, offer guidance as to the limitations of officers to seize items that are outside of their original purpose for being on the premises. As long as they are lawfully at the place, they can see the items with their eyes (or with enhancements such as flashlights or binoculars), and they do not "search" the item to determine whether it is contraband, their actions fall within the plain view doctrine.

6.3 Open Fields

Another area that is not protected by the Fourth Amendment is open fields. According to the Court, an **open field** is any privately owned property that is located too far from the home to be considered within the curtilage. The farther the property gets from the home, the less protection that property enjoys. Furthermore, posting signs and putting fences around an open field cannot necessarily change it to property that has a protected privacy interest. "No Trespassing" signs do not effectively bar the public from viewing open fields; therefore, the expectation of privacy by the owner of an open field does not exist. The police may enter and investigate unoccupied or undeveloped areas outside the curtilage without either a warrant or probable cause.

Oliver v. United States, 466 U.S. 170 (1984)

Facts Acting on reports that marijuana was being grown on the petitioner's farm, but without a search warrant, probable cause, or exigent circumstances, police officers went to the farm to investigate. They drove past Oliver's house to a locked gate with a "No Trespassing" sign, and with a footpath around one side. Officers followed the footpath around the gate and found a field of marijuana more than one mile from the petitioner's house. Oliver was charged and convicted of manufacturing a controlled substance.

Issue Does the open fields doctrine apply when the property owner attempts to establish a reasonable expectation of privacy by posting a "No Trespassing" sign, using a locked gate, and planting marijuana more than one mile from the house? YES

Supreme Court Decision Because open fields are accessible to the public and the police in ways that a home, office, or commercial structure would not be, and because fences or "No Trespassing" signs do not effectively bar the public from viewing open fields, the expectation of privacy by an owner of an open field does not exist. Consequently, the police may enter and search unoccupied or underdeveloped areas outside the curtilage without either a warrant or probable cause.

Reason The test of a reasonable expectation of privacy is not whether the individual attempts to conceal criminal activity, but whether the government's intrusion infringes upon the personal and societal values protected by the Fourth Amendment. Because open fields are accessible to the public and because fences or "No Trespassing" signs, etc., are not effective bars to public view of open fields, the expectation of privacy does not exist and police are justified in investigating these areas without a warrant.

Case Significance This case makes clear that the "reasonable expectation of privacy" doctrine under the Fourth Amendment, as established in *Katz v. United States,* 389 U.S. 347 (1967), does not apply when the property involved is an open field. The Court stressed that steps taken to protect privacy, such as planting the marijuana on secluded land and erecting a locked gate (but with a footpath along one side) and posting "No Trespassing" signs around the property, do not establish any reasonable expectation of privacy. This case allows law enforcement officers to make warrantless entries and observations without probable cause in open fields, thus affording them greater access to remote places where prohibited plants or drugs might be concealed.

Based on the Supreme Court ruling, the nature of the property itself, more than the intentions of the property owner, determines whether property is an open field or a protected area. When a place is public, a person cannot convert it to private, by signs or fences. If the public can see the space, they can see the activity and it is not protected. Areas immediately surrounding a home, such as garages, patios, and pools, are not considered open fields because those areas are where families congregate and other private activities occur. In *United States v. Dunn*, 480 U.S. 294 (1987), the Supreme Court laid out the criteria for determining whether something is within the curtilage of a home: (1) the proximity of the area to the home, (2) whether the area is in an enclosure surrounding the home, (3) the nature and uses of the area, and (4) the steps taken to conceal the area from public view. These four criteria help separate space close to the home from space that is in an open field. Although they continue to be subjective and open to broad interpretation, they provide minimal guidance in determining whether a reasonable expectation of privacy exists in a specific place and whether a warrant is required before officers can search that place.

6.4 Abandoned Property

Like open fields, **abandoned property** has no reasonable expectation of privacy. The determination of whether something has been abandoned is often a significant part of the debate. The Supreme Court has adopted a totality of the circumstances test to determine whether or not property has been abandoned. Some of the considerations involve physically giving up possession of something and the intent to give up the expectation of privacy. The Court looks at all of the facts in each case to determine the intent to abandon, the actions indicating abandonment, and the termination of a reasonable expectation of privacy. In *California v. Greenwood*, 486 U.S. 35 (1988), the Supreme Court applied the totality of the circumstances test to determine whether Greenwood had abandoned his trash when he left it at the curb for collection.

The concept of abandoned property would likely apply to items that a defendant throws from his or her pants or coat pocket just before being seized by the police. Additionally, any vehicle left unattended on the side of the roadway for an extended period of time would likely be abandoned. Once the property is abandoned, the owner of the property has no more

California v. Greenwood, 486 U.S. 35 (1988)

Facts Police received information indicating that respondent Greenwood might be engaged in narcotics trafficking. Police conducted surveillance of Greenwood's home. Observations revealed several vehicles making stops at the home during the late night and early morning hours, as well as association with known narcotics traffickers. Police asked the local trash collector to pick up the garbage that Greenwood left at the curb in front of his house, to keep it separate from any other trash, and to turn it over to police. They did that on two different occasions and found evidence of narcotics use in the trash. Based on the evidence from the trash, officers secured two different warrants, conducted two different searches, and found narcotics both times. Greenwood was arrested two different times.

Issue Did the respondents maintain a reasonable expectation of privacy in the garbage that was left at the curb for pickup? NO

Supreme Court Decision Respondents exposed their garbage to the public sufficiently to defeat their claim to Fourth Amendment protection. It is common knowledge that plastic garbage bags left on or at the side of a public street are readily accessible to animals, children, scavengers, snoops, and other members of the public. Moreover, respondents placed their refuse at the curb for the express purpose of conveying it to a third party, the trash collector, who might himself have sorted through the trash. Accordingly, having deposited their garbage in an area particularly suited for public inspection and, in a manner of speaking, public consumption, for the express purpose of having strangers take it, respondents could have no reasonable expectation of privacy in the discarded items.

Case Significance The warrantless search and seizure of the garbage bags left at the curb outside the Greenwood house would violate the Fourth Amendment only if respondents manifested a subjective expectation of privacy in their garbage that society accepts as objectively reasonable. This case holds that society is not prepared to recognize any privacy interest in garbage that is at the curb. That property is considered abandoned for Fourth Amendment purposes, and no search warrant is required.

expectation of privacy in the item, and police do not need a search warrant to conduct a search.

6.5 Consent

Consent searches are another area where officers do not need probable cause or a warrant to conduct a valid search. The only thing they need is for the person to give consent. Cases in this area revolve around what constitutes valid consent. Two basic requirements must be met for consent to be valid. First, consent must be voluntarily and intelligently given, and, second, consent must be given by someone who has authority to give it. These types of searches make law enforcement officers' jobs easier because they do not have to take the time to get a warrant and they do not have to articulate probable cause.

As to the **voluntary and intelligent consent** requirement, consent must be given without force, duress, or anything that would make the person feel obligated to give it, and the person giving it must know what he or she is doing. Police cannot intentionally misrepresent their authority to get consent. For example, in *Bumper v. North Carolina,* 391 U.S. 543 (1968), the police said they had a warrant when, in fact, they did not. On the basis of that deception, they obtained consent. The consent was not considered voluntarily, thus the search was unlawful.

The Supreme Court has identified circumstances surrounding the voluntariness of the search to include knowledge of constitutional rights, sufficient age and maturity to make an independent decision, intelligence to understand the significance of consent, knowledge of the criminal justice system, length of detention, nature of questioning regarding consent, and coercive police behavior surrounding the consent. The Supreme Court has created a totality of the circumstances test of voluntariness to examine the circumstances surrounding consent. Although whether someone has the right to refuse to give consent is one of the considerations in the totality of the circumstances analysis, the Court has not gone so far as to require police to tell citizens that they do not have to give consent for it to be intelligently given.[a] Mere silence or failure to object to a search, however, does not necessarily indicate valid consent. Finally, although written consent is not constitutionally required, it goes a long way toward proving the validity of the consent if later challenged in court.

Aside from the need for the consent to be voluntary and intelligent, consent must be given by someone who has authority to give it. The general rule is that one who has common authority over an area may consent to the search of that area. Spouses may only give consent for a search of common areas of the premises if the other spouse is not present. One spouse may not give consent to search an area privately used by the absent party. Consent may be given to a private container if it is in a common area used by both parties. A parent may give consent to police to search a child's area in the home of the parents. If the child has a private room and pays rent for the space, then the parent can no longer give consent for a search of that area unless the parent is allowed access to the room. If an individual borrows a car, he or she may give consent to a search of the car

[a]*Schneckloth v. Bustamonte,* 412 U.S. 218 (1973).

without the owner's knowledge. School officials are allowed to search students or their bags as long as there is reasonable suspicion that the student has violated a law or a school policy.[b] The search or consent to a search of a student's locker by school officials is determined by rules of the school stating they can do so or whether the locker and lock are owned by the school or a private individual. On the other hand, a hotel clerk cannot give consent to search the room of a hotel guest.[c] A hotel guest has a reasonable expectation of privacy that cannot be waived by the hotel management simply because the management has the key.

Circumstances can arise in which officers believe one has **authority to consent** but later finds out that the person did not have the authority to consent. Generally, if police can reasonably rely on the **apparent authority** of the one giving the consent then the search will be valid.

Illinois v. Rodriguez, 497 U.S. 177 (1990)

Facts After being summoned to a house, the police were met by Gail Fischer, who showed signs of a severe beating. She informed the officers that she had been assaulted by Rodriguez earlier that day in an apartment. Fischer and the police subsequently drove to the apartment of Rodriguez because she stated that Rodriguez would be asleep at that time and that she could let them into the apartment with her key so that they could arrest him. Several times she referred to the apartment as "our" apartment and stated that she had clothes and furniture there. She did not tell the police, however, that she was no longer living there. Upon entrance, without a warrant but with a key and permission provided by Fischer, the police saw in plain view drug paraphernalia and containers filled with cocaine. The officers seized these and other drug paraphernalia found in the apartment where Rodriguez was sleeping. Rodriguez was arrested and charged with possession of a controlled substance with intent to deliver. On appeal, the Circuit Court suppressed the evidence, holding that at the time Fischer consented to the entry of the apartment she did not have common authority over it because she had actually moved out several weeks earlier.

Issue Is a warrantless entry and subsequent search, based on the consent of a person whom the police believed to have possessed common authority over the premises, but who in fact did not have such authority, valid? YES

Supreme Court Decision The warrantless entry of private premises by the police is valid if based on the consent of a third party whom the police reasonably believed to possess common authority over the premises, but who in fact did not have such authority.

Reason The appellate court was correct in determining that Fischer had no common authority over the apartment; however, the State contended that even if she did not have the authority to consent, it should suffice to validate the entry that the law enforcement officers reasonably believed she did. Furthermore, the Fourth

[b]*New Jersey v. T.L.O.*, 468 U.S. 1214 (1984).
[c]*Stoner v. California*, 376 U.S. 483 (1964).

Amendment only protects against unreasonable searches, not searches performed without the owner's consent. The reasonableness clause of the Fourth Amendment "does not demand that the government be factually correct in its assessment." Furthermore, "The Constitution is no more violated when officers enter without a warrant because they reasonably (though erroneously) believe that the person who has consented to their entry is a resident of the premises, than it is violated when they enter without a warrant because they reasonably (though erroneously) believe they are in pursuit of a violent felon who is about to escape."

Case Significance This case reiterates the "apparent authority" rule in searches with consent. The rule says that consent given by a third party whom the police reasonably believe to possess common authority over the premises is valid even if it is later established that the person did not in fact have that authority. In this case, the girlfriend, who gave consent and provided the key, had moved out of the apartment. She led the police to the house and allowed them entry by using her key. She did not tell them that she no longer lived there. The officers reasonably believed that she had authority to give consent; hence, the entry was valid, and the evidence subsequently obtained was admissible. It is important to note, however, that for the "apparent authority" rule to apply, the belief by the police must be reasonable, considering the circumstances.

When officers rely on the apparent authority of the person giving consent, the search will be valid and the evidence will be allowed in the trial. When, however, one party consents to a search and the other party, who is present, refuses the search, the search is not considered valid. Consider the case of *Georgia v. Randolph*, 547 U.S. 103 (2006), in which one spouse consented to the search over the objection of the other spouse.

Georgia v. Randolph, 547 U.S. 103 (2006)

Facts After a separation between Randolph and his wife and her return to the household, the wife notified police of a domestic dispute when Randolph took their son away. When officers responded, the wife told them that her husband was a cocaine user. Shortly after the police arrived, Randolph returned. Randolph denied cocaine use and countered that it was his wife who abused drugs. Later, the wife reaffirmed Randolph's drug use and told police there was "drug evidence" in the house. An officer asked Randolph for permission to search the house, which he unequivocally refused. The officer then asked the wife for consent to search, which she readily gave. She led the officer to a bedroom that she identified as Randolph's, where officers found a section of a drinking straw with a powdery residue suspected to be cocaine. Officers then contacted the district attorney's office, which instructed him to stop the search and apply for a warrant. When the officers returned to the house, the wife withdrew her consent. The police took the straw to the police station, along with the Randolphs. After obtaining a search warrant, officers returned to the house and seized further evidence of drug use. Randolph was indicted for possession of cocaine.

Issue Is a warrantless search of a shared dwelling valid when one occupant gives consent but another occupant who is present expressly refuses to consent? NO

Supreme Court Decision "We therefore hold that a warrantless search of a shared dwelling for evidence over the express refusal of consent by a physically present resident cannot be justified as reasonable as to him on the basis of consent given to the police by another resident."

Reason In previous cases, the Court recognized the validity of searches based on voluntary consent of an individual who shares common authority over the property to be searched. None of the co-occupant consent-to-search cases, however, included the circumstances of a second occupant physically present and refusing permission to search. "[I]t is fair to say that a caller standing at the door of shared premises would have no confidence that one occupant's invitation was a sufficiently good reason to enter when a fellow tenant stood there saying, 'stay out.' Without some very good reason, no sensible person would go inside under those conditions. . . .Such reticence would show not timidity but a realization that when people living together disagree over the use of their common quarters, a resolution must come through voluntary accommodation, not by appeals to authority. . . .Since the co-tenant wishing to open the door to a third party has no recognized authority in law or social practice to prevail over a present and objecting co-tenant, his disputed invitation, without more, gives a police officer no better claim to reasonableness in entering than the officer would have in the absence of any consent at all. . . .So long as there is no evidence that the police have removed the potentially objecting tenant from the entrance for the sake of avoiding a possible objection, there is practical value in the simple clarity of complementary rules, one recognizing the co-tenant's permission when there is no fellow occupant on hand, the other according dispositive weight to the fellow occupant's contrary indication when he expresses it."

Case Significance Consent is an exception to the Fourth Amendment rule requiring probable cause and a warrant in search and seizure cases. This case resolves an issue that was not previously addressed by the Court: whether consent by an occupant of a dwelling over the expressed objection of another occupant authorizes the police to conduct a warrantless search. Previous Supreme Court cases held that one consent sufficed. Those cases, however, did not involve similar circumstances, as in this case where the other occupant, the husband, was present and specifically refused to give consent. In previous cases, the other occupant either was away or did not expressly refuse consent. In this case, the Court held the search invalid as to the occupant who specifically refused consent. The majority stated, however, that this ruling does not apply to instances when: (1) the police must enter a dwelling to protect a resident from domestic violence, as long as they have good reason to believe that such a threat exists; and (2) in cases where the purpose of the entry is "to give a complaining tenant the opportunity to collect belongings and get out safely, or to determine whether violence (or threat of violence) has just occurred or is about to (or soon will) occur, however much a spouse or other co-tenant objected." The Court also held that this ruling does not apply to cases where the person giving consent is in a position of authority in a "recognized hierarchy," such as parent and child. Finally, the Court ruled that the police could not remove one of the occupants deliberately to prevent the person from refusing consent. Despite this ruling, other issues remain unresolved, such as: Must the police expressly inform all the occupants that they have a right to refuse consent? How is that consent expressed? Does silence mean consent or refusal? The safer practice is for police officers to make sure occupants of equal status in the house give their expressed consent and obtain that consent in writing.

Based on this case, two people who have equal authority over a place must both give consent or the police must obtain a warrant before they can conduct a valid search. Other considerations regarding consent are that consent may be limited by the person who gives it. If consent is given to search a certain room, then officers are limited to that room and may not search the entire premises. The limits to what is searchable based on consent comes from the wording of the consent. If the person states that police can search his house, then they are allowed to search anything in the house, including closed containers. Any individual who gives consent to an officer may also take it away at any time during the search. The officers performing the search must abide by the request and stop immediately. Any evidence found prior to the withdrawal of consent may still be used in court against the suspect.

6.6 Summary

This chapter examined four circumstances in which police officers can search without a warrant and without violating the Fourth Amendment. In each circumstance, specific criteria are required before the search is valid. The plain view doctrine was the first type of warrantless search identified. For plain view to be valid, the officers must be lawfully on the premises, they must be able to see the items with their own sense of sight, and the items must be readily identifiable as contraband without any movement or manipulation. If these elements are met, officers may seize the items without a warrant and the seizure will be valid.

The next issue addressed was open fields. The open fields doctrine states that items in open fields are not protected by the Fourth Amendment and may be properly seized by an officer without a warrant or probable cause. Generally, areas outside of the curtilage of the home are not covered by a reasonable expectation of privacy. As such, the owner of the property cannot create a protected interest in the property. They are treated as public space and officers do not need a search warrant to search them.

Plain view and open fields are similar in that, in both situations, there is no need for a search warrant or probable cause for the police to be able to seize the items. They are different, however, in two ways:

1. Under the plain view doctrine, the seizable property is usually in a house or another enclosed place (such as a car);

whereas, under the open fields doctrine, the item is found in a non-enclosed area, such as in a parking lot, a public street, or a park that is accessible to the public.

2. Under the plain view doctrine, the item seized is limited to what is in the officer's sight. By contrast, items known or observed through the use of the officer's other senses (smell, hearing, touch, and taste) also fall under the open fields doctrine.

Abandoned property, like open fields, does not retain a protected privacy interest. The determination of whether property has been abandoned hinges on whether the owner has given up possession of the property and whether the owner has intended to relinquish the expectation of privacy. Generally, if the property has been left outside the curtilage of the home for a period of time, the property is considered abandoned.

The final area of warrantless searches included in this chapter were those involving consent. For consent to be valid, it must be voluntarily and intelligently given by someone who has authority to give it. As a general rule, police cannot coerce consent through any threats or promises or misrepresentations. The authority to consent is determined by determining who has common authority over areas of property subjected to the search. Although one can consent to a search of common areas of a home or apartment, one cannot consent over the expressed refusal of a co-tenant who is present at the time of the search. In each of these cases, warrantless searches are permissible and do not violate the requirements of the Fourth Amendment.

Further Reading

Arizona v. Hicks, 480 U.S. 321 (1987).
Bumper v. North Carolina, 391 U.S. 543 (1968).
California v. Ciraolo, 476 U.S. 207 (1986).
California v. Greenwood, 486 U.S. 35 (1988).
Georgia v. Randolph, 547 U.S. 103 (2006).
Horton v. California, 496 U.S. 128 (1990).
Illinois v. Rodriguez, 497 U.S. 177 (1990).
Katz v. United States, 389 U.S. 347 (1967).
Kyllo v. United States, 533 U.S. 27 (2001).
New Jersey v T.L.O., 468 U.S. 1214 (1984).
Oliver v. United States, 466 U.S. 170 (1984).
Schneckloth v. Bustamonte, 412 U.S. 218 (1973).
Stoner v. California, 376 U.S. 483 (1964).
United States v. Dunn, 480 U.S. 294 (1987).
Washington v. Chrisman, 455 U.S. 1 (1982).

7

SEARCH INCIDENT TO A LAWFUL ARREST AND HOT PURSUIT

CHAPTER OUTLINE

KEY TERMS

Area within immediate control
Hot pursuit
Lawful arrest
Mere evidence
Wingspan

LEARNING OBJECTIVES

- Understand the permissible scope of searches incident to lawful arrest.
- Understand the rationale for allowing warrantless searches incident to lawful arrests.
- Identify the differences between searches incident to lawful arrests and protective sweeps.
- Understand the meaning of hot pursuit.

7.1 Introduction

As discussed earlier, any search without a warrant is presumed to be unreasonable. Obtaining search warrants in every situation, however, is not practical. The reality of police work is that most searches occur without a warrant. This chapter examines in detail two situations in which obtaining a search warrant is not practical: search incident to a lawful arrest and hot pursuit. In both of these situations, officers may search without a warrant without violating the Fourth Amendment.

7.2 Search Incident to Arrest

Search incident to a **lawful arrest** is one of the exceptions to the warrant requirement upheld by the Supreme Court. The Court has identified three reasons why these types of searches are lawful. First, they protect officers from suspects who may be able to access weapons they may use to injure or kill the officer while being transported. Next, they help prevent arrested persons from being able to escape. Finally, they preserve evidence that suspects might destroy or damage if officers had to leave to obtain a search warrant. As a further consideration, the arrested person's privacy rights have already been significantly reduced by the arrest; thus, a search involves only minimally greater intrusion, and the benefits of the search outweigh the additional intrusion into the privacy rights of the arrested person.

Valid searches incident to lawful arrests require two elements to be lawful: the arrest must be valid from the start, and the search must be limited to the person and the **area within his or her immediate control**. The Supreme Court discussed the purposes and the scope of this practice in *Chimel v. California*, 395 U.S. 752 (1969). In that case, the Court determined that the search of the area within an arrestee's immediate control is permissible.

Chimel v. California, 395 U.S. 752 (1969)

Facts Chimel was suspected of having robbed a coin shop. Armed with an arrest warrant (but without a search warrant), police officers went to Chimel's house and were admitted by his wife. Chimel was not at home, so the officers waited for him inside the home. He was immediately arrested when he arrived. The police asked Chimel if they could "look around." Chimel denied the request, but the officers searched the entire house anyway and discovered some stolen coins. At the trial, the coins were introduced as evidence over Chimel's objection. Chimel was convicted of robbery.

Issue In the course of making a lawful arrest, may officers search the immediate area where the person was arrested without a search warrant? YES

Supreme Court Decision After making an arrest, the police may search the area within the person's immediate control. The purpose of such a search is to discover and remove weapons and to prevent the destruction of evidence.

Reason "When an arrest is made, it is reasonable for the arresting officer to search the person arrested in order to remove any weapons that the latter might seek to use in order to resist arrest or effect his escape. Otherwise, the officer's safety might well be endangered, and the arrest itself frustrated. In addition, it is entirely reasonable for the arresting officer to search for and seize any evidence on the arrestee's person in order to prevent its concealment or destruction. And the area into which an arrestee might reach in order to grab a weapon or evidentiary items must, of course, be governed by a like rule.... There is ample justification, therefore, for a search of the arrestee's person and the area within his immediate control."

Case Significance Chimel states that the police may search the area in the arrestee's immediate control when making a valid arrest, whether the arrest takes place with or without a warrant. That area of immediate control is defined by the Court as "the area from within which he might gain possession of a weapon or destructible evidence." Thus, police may search the area around the arrestee without a warrant after an arrest, but the extent of the search is limited to the area of the arrestee's immediate control.

In *Chimel,* the Court authorized the search of the area within a person's immediate control after an arrest. The problem, however, is that the opinion does not clearly indicate what is meant by the "area of immediate control." Interpretation of this holding has determined that the **wingspan** of the individual is the searchable area; however, how far the wingspan extends has not been addressed, other than to suggest that any area from which the arrested person may obtain weapons or destroy evidence is covered. Thus, for example, if a person is arrested in the living room, a search of the living room area is most likely acceptable, but that search could not extend to the attic or basement.

The Court in *Chimel* addressed the area around the arrestee that could be searched but did not address the physical body of the arrestee. The prevailing rule about searching the arrested person had been that officers could conduct a pat down search for officer safety. Officers were not previously authorized to retrieve anything from the arrested person unless they believed the item to be a weapon. In *United States v. Robinson,* 414 U.S. 218 (1973), the Court determined that a full body search is valid without a search warrant when a custodial arrest is made.

United States v. Robinson, 414 U.S. 218 (1973))

Facts Based on a previous investigation, a police officer stopped Robinson on the suspicion that he was operating a motor vehicle after his license had been revoked. The officer made a full custodial arrest of Robinson based on probable cause, and incident to the arrest the officer searched Robinson's person. He felt an unrecognizable object in Robinson's left breast pocket, but admitted in court that he knew it was not a weapon. The officer removed the object, which turned out to be a "crumpled up cigarette package" that contained 14 gelatin capsules of heroin. The capsules were admitted as evidence in Robinson's trial, and he was convicted of possession of heroin.

Issue Is it constitutional for a police officer to search (as opposed to merely frisking) a person's body after a lawful custodial arrest even though the officer does not fear for his or her personal safety or believe that evidence will be destroyed? YES

Supreme Court Decision A full search of the person's body is valid in any situation in which a full-custody arrest occurs. There is no requirement that officers fear for their safety or believe that they will find evidence of a crime before the body search can be made.

Reason "A custodial arrest of a suspect based on probable cause is a reasonable intrusion under the Fourth Amendment; that intrusion being lawful, a search incident to the arrest requires no additional justification. The lawful arrest establishes the authority to search, and we hold that in the case of a lawful custodial arrest a full search of the person is not only an exception to the warrant requirement of the Fourth Amendment, but is also a 'reasonable' search under that Amendment."

Case Significance *Robinson* allows the search of a person's body after a lawful arrest. Prior to *Robinson*, courts allowed a full-body search (as opposed to a frisk) only if the officer feared for his or her personal safety. This case changed that rule to allow a full search of the person in any custodial arrest.

The *Robinson* holding extended the scope of the search incident to a lawful arrest by allowing officers to conduct full body searches in incidents where they were not in fear of their safety and had no additional probable cause to believe that the offender was armed. The case differs from *Chimel* in that the *Chimel* case deals with the "area within the arrestee's immediate control," whereas Robinson specifically refers to the search of the arrestee's body. The suspect's body is obviously within the area of immediate control, but the authority to search it was not necessarily included in *Chimel* because a person's body enjoys greater protection from governmental intrusion than the area around the person.

In a similar case, police officers are authorized to seize the clothing and effects of the arrested person either at the scene of the arrest, or at some time later. In *United States v. Edwards*, 415 U.S. 800 (1974), the Court determined that, after a lawful arrest and detention, any search conducted at the place of detention that would have been lawful at the time of the arrest may be conducted without a warrant, even though a substantial period of time had elapsed between the arrest and the search. In that case, Edwards was arrested shortly after 11:00 p.m. for attempting to break into a post office. He was taken to jail and charged. Subsequent investigation at the scene of the crime revealed that the attempted entry was made through a wooden window that had been forced open with a pry bar, leaving paint chips on the window sill. Because they believed that the paint chips might be found on Edwards clothing, the next morning officers gave Edwards a different set of clothes, asked him to change, and examined the clothes he had on for paint chips. Paint chips were found on his clothes and they were held as evidence. Edwards argued that officers needed a warrant to take his clothing. The Court disagreed. They held that after being lawfully arrested and placed in custody, any search conducted at the place of detention that would have been lawful at the time of the arrest may be conducted without a warrant, even though a substantial period of time may have elapsed between the arrest and the search. A reasonable delay in completing the search does not change the fact that Edwards was no more imposed upon the next day than he would have been at the time and place of the arrest. Based on this case, a search incident to an arrest does not have to take place immediately after the arrest as long as the arrest is lawful. The key is whether the arrest was valid. If the arrest was valid and the suspect is in custody, the search may take place at a later time and the evidence will be admissible in court.

Searches incident to lawful arrests can also involve automobile searches once the driver has been arrested. This information is covered in Chapter 5 of this book. The leading case in that area is *New York v. Belton*, 453 U.S. 454 (1981), in which the Court determined that the police may search the passenger compartment of a car if it is incident to a lawful arrest. Furthermore, in *Brendlin v. California*, 551 U.S. 1 (2007), the Court ruled that all of the occupants of a vehicle are seized within the meaning of the Fourth Amendment during a valid traffic stop.

In a somewhat different case, the question arose as to whether the police can conduct a protective sweep of a home after a valid arrest. In this circumstance, officers are not searching for a particular thing but are mainly checking to make sure that no additional suspects are present in the home that would create a danger to officers or cause evidence to be destroyed. In *Maryland v. Buie*, 494 U.S. 325 (1990), the Court determined that the protective sweep was valid under certain circumstances.

Maryland v. Buie, 494 U.S. 325 (1990)

Facts After surveillance, six or seven police officers obtained and executed arrest warrants for Buie and an accomplice in connection with an armed robbery. Upon reaching Buie's house, the officers "fanned out through the first and second floors." One of the officers observed the basement so that no one would surprise the officers.

This officer shouted into the basement and ordered anyone there to come out. A voice asked who was there. The officer ordered the person to come out three more times before Buie emerged from the basement. After placing Buie under arrest, another officer entered the basement to see whether there was anyone else down there. Once in the basement, the officer noticed in plain view a red running suit similar to the one worn by one of the suspects in the robbery. The running suit was admitted as evidence at Buie's trial over his objection, and he was convicted of robbery with a deadly weapon and using a handgun in the commission of a felony.

Issue May officers conduct a warrantless protective sweep of the area in which a suspect is arrested in order to determine whether another person might be there who would be a danger to the officers? YES

Supreme Court Decision "The Fourth Amendment permits a properly limited protective sweep in conjunction with an in-home arrest when the searching officer possesses a reasonable belief based on specific and articulable facts that the area to be swept harbors an individual posing a danger to those on the arrest scene."

Reason "We. . .hold that as an incident to the arrest the officers could, as a precautionary matter and without probable cause or reasonable suspicion, look in closets and other spaces immediately adjoining the place of arrest from which an attack could be immediately launched. Beyond that, however, we hold that there must be articulable facts which, taken together with the rational inferences from those facts, would warrant a reasonably prudent officer in believing that the area to be swept harbors an individual posing a danger to those on the arrest scene.. . . We should emphasize that such a protective sweep, aimed at protecting the arresting officers, if justified by the circumstances, is nevertheless not a full search of the premises, but may extend only to cursory inspection of those spaces where a person may be found. The sweep lasts no longer than is necessary to dispel the reasonable suspicion of danger and in any event no longer than it takes to complete the arrest and depart the premises."

Case Significance This case is significant because it authorizes the practice in some police departments of conducting a "protective sweep" during an arrest. It is important for police officers to note, however, that Buie does not give the police unlimited authority when making an arrest to search the whole house. The protective sweep allowed by Buie is limited in scope, and the following limitations must be observed: "There must be articulable facts which. . .would warrant a reasonably prudent officer in believing that the area to be swept harbors an individual posing a danger. Such a protective sweep is not a full search of the premises, but may extend only to a cursory inspection of the spaces where a person may be found. The sweep lasts no longer than is necessary to dispel the reasonable suspicion of danger and in any event no longer than it takes to complete the arrest and depart the premises." The police must be careful to observe these limitations; otherwise, the search becomes invalid.

The *Buie* decision does not broaden the holding from *Chimel*. The Court maintains that a full search can only extend to the person and the area within his or her immediate control. The sweep allowed in *Buie* is only for the protection of officer safety. The Court itself distinguished *Chimel* from *Buie* as follows:

1. *Chimel* was concerned with a full-blown, top-to-bottom search of an entire house for evidence of the crime for which the arrest was made, not the more limited intrusion contemplated by a protective sweep.

2. The justification for the search incident to arrest in *Chimel* was the threat posed by the arrestee, not the safety threat posed by the house or more properly by unseen third parties in the house.

The concept of a protective sweep for officer safety also extends to the occupants of a vehicle. In *Maryland v. Wilson*, 519 U.S. 408 (1997), the Court ruled that all occupants of a car may be ordered out of the vehicle after a valid traffic stop. The rationale for the holding was that officer safety was paramount in traffic stops and all of the occupants in a car, not just the driver, could cause harm to the officer. Thus, similar to the concept of a protective sweep, officers may order occupants out of the car.

Based on the Court's ruling in the three cases outlined in this section, when officers have conducted a valid arrest, they are authorized to conduct a full search of the body of the person, a full search of the area within the immediate control of the person, and a limited protective sweep for the officer's safety. Whether the arrest occurs in a home or in an automobile, the concepts are applied the same.

7.3 Hot Pursuit

Another area in which warrantless searches are allowed is that of **hot pursuit**. Hot pursuit is an emergency situation in which some sort of a chase is involved, usually officers chasing a fleeing suspect. When officers have probable cause to arrest a suspect, and they follow the suspect into a house without getting a warrant, that entry and subsequent arrest are valid.[a] Although not much doubt exists over the officer's ability to enter into the home without a warrant to apprehend the fleeing felon, some concern arises as to how extensive the search can be once inside the home. The Court has determined that a search based on hot pursuit can only be as extensive as necessary to prevent the suspect from escaping or resisting arrest. Consider *Warden v. Hayden*, 387 U.S. 294 (1988).

Based on the *Warden* holding, if officers are immediately on the heels of a fleeing felon who darts into a home, they are not required to take a break from the pursuit to get a warrant. Furthermore, they are authorized to search any area of the property where the person may be located and where weapons may be kept. The basic premise for the exigency in this case is

[a] *United States v. Santana*, 427 U.S. 38 (1976).

Warden v. Hayden, 387 U.S. 294 (1967)

Facts Police arrived at the home of an armed robbery suspect less than five minutes after he reportedly had dashed into the premises after fleeing the scene of the hold-up. Several officers made a warrantless entry into the home after the suspect's wife answered their knock on the door. The officers fanned throughout the house in search of the robber. The defendant was found feigning sleep in an upstairs bedroom. One of the officers, attracted by the sound of running water in the bathroom, discovered a shotgun and a pistol in the flush tank of the commode. Ammunition for the guns was found under the bed's mattress and in a bureau drawer. Meanwhile, another officer, searching the basement for either a man or the money from the robbery, found a jacket and pair of pants in the washing machine that fit the description of those worn by the robber. Hayden was arrested when it was determined that he was the only man in the house. All items of evidence were admitted at the trial. Hayden was convicted of armed robbery.

Issues

1. Was the search without a warrant valid? YES
2. Are items considered **mere evidence** (the pistol, shotgun, and clothes), as distinguished from contraband and instrumentalities of crimes, seizable by the police for use as evidence? YES

Supreme Court Decisions

1. The warrantless seizure in this case was valid because of probable cause and because officers were in hot pursuit of a fleeing felon.
2. There is no difference between "mere evidence" and contraband or instrumentalities of a crime under the provisions of the Fourth Amendment. "Mere evidence" may be searched for, seized, and admitted in court as evidence.

Reason The police acted reasonably when they entered the house and began to search for a person matching the description of an armed robber who was reported to have entered the premises less than five minutes before they arrived. The Fourth Amendment does not require police officers to delay in the course of an investigation if to do so would gravely endanger their lives or the lives of others. "Speed here was essential, and only a thorough search of the house for persons and weapons could have insured that Hayden was the only man present and that the police had control of all weapons which could be used against them or to affect an escape.. . .It is argued that, while the weapons, ammunition, and cap may have been seized in the course of a search for weapons, the officer who seized the clothing was searching neither for the suspect nor the weapons when he looked into the washing machine." However, weapons and ammunition could have been found in the washing machine. The officer knew the suspect had been armed, but he did not know that some ammunition had already been found at the time he opened the machine. The search was valid. The Court also discarded the "mere evidence" rule in this case, holding that nothing in the Fourth Amendment required a distinction between instrumentalities and fruits from other evidence.

Case Significance This case establishes that a warrant is not needed if there are probable cause and "exigent" (emergency) circumstances. Hot pursuit is an exigent circumstance that justifies a warrantless search and seizure. The Court also settled the issue of whether "mere evidence" (as opposed to contraband or illegal items) can be seized by the police. Under this ruling, any evidence, not just contraband, that can help prove the case against the defendant can be seized by the police when they make a warrantless entry based on hot pursuit.

to protect the safety of the officers and to protect the public from the offender.

The concept of hot pursuit involves some form of chase of a suspect. In *United States v. Santana*, 427 U.S. 38 (1976), the Court determined that the "chase" could be very limited yet still be considered a hot pursuit. In that case, the police responded to a call. When they pulled up, the defendant was standing in her doorway but she retreated into the home when police emerged from their vehicle and shouted "Police!" An officer followed the defendant into her home and seized her in the vestibule area. Two packets of heroin fell from the defendant's person to the floor during this action. The court held the officer's warrantless entry into the home to be reasonable under the circumstances.

The Court held that the act of retreating into the home could not stop officers from making an otherwise lawful arrest. The Court determined that the principles of *Warden v. Hayden* governed this case. The need to act quickly was even greater than in the case of *Warden* and the intrusion was much less. Instead of fanning out throughout the home, police apprehended the suspect in the vestibule area. They did not continue to search throughout her house. The argument in the case revolved around whether or not hot pursuit was a valid justification when the defendant only retreated from her doorway into her home. The Court determined, however, that although hot pursuit involves some sort of chase, it need not be an extended chase around the neighborhood or through the streets. The fact that the pursuit in this case ended almost as soon as it began did not render it any less a hot pursuit sufficient to justify the warrantless entry into Santana's house. Once Santana saw the police, there was likewise a realistic expectation that any delay would result in destruction of evidence. Once she had been arrested, the search incident to that arrest and that produced the drugs and money was clearly justified.

These cases taken together indicate that police are justified in entering a home to apprehend a fleeing felon if they are already involved in some sort of pursuit of the person prior to that person entering the home. The chase need not be extended, nor must the chase be contemporaneous with the entry into the home. The threshold issues are whether evidence will be destroyed and whether the fleeing felon will escape if officers do not continue the pursuit. The extent to which they can search after entering the home depends on the circumstances of each case. Officers are authorized to search any area to which they believe probable cause extends, including where the fleeing felon may be hiding or where the fleeing felon may have stashed the proceeds of the crime.

7.4 Summary

This chapter identifies two specific exceptions to the search warrant requirement: search incident to a lawful arrest and hot pursuit. In both of these instances, officers must act quickly to keep the suspect from escaping, to secure the premises to protect officer safety, and to preserve evidence. In the first situation, search incident to a lawful arrest requires that the arrest be valid for the ensuing search to be valid. Once the valid arrest is made (either with a warrant or probable cause), officers are authorized to search the body of the arrested person and the area within his or her immediate control. To be able to conduct a body search, officers are not required to fear for their lives or believe that the suspect is armed. Likewise, they are not required to articulate additional probable cause for the search of the immediate surroundings to be valid.

In addition to searches of the person and the area within his or her immediate control, officers may conduct a protective sweep of the premises to make certain that no additional people are hiding who could cause harm or destroy evidence. These types of sweeps are valid only when circumstances indicate they are necessary. Further, they must be limited to the equivalent of a pat-down search, only for officer safety, and may not be used as general fishing expeditions to search for evidence that would not be obtainable through other means.

Finally, hot pursuit cases allow officers to enter into homes to apprehend fleeing felons when they would otherwise need to secure a warrant to do so. In these cases, some sort of chase has already begun prior to the suspect darting into a home. The chase need not be long and need not involve the use of public streets. Once officers begin pursuing a suspect, however, they are authorized to continue that pursuit until the suspect is apprehended, even if they have to enter into a home to do so.

Further Reading

Brendlin v. California, 551 U.S. 1 (2007).
Chimel v. California, 395 U.S. 752 (1969).

Maryland v. Buie, 494 U.S. 325 (1990).
Maryland v. Wilson, 519 U.S. 408 (1997).
New York v. Belton, 453 U.S. 454 (1981).
United States v. Edwards, 415 U.S. 800 (1974).
United States v. Robinson, 414 U.S. 218 (1973).
United States v. Santana, 427 U.S. 38 (1976).
Warden v. Hayden, 387 U.S. 294 (1967).

8

AIRPORT, BORDER, AND OTHER EXIGENCIES

CHAPTER OUTLINE

KEY TERMS

Body scans	National security
Destruction of evidence	Non-routine searches
Exigent circumstances	Regulated businesses
Functional equivalent of the border	Routine searches and inspections
Magnetometers	

LEARNING OBJECTIVES

- Understand the meaning of exigent circumstances.
- Understand the necessity for searches at the airport.
- Understand the necessity for searches at the borders.
- Identify the types of emergency circumstances that do not require a search warrant.

8.1 Introduction

Searches of any sort involve a certain amount of invasion of personal space of the person being searched. The laws of criminal procedure attempt to balance the need for public safety against the expectation of privacy enjoyed by citizens. Only when public safety concerns are greater and the invasion of privacy minimal are courts willing to allow searches to proceed without a search warrant. These searches are often conducted without probable cause or reasonable suspicion, but instead are random in nature and apply equally to all types of people who come to a particular place. Two specific types of searches that benefit public safety are airports and borders. These two types of searches will be addressed in this chapter. After discussing those, other types of exigencies will be identified and addressed.

8.2 Airport Searches

Searches of personal belongings at an airport are an exception to the search warrant requirement of the Fourth Amendment. Since a series of airline hijackings and terrorist bombings in the 1970 s, travelers have had to pass through detectors before they can board airplanes. Passengers also must pass their luggage through x-ray machines for examination. Additionally, sometimes inspectors open and look through baggage. If they discover suspicious items, they investigate further. Applying the balancing test of the Fourth Amendment reasonableness, courts have held that airport searches are reasonable even without warrants or probable cause. According to the court, airport searches serve an extremely important special need—maintaining the security and safety of air travelers. These special needs clearly outweigh the minimal invasion of privacy caused by having passengers pass through metal detectors and allowing their luggage to be observed by x-ray. Further, these invasions apply equally to all passengers, who are notified in advance that they are subject to them; thus, passengers are free not to board the airplane if they do not want to subject their person and luggage to these intrusions. Alternative avenues of travel are available (LaFave and Isreal, 1984).

In the earlier cases involving searches at airports, authorities were mostly concerned with hijackers on airlines. Regulations that were put into place to prevent hijacking largely required passengers who were subjected to screening to meet some sort of hijacker profile. In *United States v. Epperson*, 454 F.2d 769 (4th Cir. 1972), cert. denied, 406 U.S. 947 (1972), however, the Fourth Circuit allowed the search of an airline passenger to be carried out solely on the basis of the activation of a **magnetometer**, without any regard to whether the passenger met the criteria of the hijacker profile. In so holding, the court noted that,

"The danger is so well known, the governmental interest so overwhelming, and the invasion of privacy so minimal, that the warrant requirement is excused by exigent national circumstances." The court also found that the scope of the search was reasonably related to its purpose, and "fully justified the minimal invasion of personal privacy by [the] magnetometer. . .[and] the person scrutinized is not even aware of the examination." It was clear to the court "that to innocent passengers the use of a magnetometer to detect metal on those boarding an aircraft is not a resented intrusion on privacy, but, instead, a welcome reassurance of safety. Such a search is more than reasonable; it is a compelling necessity to protect essential air commerce and the lives of passengers."

In *United States v. Bell,* 464F.2d 667 (2nd Cir. 1972), cert. denied, 409 U.S. 991 (1972), the Second Circuit expanded the scope of the search allowed at airports beyond weapons that might be used against the officer personally. In that case, Bell not only met the hijacker profile and activated a magnetometer but also had no identification and admitted to the security official that he was out on bail for attempted murder and narcotics charges. In upholding the search, the court noted there is an "apprehension of the officer for the safety of others as well as himself." A more thorough search of Bell was allowed because the court recognized that, "[T]he weapon of the skyjacker is not limited to the conventional weaponry of the bank robber or of the burglar. His arsenal may well include explosives."

In *United States v. Edward,* 498F.2d 496 (2nd Cir. 1974), a Deputy U.S. Marshal searched a woman's carry-on luggage after she set off the magnetometer. The Marshal found packages inside a pair of slacks as well as in the pockets of the bag, ultimately finding over 1600 envelopes that were found to contain heroin. In the appeal of the search, the circuit court ruled that the search was lawful and did not violate the Fourth Amendment because it was performed to prevent further criminal laws from being broken and to protect human life that may be at risk, and no abuse of power was evident.

The issue involved in the *Edwards* case, was that of whether carry-on luggage could be searched without probable cause. The Second Circuit allowed such searches because of the minimal invasion of privacy. Passengers could choose to check their luggage and not bring it on to the plane. To require all carry-on luggage to be searched did not put passengers in a position of choosing between not flying and not being searched; instead, they could choose not to have their luggage on the plane with them.

United States v. Edwards, 498 F.2d 496 (2nd Circuit, 1974)

Facts Defendant Cynthia Edwards arrived at La Guardia Airport in New York City on the evening of August 23, 1972, to take an Eastern Air Lines shuttle flight to Boston. The relevant regulations of the Federal Aviation Administration (FAA) then in effect with respect to non-reservation flights such as the shuttle required that: (A) each certificate holder shall prevent the carriage aboard its aircraft of baggage on or about the person of passengers unless that baggage has been examined by a responsible representative of the certificate holder or a law enforcement officer, and (B) the certificate holder shall require each passenger to clear through a metal detector without indication of unaccounted for metal on his person prior to boarding. Near the entrance to the boarding gate were two large printed signs, plainly warning, among other things, "PASSENGERS AND BAGGAGE SUBJECT TO SEARCH." When an Eastern employee announced over a loudspeaker that the flight could be boarded, he also announced that all carry-on luggage would be searched. At this time, Edwards was in the line of boarding passengers, carrying a pocketbook and what she described as a "beach bag." When she activated the magnetometer, the Deputy U.S. Marshal examined the beach bag and found that it contained a pair of slacks wrapped around a package. Upon examination, the Marshal found that the package contained a large number of glassine envelopes, each containing a white powder. He later found other such envelopes in three pockets in the beach bag, bringing the total to 1664. Edwards testified that she knew that there were about 1600 envelopes in the bag and that the white powder was heroin. The alleged illegality of the search is thus the sole ground of the appeal.

Issue Was the warrantless search of the carryon bag at the airport a violation of the Fourth Amendment? NO

Supreme Court Decision

Reason Signs and announcements clearly posted gave citizens fair warning that they were going to be searched pursuant to airport policy. Passengers had ample opportunity to turn back before entering the search area. To continue beyond that point could be considered implied consent on the part of the passenger to the search that was part of routine practice at the airport. Further, the reasonableness of a warrantless search depends on balancing the need for a search against the offensiveness of the intrusion. In this instance, the search was conducted pursuant to the FAA's anti-hijacking program designed to prevent dangers from terrorists, ordinary criminals, or the demented. "The search of carry-on baggage, applied to everyone, did not involve any stigma. More than a million Americans subject themselves to it daily; all but a handful do this cheerfully, even eagerly, knowing it is essential for their protection. To brand such a search as unreasonable would go beyond any fair interpretation of the Fourth Amendment. If experience should demonstrate that the Government is abusing its authority and is using the airport search not for the purpose intended but as a general means for enforcing the criminal laws," such could be examined separately. "But unless and until there should be evidence of abuse, we hold to the traditional rule that if the search is proper," it does not matter that the object found was one other than that for which they were originally searching.

Case Significance This case affirmed the necessity of airport authority to be able to search passengers without probable cause or individualized suspicion. The need for public safety outweighs the minimal intrusion into personal privacy. Passengers are aware that they will be searched when they go through the boarding point. They have the ability to turn back. As long as airport authorities conduct searches pursuant to their stated policy, any contraband retrieved is permissible evidence.

In *United States v. Davis*, 482F.2d 893 (9th Cir. 1973), a routine security check revealed that the defendant was attempting to board an airplane with a loaded gun. The Ninth Circuit held that searches conducted in furtherance of a regulatory administrative purpose are permissible under the Fourth Amendment, despite the lack of either a warrant or probable cause. The court held that administrative searches stem from the government's need to oversee highly regulated activities. When deciding whether a search is administrative in nature, the court must make a dual determination: (1) whether the search serves a narrow but compelling administrative objective, and (2) whether the intrusion is as "limited as is consistent with satisfaction of the administrative need that justifies it." In *Davis*, the court balanced the competing interests of the government's prevention of airline hijacking and a passenger's expectation of privacy and found that the scales tipped in favor of the government. "The need to prevent airline hijacking is unquestionably grave and urgent. The potential damage to person and property from such acts is enormous." Because the security measures were not used to secure evidence in a criminal investigation, but rather as a regulatory means to thwart the threat of airplane hijackings, the search was characterized as administrative. "The essential purpose of the scheme is not to detect weapons or explosives or to apprehend those who carry them, but to deter persons carrying such material from seeking to board at all." Once the administrative search is determined to be an exception to the warrant requirement, the constitutionality of the search will be upheld if it meets the Fourth Amendment's standard of reasonableness. In *Davis*, the court concluded that a "pre-boarding screening of all passengers and carry-on articles sufficient in scope to detect the presence of weapons or explosives is reasonably necessary to meet the need" of preventing airline hijacking. A warrant is not required and would only "frustrate the governmental purpose behind the search." Because the administrative purpose was to prevent people with weapons from boarding the aircraft, the option of not flying was crucial in upholding the search in the *Davis* case. "We have held that, as a matter of constitutional law, a prospective passenger has a choice: he may submit to a search of his person and immediate possessions as a condition to being boarding; or he may turn around and leave."

Since the terrorist attacks on the United States on September 11, 2001, airport searches have become more frequent and more invasive, but so has the sense of urgency about security.

No court challenge to these security changes has yet made it to the Supreme Court. But, should a court challenge arise, it is not likely the balance will be struck against the current practice. If passengers are singled out for more frequent and more invasive measures because of their appearance, such as looking like they are of Middle Eastern descent, that may be an entirely different matter.

More recent technology requires that all persons who board commercial airplanes submit to **body scans**. The latest body scanners provide images in graphic anatomical detail that are viewed by a Transportation Security Administration (TSA) employee. Some frequent air travelers are concerned about the health risks associated with undergoing routine body scans. Those that employ these screening devices argue that they are safe and are the least invasive means to get a total picture of the person about to fly. If a person is unable or unwilling to submit to the full body scanners, that person must submit to pat-down frisking similar to that performed by law enforcement agents on suspected criminals, before being allowed to board an aircraft. Many persons, including Secretary of State Hillary Clinton, have expressed objections to the pat-down searches.

Interestingly, however, citizens have not posed major objections to the scanners. While some have objected, for the most part travelers have accepted this new process as part of the practice of flying. TSA personnel are not required to have a reason to scan or frisk travelers other than the fact that a person is traveling by commercial airliner. Persons traveling from private airports are not required to be scanned, frisked, or otherwise detained for surveillance and search before they board an aircraft.

Under other circumstances, such as if every person were required to be searched to be allowed on a public sidewalk, without any objective indication that the people posed a danger to others such action would be associated with a "police state." If freedom and personal dignity mean anything, people have the right to be left alone by others (including the government) unless there is a specific reason to interfere with that right. In the case of flying on airplanes, however, people have tried to carry dangerous objects onto airplanes, including box cutters in their carry-on bags and explosives in their shoes and underwear. As a result, the public has determined that the interest of public safety outweighs concerns about intrusive government action.

8.3 Border Searches

The border exception to the Fourth Amendment's warrant requirement has long been established in American jurisprudence. Since the founding of the United States, Congress "has granted the Executive [branch] plenary authority to conduct **routine searches and seizures** at the border, without probable cause or a warrant, in order to regulate the collection of duties and to prevent the introduction of contraband into this country."[a] This extension of police power is derived from the inherent authority of the national government to defend itself from outside threats and harmful influences, including the "power to prohibit the export of its currency, national treasures, and other assets"[b] and extends to all routine searches at the nation's borders, regardless of whether persons or property are entering or exiting from the country. Consistent with Congress' sovereign power to protect the nation by stopping and examining individuals who are trying to enter the country, the Fourth Amendment's standard of reasonableness is different at the international border than once someone or something is inside the country. Searches occurring at an international border are justified simply because they occur at the border. Those entering the country have no reasonable expectation of privacy, and routine searches of their persons and belongings are justified without the need for probable cause, reasonable suspicion, or a warrant. Searches at locations considered the "functional equivalent" of an international border are also included within the exception; for example, a nonstop international flight arriving in Chicago or St. Louis would be considered an entry at the border, even though the flight has landed well within the boundaries of the United States. As a result, routine searches conducted upon the arrival of an international flight are considered an exception to the Fourth Amendment's warrant requirement.

Although border searches are considered an exception to the search warrant requirement, to fall under the exception the searches must be routine. "Routine border inspections are those that do not pose a serious invasion of privacy and that do not embarrass or offend the average traveler."[c] Routine searches occur at the border and are minimally invasive. A routine search

[a] *United States v. Montoya de Hernandez*, 473 U.S. 531, 537 (1985).
[b] *United States v. Oriakhi*, 57 F.3d 1290, 1297 (4th Cir. 1995).
[c] *United States v. Johnson*, 991 F.2d 1287, 1291 (7th Cir. 1993).

consists of checking documents, emptying pockets, and checking vehicles and cargo.

Non-routine searches are more intrusive, with a varying style of search, and occur only with reasonable suspicion to perform such search. A non-routine search is more invasive in all forms of the search, from intensively checking everything in the vehicle, a full body search, and other means of checking anything crossing the border. Strip, body cavity, and other means such as x-ray can be used in the process of preventing unlawful items from coming into the country so long as reasonable suspicion is involved. Furthermore, if the circumstances surrounding the search give rise to reasonable suspicion, officials can hold individuals as well as property for a longer period of time.

United States v. Montoya de Hernandez, 473 U.S. 531 (1985)

Facts Respondent traveled from Colombia to the Los Angeles airport and was detained at the airport for questioning. The customs officers had discovered that respondent had made multiple trips from Colombia to either Miami or Los Angeles in recent months. In addition, upon questioning, the officers learned that respondent had no friends or family in the country and had $5000 cash. Respondent stated that she came to Los Angeles to purchase merchandise for her husband's store, but she was unable to name any vendors. Female officers searched respondent and felt hardness around her abdominal area, which made them believe she was transporting narcotics. Respondent was detained for 16 hours before officers sought a court order. During those 16 hours, she was given the option of returning to Colombia on the next available flight, agreeing to an x-ray, or remaining in detention until she produced a monitored bowel movement. She chose the first option, but the officials were unable to place her on the next flight, and she refused to use the toilet facilities. Respondent refused to x-ray and stated that she was pregnant. She also refused to eat or drink. The officers obtained a court order to test whether respondent was pregnant and for an x-ray. Upon testing, officers learned that respondent was not pregnant and, in addition, discovered balloons of cocaine in her abdomen. During the body cavity search 88 balloons containing 528 grams worth of pure Colombian cocaine were found inside of her rectum.

Issue Can custom officers detain a person at the border upon suspicion that the person is transporting narcotics? YES

Supreme Court Decision The Court reasoned that "the Fourth Amendment's balance of reasonableness is qualitatively different at the international border than in the interior. Routine searches of the persons and effects of entrants are not subject to any requirement of reasonable suspicion, probable cause, or warrant." Thus, the Court held that "the detention of a traveler at the border, beyond the scope of a routine customs search and inspection, is justified at its inception if customs agents, considering all the facts surrounding the traveler and her trip, reasonably suspect that the traveler is smuggling contraband in her alimentary canal." The Court stated that the facts and their rational inferences, known to customs inspectors in this case, clearly supported a reasonable suspicion that respondent was an alimentary canal smuggler.

Reason

Case Significance Based on this case, a routine border search can give rise to reasonable suspicion or probable cause for a more invasive detention and search. The threshold is what border agents believe based on all of the facts surrounding the incident. If these facts give rise to reasonable suspicion, detainment and search beyond a routine search may be justified.

Based on the protection of the borders and the need to discover narcotics and other illegal items entering the country, courts have ruled that it is acceptable to hold an individual for a reasonable amount of time, around 48 hours, before getting a court order for continued detainment or search. Officers are generally not allowed to perform invasive searches, such as body cavity searches or x-rays, without the court order, but no violation of rights occurs from detaining the individual and allowing nature to take its course.

If the search does not involve the length of time for a person to be detained, it might involve the scope of the allowable search. For example, the government's authority to conduct suspicionless inspections at the border has been held to include the authority to remove, disassemble, and reassemble a vehicle's fuel tank.

United States v. Flores-Montano, 541 U.S. 149 (2004)

Facts Flores-Montano attempted to enter the United States at a border crossing. A customs inspector examined the vehicle and asked Flores-Montano to leave the vehicle for secondary inspection. At the secondary station, another customs inspector tapped on the gas tank and noted that it sounded solid. The inspector then asked a mechanic to help remove the gas tank. The mechanic arrived approximately 20 minutes later. The mechanic removed the gas tank, and then the inspector hammered off the putty used to seal the top of the gas tank. When the inspector opened an access plate underneath the putty, he found 37 kilograms of marijuana. Flores-Montano sought suppression of the evidence, saying the inspectors did not have reasonable suspicion that he was engaged in criminal activity, and reasonable suspicion is required to remove a gas tank.

Issue Must officers have reasonable suspicion of criminal activity to remove the gas tank of a vehicle at an international border crossing? NO

Supreme Court Decision "The Government's authority to conduct suspicionless inspections at the border includes the authority to remove, disassemble, and reassemble a vehicle's fuel tank."

Reason "The Government's interest in preventing the entry of unwanted persons and effects is at its zenith at the international border. Time and again, we have stated that 'searches made at the border, pursuant to the longstanding right of the sovereign to protect itself by stopping and examining persons and property crossing into this country, are reasonable simply by virtue of the fact that they occur at the border.' Congress, since the beginning of our Government, 'has granted the executive plenary authority to conduct routine searches and seizures at the border, without probable cause or a warrant, in order to regulate the collection of duties and to prevent the introduction of contraband into this country.'. . .That interest in protecting the borders is illustrated in this case by the evidence that smugglers frequently attempt to penetrate our borders with contraband secreted in their automobiles' fuel tanks. Over the past 5-1/2 fiscal years, there have been 18,788 vehicle drug seizures at the southern California ports of entry. Of those 18,788, gas tank drug seizures have accounted for 4,619 of the vehicle drug seizures, or approximately 25%."

Case Significance This case involves one type of search—border searches. The rule here, therefore, does not apply to searches and seizures other than border searches. Border searches may be conducted without probable cause or reasonable suspicion because they are a special kind of search done in a different kind of place—a border. The Court noted in this case that "on many occasions, we have noted that the expectation of privacy is less at the border than it is in the interior," and "we have long recognized that automobiles seeking entry into this country may be searched." Flores-Montano argued that reasonable suspicion (a lower degree of certainty than probable cause) was required for the type of search conducted by the officers, claiming that: (1) he "has a privacy interest in his fuel tank, and that the suspicionless disassembly of his tank is an invasion of his privacy," and (2) because the Fourth Amendment "protects property as well as privacy. . .that the disassembly and reassembly of his gas tank was a significant deprivation of his property interest because it could damage the vehicle." Despite the intrusiveness of the search, the Court rejected both arguments, saying Flores-Montano "cites not a single accident involving the vehicle or motorist in the many thousands of gas tank disassemblies that have occurred at the border." The Court concluded that, "While it may be true that some searches of property are so destructive as to require a different result, this is not one of them."

Although searches in airports and at borders have been upheld, cases have also addressed searches that occur in locations that are close to borders. In *Almeida-Sanchez v. United States*, a roving patrol conducted a vehicle search about 26 miles from the border of Mexico, on a highway that did not actually go to the border. The respondent was a Mexican citizen who held a work permit for the United States and traveled frequently. The officer found marijuana and arrested him. Almeida-Sanchez claimed that the search was unlawful because he did not consent to the search, and he was too far from the border for the search to be covered under the border search exception. The Court agreed.

Based on the above cases, border searches come in different shapes and sizes. Some types of searches, those in which a

Almeida-Sanchez v. United States, 413 U.S. 266 (1973)

Facts The petitioner was stopped by the U.S. Border Patrol on State Highway 78 in California, and his car was thoroughly searched. The road is essentially an east–west highway that runs for part of its course through an undeveloped region. At about the point where the petitioner was stopped, the road meanders north as well as east, but nowhere does the road reach the Mexican border, and at all points it lies north of U.S. 80, a major east–west highway entirely within the United States that connects the Southwest with the west coast. The petitioner was some 26 air miles north of the border when he was stopped. The Border Patrol had no search warrant, and there was no probable cause of any kind for the stop or the subsequent search. Officers found marijuana and arrested the defendant.

The Border Patrol conducts three types of surveillance along inland roadways, all in the asserted interest of detecting the illegal importation of aliens. Permanent checkpoints are maintained at certain nodal intersections, temporary checkpoints are established from time to time at various places, and, finally, there are roving patrols such as the one that stopped and searched the petitioner's car. In all of these operations, it is argued, the agents are acting within the Constitution when they stop and search automobiles without a warrant, without probable cause to believe the cars contain aliens, and even without probable cause to believe the cars have made a border crossing. The only asserted justification for this extravagant license to search is § 287(a)(3) of the Immigration and Nationality Act, 66 Stat. 233, 8 U.S.C. § 1357(a)(3), which simply provides for warrantless searches of automobiles and other conveyances "within a reasonable distance from any external boundary of the United States," as authorized by regulations to be promulgated by the Attorney General. The Attorney General's regulation, 8 CFR § 287.1, defines "reasonable distance" as "within 100 air miles from any external boundary of the United States." The only justification used to validate this stop and search is the above-mentioned regulation.

Issue Did the search of defendant's automobile violate the Fourth Amendment since it was not conducted at the border or the **functional equivalent of the border** and it was conducted without probable cause or consent? YES

Supreme Court Decision

Reason "The search in the present case was conducted in the unfettered discretion of the members of the Border Patrol, who did not have a warrant, probable cause, or consent. The search thus embodied precisely the evil the Court" has sought to prevent. "Since neither this Court's automobile search decisions nor its administrative inspection decisions provide any support for the constitutionality of the stop and search in the present case, we are left simply with the statute that purports to authorize automobiles to be stopped and searched, without a warrant and 'within a reasonable distance from any external boundary of the United States.' It is clear, of course, that no Act of Congress can authorize a violation of the Constitution.. . .It is undoubtedly within the power of the Federal Government to exclude aliens from the country.. . .It is also without doubt that this power can be effectuated by routine inspections and searches of individuals or conveyances seeking to cross our borders.. . .Whatever the permissible scope of intrusiveness of a routine border search might be, searches of this kind may in certain circumstances take place not only at the border itself, but at its functional equivalents as well.. . .But the search of the petitioner's automobile by a roving patrol, on a California road that lies at all points at least 20 miles north of the Mexican border, was of a wholly different sort. In the absence of probable cause or consent, that search violated the petitioner's Fourth Amendment right to be free of 'unreasonable searches and seizures.'"

Case Significance "It is not enough to argue, as does the Government, that the problem of deterring unlawful entry by aliens across long expanses of national boundaries is a serious one. The needs of law enforcement stand in constant tension with the Constitution's protections of the individual against certain exercises of official power. It is precisely the predictability of these pressures that counsels a resolute loyalty to constitutional safeguards.... Travelers may be so stopped in crossing an international boundary because of national self protection reasonably requiring one entering the country to identify himself as entitled to come in, and his belongings as effects which may be lawfully brought in.... But those lawfully within the country, entitled to use the public highways, have a right to free passage without interruption or search unless there is known to a competent official, authorized to search, probable cause for believing that their vehicles are carrying contraband or illegal merchandise."

person is actually entering or exiting the border, or the functional equivalent of the border, do not require any probable cause or consent. In those instances, officers are justified in holding individuals for a reasonable period of time and can conduct a significantly invasive search. These searches are valid simply because the person or item is crossing the border. Other types of detentions and searches require either probable cause or consent, as when a person has crossed a border but is not lawfully found within the boundaries of the country conducting the search. Without some probable cause or consent, such a search violates the Fourth Amendment.

8.4 Other Exigencies to the Warrant Requirement

Other than airports and borders, certain circumstances arise that make obtaining a warrant to search particularly burdensome for law enforcement. If the circumstances create enough of an emergency, the Court has upheld the warrantless search. Each of these cases is determined on a case-by-case analysis of the particular facts unique to the situation. The cases generally turn on the degree of exigency presented by the facts. For example, a warrantless murder scene search, where there is no indication that evidence would be lost, destroyed, or removed during the time required to obtain a search warrant and there is no suggestion that a warrant could not easily be obtained, is inconsistent with the Fourth Amendment because the situation does not create **exigent circumstances** of the kind that would justify a warrantless search.[d]

[d]*Mincey v. Arizona*, 437 U.S. 385 (1978).

Mincey v. Arizona, 437 U.S. 385 (1978)

Facts During a narcotics raid on Mincey's apartment, an undercover officer was shot and killed and Mincey and others were wounded. Pursuant to police department policy that officers should not investigate incidents in which they are involved, officers at the scene took no action other than to look for other wounded people and to render medical assistance. About ten minutes after the shooting, homicide investigators arrived at the scene and took charge of the investigation. These officers conducted an extensive search of the apartment that lasted four days, included opening drawers and ripping up carpets, and resulted in the seizure of 200 to 300 objects. The items seized were admitted into evidence during trial. Mincey was convicted of murder, assault, and narcotics offenses.

Issue Does the scene of a homicide represent exigent circumstances that would create an additional exception to the warrant requirement of the Fourth Amendment? NO

Supreme Court Decision "The 'murder scene exception' created by the Arizona Supreme Court to the warrant requirement is inconsistent with the Fourth and Fourteenth Amendments, and the warrantless search of petitioner's apartment was not constitutionally permissible simply because a homicide had occurred there."

Reason "[W]hen the police come upon the scene of a homicide, they may make a prompt warrantless search of the area to see if there are other victims or if a killer is still on the premises.. . .And the police may seize any evidence that is in plain view during the course of their legitimate emergency activities.. . .But a warrantless search must be 'strictly circumscribed by the exigencies which justify its initiation,' *Terry v. Ohio*, 392 U.S., at 25-26, and it simply cannot be contended that this search was justified by any emergency threatening life or limb.. . .We decline to hold that the seriousness of the offense under investigation itself creates exigent circumstances of the kind that under the Fourth Amendment justify a warrantless search."

Case Significance This case is best understood as an issue under the "exigent circumstances" exception to the warrant requirement. The general rule is that a search warrant must be obtained prior to a search. Among the many exceptions, however, is the presence of exigent circumstances. In this case, the Arizona Supreme Court in previous decisions had carved out a "murder scene" exception, saying that investigations of murder scenes did not need a warrant because of the seriousness of the offense. The police conducted a warrantless search based on this exception. The importance of this case lies in the Court's statement that "the seriousness of the offense under investigation did not itself create exigent circumstances of the kind that under the Fourth Amendment justify a warrantless search, where there is no indication that evidence would be lost, destroyed, or removed during the time required to obtain a search warrant and there is no suggestion that a warrant could not easily and conveniently have been obtained."

In sum, the Court said that a warrant must be obtained for crime scene investigations, regardless of the seriousness of the offense. The only exception to this rule is if obtaining a warrant would mean that the evidence would be lost, destroyed, or removed during the time required to obtain a search warrant.

8.5 Destruction of Evidence

If police have probable cause to search, and they reasonably believe evidence is about to be destroyed, they can search without a warrant. For example, in *Cupp v. Murphy*, 412 U.S. 291 (1973), the Supreme Court held that police officers who had probable cause to believe Daniel Murphy had strangled his wife did not need a warrant to take scrapings of what looked like blood under his fingernails. The rationale for the holding was that Murphy knew the officers suspected he was the strangler; thus, he had a motive to destroy the short-lived bloodstain evidence. Because of the urgency of collecting that specific evidence, to go through the process to obtain a search warrant would thwart police officer efforts to conduct a thorough investigation. In a similar case, in *Schmerber v. California*, 384 U.S. 757 (1966), the Supreme Court held that rapidly declining blood alcohol levels justified giving a blood alcohol test to Schmerber without a warrant. Again, if police had waited to obtain a search warrant, the evidence would not have been available. Finally, the likelihood that suspects will destroy or hide drugs has been held by the Court to justify a warrantless entry into a home.[e] Considering these cases together, the Court has been open to the exigency of collecting evidence that might easily be removed or destroyed. In those cases, officers may collect the evidence without a search warrant.

8.6 Danger to the Community

Another area in which the Court has been more lenient in requiring a search warrant are those cases in which either the officers' safety or the safety of the community is at risk. If officers have probable cause to believe that a suspect has committed a violent crime or that they or others in the community are in immediate danger, they may enter and search a house. In *United States v. Lindsey*, 877F. 2d 777 (1989), officers reasonably believed guns and bombs were in the house. The Court also determined that officers acted reasonably in reentering a house without a warrant to search for a weapon when police found a dead body on the front porch.[f] Fires and explosions present a particular danger to the public and to officers investigating them. If police officers respond to the scene of a fire, they do not need a warrant to stay inside a burned building long

[e] *Ker v. California*, 374 U.S. 23 (1963).
[f] *United States v. Doe*, 465 U.S. 605 (1984).

enough to look for possible injured victims and to investigate the cause of the fire or explosion. Once they determine the cause of the fire, however, they must obtain a warrant before continuing to search for evidence of a crime.[g] Furthermore, officers are not authorized to enter a home without a warrant because they think that a suspect is planning a fire or explosion. For example, a court ruled that the entry and search of a house was not lawful just because officers knew that a man kept dangerous chemicals in his house and that he was not home.[h]

8.7 Regulated Business Searches

Businesses that are regulated, such as places that serve alcohol or sell guns, are not protected by the same rights as other non-regulated businesses. Warrantless searches are not prohibited in **regulated businesses** because it is necessary to prevent any illegal operations by such highly regulated businesses. The owners of the business understand they are subject to searches based on the type of services they provide. In *United States v. Biswell*, 406 U.S. 311 (1972), an official asked for entrance into a locked gunroom based on provisions allowing officers to inspect weapons being sold. Upon entrance, the officer found and seized illegal weapons. The Supreme Court upheld the seizure based on the right that officials have to regularly inspect businesses that have special permits to sell firearms. Government agents have to inspect businesses that sell weapons and alcoholic beverages to ensure that they are following legal guidelines in doing so and therefore no warrant is required to search such a place.

8.8 Summary

This chapter identifies and examines circumstances considered to be emergency situations, or exigencies, in which obtaining a search warrant would be detrimental to either the investigation, or the safety of the officers or the public. Two of the more obvious examples of exceptions to the search warrant requirement involve airport searches and border searches. In both of these instances, the interest of public safety is thought to outweigh the minimal invasion of privacy to which travelers are subjected.

[g]*Michigan v. Clifford*, 464 U.S. 287 (1984).
[h]*United States v. Warner*, 843 F. 2d 401 (1988).

In airport searches, all passengers who travel on public airlines are required to submit to suspicionless searches prior to boarding. Likewise, all people entering the borders of the United States are subjected to routine stops and searches. In cases where additional searches or detentions are required, to promote the interest of public safety some type of suspicion is required and can rise to the level of needing a court order. For example, when a traveler is detained for a longer period of time, it might be necessary to obtain a court order to continue to hold the person or to conduct a more extensive search.

Other types of exigencies can arise that make obtaining a search warrant impractical. In situations in which evidence will likely be destroyed or lost, police are authorized to search without a warrant. Likewise, if the safety of police or the public would be compromised by obtaining a search warrant, warrantless searches are justified. Finally, businesses that are subjected to regulations because of the nature of the products sold or business performed may be searched without search warrants.

References

[1] Lafave W, Isreal J. Criminal Procedure. West: St. Paul, MN; 1984.

Further reading

Almeida-Sanchez v. United States, 413 U.S. 266 (1973).
Cupp v. Murphy, 412 U.S. 291 (1973).
Ker v. California, 374 U.S. 23 (1963).
Michigan v. Clifford, 464 U.S. 287 (1984).
Mincey v. Arizona, 437 U.S. 385 (1978).
On Lee v. United States, 343 U.S. 747 (1952).
Schmerber v. California, 384 U.S. 757 (1966).
United States v. Bell, 464F.2d 667 (2nd Cir. 1972), cert. denied, 409 U.S. 991 2).
United States v. Biswell, 406 U.S. 311 (1972).
United States v. Davis, 482F.2d 893 (9th Cir. 1973).
United States v. Doe, 465 U.S. 605 (1984).
United States v. Edward, 498F.2d 496 (2nd Cir. 1974).
United States v. Epperson, 454F.2d 769 (4th Cir. 1972), cert. denied, 406 U.S. (1972).
United States v. Flores-Montano, 541 U.S. 149 (2004).
United States v. Johnson, 991F.2d 1287 (7th Cir. 1993).
United States v. Lindsey, 877F. 2d 777 (1989).
United States v. Montoya de Hernandez, 473 U.S. 531 (1985).
United States v. Oriakhi, 57F.3d 1290 (4th Cir. 1995).

9

SPECIAL PROBLEMS: LOCATION OF TRIAL AND DOUBLE JEOPARDY

CHAPTER OUTLINE

KEY TERMS

Custodial interrogation
Miranda warnings
Physical evidence
Public safety exception
Transactional immunity
Use immunity
Verbal testimony

LEARNING OBJECTIVES

- Understand custodial interrogation that triggers the protection against self-incrimination.
- Identify the difference between verbal testimony and physical evidence.
- Understand the *Miranda* warnings and when they apply.
- Understand when and how the right to remain silent can be waived.

> *. . . nor shall [any person] be compelled in any criminal case to be a witness against himself, nor be deprived of life, liberty, or property, without due process of law.*
>
> **—Fifth Amendment (*Miranda* issues)**

9.1 Introduction

The Fifth Amendment to the U.S. Constitution provides, in pertinent part, that no person shall be compelled to testify against himself in a criminal case. Although the words seem straightforward upon first glance, considerable discussion has resulted with regard to the exact interpretation of this provision. The Fifth Amendment has been interpreted only to prevent compelled **verbal testimony** of a suspect against him or herself; thus, **physical evidence**, even if it can be used to convict a suspect, is not protected by the Fifth Amendment. Items that are not protected include hair samples, fingerprints, photographs, blood samples, urine samples, weapons, and contraband. In the case of physical evidence, the analysis falls under the Fourth Amendment; that is, were the items seized in a reasonable manner that complied with the requirements of the Fourth Amendment? If, however, the defendant is making statements to law enforcement that are likely to be used at trial to prove guilt, the Fifth Amendment protection applies.

9.2 *Miranda* Warnings

One of the most significant issues related to Fifth Amendment protections is understanding the point in the criminal process at which the right actually becomes applicable. It seems clear that if someone is sworn in on the witness stand in an active criminal trial then that person cannot be required to give testimony that directly incriminates himself. But, what about situations that occur before trial, particularly in interactions with police? When police are questioning suspects about the crime, with the purpose of extracting evidence, those people are also protected by the Fifth Amendment's protection against self-incrimination. The Court laid out the specific requirements that police officers must follow to comply with the protection in *Miranda v. Arizona*, 384 U.S. 436 (1966).

Miranda v. Arizona, 384 U.S. 436 (1966)

Facts Ernesto *Miranda* was arrested at his home and taken to a police station for questioning in connection with a rape and kidnapping. *Miranda* was 23 years old and poor and had completed only one-half of the ninth grade. The officers interrogated him for two hours, and eventually they obtained a written confession. The officers admitted at trial that *Miranda* was not advised that he had a right to have an attorney present. *Miranda* was convicted of rape and kidnapping on the basis of the confession.

Issue Must the police inform a suspect who is subject to a **custodial interrogation** of his or her constitutional rights involving self-incrimination and right to counsel prior to questioning? YES

Supreme Court Decision An individual who is being held and interrogated must be informed of the following specific rights before any evidence will be admissible in court:

1. The right to remain silent
2. That any statement made can and will be used against him or her in a court of law
3. The right to have an attorney present during questioning
4. If the suspect cannot afford an attorney, one will be appointed for him or her prior to questioning

Reason Suspects have a right against self-incrimination guaranteed by the Fifth Amendment. "The Fifth Amendment privilege is so fundamental to our system of constitutional rule and the expedient of giving an adequate warning as to the availability of the privilege so simple, we will not pause to inquire in individual cases whether the defendant was aware of his rights without a warning being given. Assessments of the knowledge the defendant possessed, based on information as to his age, education, intelligence, or prior contact with authorities, can never be more than speculation; a warning is a clear-cut fact. More important, whatever the background of the person interrogated, a warning at the time of the interrogation is indispensable to overcome its pressures and to insure that the individual knows he is free to exercise the privilege at that point in time.. . .The warning of the right to remain silent must be accompanied by the explanation that anything said can and will be used against the individual in court. This warning is needed to make him aware not only of the privilege, but also of the consequences of forgoing it. Only through awareness of these consequences can there be any assurance of real understanding and intelligent exercise of the privilege. Moreover, this warning may serve to make the individual more acutely aware that he is faced with a phase of the adversary system—that he is not in the presence of persons acting solely in his interest.. . .The circumstances surrounding in-custody interrogation can operate very quickly to overbear the will of one merely made aware of his privilege by his interrogators. Therefore, the right to have counsel present at interrogation is indispensable to the protection of the Fifth Amendment privilege under the system we delineate today. Our aim is to assure the individual's right to choose between silence and speech remains unfettered throughout the interrogation process.. . .The presence of counsel at the interrogation may serve several significant subsidiary functions as well. If the accused decides to talk to his interrogators, the assistance of counsel can mitigate the dangers of untrustworthiness. With a lawyer present the likelihood that the police will practice coercion is reduced, and if coercion is nevertheless exercised the lawyer can testify to it in court. The presence of a lawyer can also help to guarantee that the accused gives a fully accurate statement to the police and that the statement is rightly reported by the prosecution at trial.. . .We have concluded that without proper safeguards the process of in-custody interrogation of persons suspected or accused of crime contains inherently compelling pressures which work to undermine the individual's will to resist and to compel him to speak where he would not otherwise do so freely. In order to combat these pressures and to permit a full opportunity to exercise the privilege against self-incrimination, the accused must be adequately and effectively apprised of his rights and the exercise of those rights must be fully honored."

Case Significance *Miranda v. Arizona* is, arguably, the most widely known case ever decided by the Supreme Court. It also has had the deepest impact on the day-to-day crime investigation phase of police work and has led to changes that have since become an accepted part of routine police procedure. Supporters of the *Miranda* decision hail it as properly protective of individual rights, whereas critics have accused the Supreme Court of being soft on crime and coddling criminals. The 5-4 split among the justices served to fan the flames of the controversy in its early stages, with opponents of the ruling hoping that a change in Court composition would hasten its demise. That has not happened, and neither is it likely to happen in the immediate future. *Miranda* has survived the test of time and, although the process of erosion has begun in recent years, a complete overruling of *Miranda*, even by a conservative Court, appears remote.

The protections covered by *Miranda* are often confusing to the public and students of criminal procedure. The words of the ***Miranda* warnings** state that the accused has the right to an attorney and that one will be appointed for him if he cannot afford one. This right is often confused with the Sixth Amendment's "right to counsel." Clear distinctions should be drawn between the two rights. One is a trial right (the Sixth Amendment) and attaches at the point where the accused has been formally charged with an offense in the court.[a] The other (Fifth Amendment) protects the accused from compelled verbal self-incrimination. The presence of an attorney at this pre-trial stage is for the specific purpose of protecting the accused from offering testimonial evidence that will incriminate him. Because police-citizen encounters often occur in an intimidating environment, the opportunity for an accused person to unknowingly, or unwillingly, offer evidence that implicates himself in an event is ever present. *Miranda* warnings are intended to minimize that opportunity and work to ensure that any confession made by an accused is freely and voluntarily made. To get a confession, or evidence that leads to an arrest, from the wrong person is not an acceptable outcome. The end does not justify the means if the wrong person is prosecuted.

Often, citizens are confused about when the *Miranda* warnings are actually required. Many people believe they are required any time an arrest is made. Others believe they are required any time a citizen speaks to the police in any circumstances. Neither of these instances is actually accurate. *Miranda* warnings must be given whenever there is a custodial interrogation. That phrase is best understood if discussed as two separate requirements. The first is a determination of whether a person is "in custody." Three specific elements should be examined to determine whether someone is in custody:

1. Is the person a suspect in the case as opposed to a witness or the victim?

[a]*Fellers v. United States*, 540 U.S. 519 (2004).

2. Did the person voluntarily come to speak to the police as opposed to being brought in for questioning?
3. Is the person free to leave at any point?

Examining those factors indicates that a person who walks into the police station off of the street to offer information about a crime is free to speak to the police without any warnings being given. Likewise, a person can start out speaking to the police as a witness and change to a suspect within the course of the conversation. In that instance, *Miranda* warnings should be read at the point where the status changes.

One of the most interesting discussions of whether a person is "in custody" for purposes of *Miranda* involves roadside questioning for a routine traffic stop. Although arguable a citizen is not "free to leave" in such an encounter, the Court ruled that such brief encounters do not require *Miranda* warnings to be read.[b] In the same case, the Court determined that *Miranda* applies equally to misdemeanor and felony offenses.

The other critical element in the determination is the word "interrogation." Interrogation denotes that the police are actively asking the suspect questions that are likely to elicit an incriminating response (typically linking the suspect to a crime). Under this logic, if police arrest a suspect, put that suspect in the back of a police car, and do not ask her any questions on the drive to the police station, they have not interrogated her and *Miranda* is not required. If the suspect becomes chatty and tells the officers all about the crime and implicates herself when they have not asked her any questions, likely the information is permissible because she was not being interrogated within the requirements of *Miranda.*

9.3 Invoking the Right to Counsel or to Remain Silent

Discussions related to *Miranda* warnings include what the police are responsible for doing once a person has invoked the right to counsel, or the right to remain silent. The most significant case in this area is that of *Edwards v. Arizona,* 451 U.S. 477 (1981), in which the Court determined that, once the defendant asks for an attorney, all questioning must stop until the defendant has been allowed to speak to an attorney.

[b]*Berkemer v. McCarty,* 468 U.S. 420 (1984).

Edwards v. Arizona, 451 U.S. 477 (1981)

Facts Edwards was arrested pursuant to a warrant. At the police station, he was read his *Miranda* warnings and indicated that he understood them and would answer questions. The police told Edwards that an accomplice had made a sworn statement implicating him in the crime, and Edwards tried to "make a deal." Later, he changed his mind and wanted to speak to an attorney before making a deal. Once he said he wanted the attorney, police stopped questioning him. The next morning, two other officers went to the jail and asked to see Edwards. Edwards told the detention officer that he did not want to speak to the officers but was told that he had no choice in the matter. Edwards was again informed of his *Miranda* rights. He indicated that he would talk if they would let him hear the taped statement of the accomplice which they did. After he heard the statement, he talked to the officers and implicated himself in the crimes. Edwards was charged and convicted of several state criminal offenses.

Issue If a suspect has been given the *Miranda* warnings and invokes the right to remain silent or to have counsel, may that suspect be interrogated at a later point if the *Miranda* warnings are given again? NO

Supreme Court Decision An accused, who, after having being given the *Miranda* warnings, invokes the right to silence and to have a lawyer, cannot be interrogated further by the police until a lawyer has been made available. The only exception to this rule is if the accused initiates further communication, exchanges, or conversations with the police.

Reason "When an accused asks for counsel, a valid waiver of that right cannot be established by showing only that he responded to further police-initiated custodial interrogation, even if he has been advised of his rights. We further hold that an accused, such as Edwards, having expressed his desire to deal with the police only through counsel, is not subject to further interrogation by the authorities until counsel has been made available to him, unless the accused himself initiates further communication, exchanges, or conversations with the police.. . .We think it clear that Edwards was subjected to custodial interrogation on January 20 within the meaning of [*Rhode Island v.*] *Innis* and that this occurred at the insistence of the authorities. His statement, made without having access to counsel, did not amount to a valid waiver and hence was inadmissible."

Case Significance The principle is clear: Once a suspect invokes his or her rights after having been given the *Miranda* warnings, interrogation must cease. Further, the police cannot later interrogate the suspect again, even with another reading of the *Miranda* warnings, until the suspect has been provided with a lawyer. If the suspect, however, on his or her own, initiates further communication or conversation with the police, the confession will be admissible. In such instances, there is a need for the suspect to be given the *Miranda* warnings again.

Although the *Edwards* rule sets forth the proposition that the defendant can re-initiate conversation about the crime that overcomes the need to have a lawyer present, the exact nature of that communication is still questionable. Several cases have occurred after the *Edwards* case that have interpreted the ruling further. For example, the police cannot question a suspect after the arrangement when the suspect asked for an attorney at the arrangement, one was appointed, but the suspect had not had a chance to consult with the attorney prior to the subsequent questioning. Even though *Miranda* warnings were read prior to the subsequent questioning, the defendant's statements could not be used against him because that was a violation of the Edwards rule.[c] Further, once a defendant has asked for an attorney and questioning has stopped, police cannot ask the defendant questions about a different crime even if they read *Miranda* warnings before the questioning.[d]

If a significant break in the questioning occurs, however, during which time the defendant is not being held in an interrogation room or prohibited from communication with other people, the protections of *Edwards* can be overcome. See the case of *Maryland v. Shatzer*, 559 U.S. ___ (2010) (No. 08-680).

Maryland v. Shatzer, 559 U.S. ___ (2010) (No. 08-680)

Facts In 2003, a police detective attempted to question Shatzer, who was in prison on a different conviction, about allegations that he sexually abused his son. Shatzer invoked his *Miranda* rights, so the detective terminated the interview and closed the investigation. Shatzer was released back into the general prison population. Because of new information, the case was reopened in 2006. A different detective again attempted to interview Shatzer, who was still incarcerated. This time, Shatzer waived his *Miranda* rights and made statements incriminating himself. After making the statements, Shatzer asked for an attorney and the detective ended the interview. The trial court refused to suppress the statements over Shatzer's argument that *Edwards v. Arizona*, 451 U.S. 477 (1987), prevented officers from re-interviewing Shatzer without an attorney present. The court held that *Edwards* did not apply because Shatzer had experienced a break in *Miranda* custody between the 2003 and 2006 interviews. Shatzer was convicted of sexual child abuse.

Issue Does a break in custody end the presumption of involuntariness established in Edwards? YES

Supreme Court Decision "Because Shatzer experienced a break in *Miranda* custody lasting more than two weeks between the first and second attempts at interrogation, *Edwards* does not mandate suppression of his March 2006 statements."

Reason In *Edwards v. Arizona*, the Court created a presumption that once a suspect invokes *Miranda* rights, any waiver of those rights can only come from the suspect. If the police attempt a subsequent custodial interrogation, it is presumed to be involuntary. In *Shatzer*, the Court reiterated that Edwards' "fundamental purpose is to '[p]reserv[e] the integrity of an accused's choice to communicate with police only through counsel,' *Patterson v. Illinois*, 487 U.S. 285, 291 (1988), by 'prevent[ing] police from badgering a defendant into waiving his previously asserted *Miranda* rights,' [*Michigan v.*] *Harvey* [494 U.S. 344, 350 (1990)]." In *Edwards*, the Court reasoned that a suspect's subsequent

[c] *Michigan v. Jackson*, 475 U.S. 625 (1986).
[d] *Arizona v. Roberson*, 486 U.S. 675 (1988).

waiver was considered coerced if the suspect had been held uninterrupted in custody since the first refusal because "he remains cut off from his normal life and companions, 'thrust into' and isolated in an 'unfamiliar, police-dominated atmosphere,' *Miranda*, 384 U. S., at 456-457, where his captors 'appear to control [his] fate,' *Illinois v. Perkins*, 496 U.S. 292, 297 (1990)." However, when "a suspect has been released from his pretrial custody and has returned to his normal life for some time before the later attempted interrogation, there is little reason to think that his change of heart regarding interrogation without counsel has been coerced." If a break in custody did not terminate *Edwards*, police would be prevented from ever interviewing a suspect who has invoked *Miranda*, even if they knew nothing of the invocation and the later crime was completely removed from the earlier one. As a result, "We conclude that such an extension of *Edwards* is not justified; we have opened its 'protective umbrella,' *Solem* [v. Helm] 465 U.S., at 644, n. 4, far enough. The protections offered by *Miranda*, which we have deemed sufficient to ensure that the police respect the suspect's desire to have an attorney present the first time police interrogate him, adequately ensure that result when a suspect who initially requested counsel is re-interrogated after a break in custody that is of sufficient duration to dissipate its coercive effects."

Case Significance The extension of *Edwards* to *Miranda* mandated that once a suspect invoked his or her *Miranda* rights police could not initiate another interview, even for another crime, without the suspect's attorney present. The only way a subsequent interview could take place was if the suspect initiated the contact with police. This prevented police from badgering a suspect with repeated requests for interviews while the suspect was still in custody, but also often prevented police from interviewing the suspect in wholly unrelated cases and where the request for an interview was substantially separated by time. The Court ruled in this case that a break in custody of 14 days is sufficient to dissipate *Edwards*, reasoning that it "provides plenty of time for the suspect to get reacclimated to his normal life, to consult with friends and counsel, and to shake off any residual coercive effects of his prior custody." This case was somewhat complicated because Shatzer remained in prison between the interviews, but the Court reasoned that "when previously incarcerated suspects are released back into the general prison population, they return to their accustomed surroundings and daily routine.. . .Their continued detention is relatively disconnected from their prior unwillingness to cooperate in an investigation." Therefore, Shatzer's release back into the general prison population constituted a sufficient break in *Miranda* custody.

9.4 Knowing and Voluntary Waiver of *Miranda* Rights

The rights afforded by *Miranda* can be waived by the defendant and questioning by law enforcement can continue without Fifth Amendment penalties. Assessment of whether the rights have been waived hinges on the determination of a "knowing and voluntary" waiver. As a general rule, if the *Miranda* rights have been read and if the defendant acknowledges these rights either orally or in writing and still agrees to talk to the police, then the waiver is presumed to be knowingly and voluntarily made. The Supreme Court, however, does not require that the waiver be expressed, which means that the defendant is not required to say or write that he or she waives the rights. The Court, instead, adopted an implied waiver test based on the totality of the circumstances in a given case. Some of the considerations in determining if the defendant made a knowing waiver include the intelligence, education level, and age of the defendant; familiarity with the criminal justice system; mental ability; ability to understand English; and physical condition at the time of the waiver. A recent case addressed whether remaining silent after *Miranda* rights have been read is equivalent to a knowing and voluntary waiver of the right.

Berghuis v. Thompkins, 560 U.S. ___ (2010) (No. 08-1470)

Facts Police interviewed Thompkins concerning a shooting in which one person was killed and another injured. Officers presented Thompkins with a form that listed the elements of *Miranda.* The officer asked Thompkins to read the statement that he could decide at any time during questioning to remain silent or ask for an attorney, and the officer read the rest of the form. Thompkins refused to sign the form, and there was conflicting testimony about whether the officer asked Thompkins if he understood his rights. About 2 hours and 45 minutes into the interrogation, one officer asked Thompkins, "Do you believe in God?" Thompkins made eye contact with the officer and said a tearful "Yes." The officer then asked, "Do you pray to God?" to which Thompkins said "Yes." The officer then asked, "Do you pray to God to forgive you for shooting that boy down?" Thompkins answered "Yes" and looked away. Thompkins refused to make a written confession, and the interrogation ended about 15 minutes later. At trial, Thompkins contended he had not waived his right to remain silent and that his statements were involuntary.

Issue Does a suspect's silence after being read the *Miranda* warnings combined with statements made during an interview represent a valid waiver of the right to remain silent? YES

Supreme Court Decision "Thompkins did not say that he wanted to remain silent or that he did not want to talk with the police. Had he made either of these simple, unambiguous statements, he would have invoked his 'right to cut off questioning.'. . .Here he did neither, so he did not invoke his right to remain silent."

Reason In this case, Thompkins argued he invoked his right to remain silent by not speaking for an extended period of time during the interview. The Court rejected this argument, relying on the decision in *Davis v. United States,* 512 U.S. 452 (1994), that a suspect must make an "unambiguous" request for an attorney and that "if an accused makes a statement concerning the right to counsel 'that is ambiguous or equivocal' or makes no statement, the police are not required to end the interrogation. . .or ask questions to clarify whether the accused wants to invoke his or her *Miranda* rights." The Court further stated, "The Court has not yet stated whether an invocation of the right to remain silent can be ambiguous or equivocal, but there is no principled reason to adopt different standards for determining when an accused has invoked the *Miranda* right to remain silent and the *Miranda* right to counsel at issue in Davis. A corollary issue was, in addition to not invoking his rights, whether Thompkins waived his rights without an explicit oral or written waiver. This was an issue because of the statement from *Miranda* that "a valid waiver will not be presumed simply from the silence of the accused after warnings are given or simply from the fact that a confession was in fact eventually obtained." Drawing on *North Carolina v. Butler*, 441 U.S. 369 (1979), the Court stated that "a waiver of *Miranda* rights may be implied through the defendant's silence, coupled with an understanding of his rights and a course of conduct indicating waiver." The prosecution's showing that *Miranda* warnings were given and Thompkins made several uncoerced statements established an implied waiver of the right to remain silent, as long as the prosecution made the additional showing that Thompkins understood these rights since he made no verbal or written indication that he did. Here the Court argued, "There was more than enough evidence in the record to conclude that Thompkins understood his *Miranda* rights. Thompkins received a written copy of the *Miranda* warnings; [the officer] determined that Thompkins could read and understand English; and Thompkins was given time to read the warnings. Thompkins, furthermore, read aloud the fifth warning." Based on these findings, the Court ruled that the statement was valid.

Case Significance This case continues to clarify several issues for police related to *Miranda* warnings and confessions. Here, "All concede that the warning given in this case was in full compliance with these requirements. The dispute centers on the response—or nonresponse—from the suspect." To this, the Court stated, "There is good reason to require an accused who wants to invoke his or her right to remain silent to do so unambiguously. A requirement of an unambiguous invocation of *Miranda* rights results in an objective inquiry that 'avoid[s] difficulties of proof and. . .provide[s] guidance to officers' on how to proceed in the face of ambiguity. *Davis*, 512 U.S., at 458-459. If an ambiguous act, omission, or statement could require police to end the interrogation, police would be required to make difficult decisions about an accused's unclear intent and face the consequence of suppression 'if they guess wrong.'" So, police officers can rely on the fact that a suspect must make an unambiguous request to remain silent. Of course, the suspect can simply remain silent for the duration of the interview, but if the suspect does speak after being given the *Miranda* warnings (and there is evidence to believe the suspect understood the rights), it is considered a valid waiver of the rights and a voluntary statement.

Whether confessions are both knowingly and voluntarily made is an important consideration for criminal procedure. Because of the unequal relationship that is evident in police and citizen encounters, courts are called upon to ensure that police do not abuse their power in attempting to discover the facts of any given case. The most common circumstances courts consider in determining whether coercive police action occurred involve issues such as the length of questioning, whether food, water, and toilets were denied; whether the police used threats, promises, lies, or tricks; and whether the requirements of the *Miranda* warnings were actually provided. Overall, courts use the totality of the circumstances in each case to determine the validity of the waiver.

9.5 Public Safety Exception to *Miranda* Warnings

The essence of the *Miranda* warnings is that police are required to tell suspects that they do not have to respond to questions about a specific criminal incident. At times, however, police need information to protect others who might be injured if a delay occurs in discovering the whereabouts of a weapon or other criminal elements. In such situations, the Court has identified a **public safety exception** to the *Miranda* warnings that allows police to question a suspect without reading *Miranda* warnings.

New York v. Quarles, 467 U.S. 649 (1984)

Facts Officers were approached by a woman claiming that she had just been raped by an armed man. She described him and said that he had entered a nearby supermarket. The officers drove the woman to the supermarket and one officer went in while the other radioed for assistance. The officer in the supermarket quickly spotted Quarles, who matched the description provided by the woman, and a chase ensued. The officer ordered Quarles to stop and place his hands over his head. The officer frisked Quarles and discovered an empty shoulder holster. After handcuffing Quarles, the officer asked him where the gun was. Quarles nodded in the direction of some empty cartons and responded, "The gun is over there." The gun was retrieved from the cartons and Quarles was placed under arrest and was read his *Miranda* warnings. Quarles indicated that he would answer questions without an attorney present and admitted that he owned the gun.

Issue Were the suspect's initial statements and the gun admissible in evidence despite the failure of the officer to give him the *Miranda* warnings prior to asking questions that led to the discovery of the gun? YES

Supreme Court Decision Responses to questions asked by a police officer that are reasonably prompted by concern for public safety are admissible in court even though the suspect was in police custody and was not given the *Miranda* warnings.

Reason "We hold that on these facts there is a 'public safety' exception to the requirement that *Miranda* warnings be given before a suspect's answers may be admitted into evidence, and that the availability of that exception does not depend upon the motivation of the individual officers involved. In a kaleidoscopic situation such as the one confronting these officers, where spontaneity rather than adherence to a police manual is necessarily the order of the day, the application of the exception which we recognize today should not be made to depend on post hoc findings at a suppression hearing concerning the subjective motivation of the arresting officer. Undoubtedly most police officers, if placed in [the officer's] position, would act out of a host of different, instinctive, and largely unverifiable motives—their own safety, the safety of others, and perhaps as well the desire to obtain incriminating evidence from the suspect."

Case Significance *New York v. Quarles* carves out a "public safety" exception to the *Miranda* rule. The Supreme Court said that the case presents a situation in which concern for public safety must be paramount to adherence to the literal language of the rules enunciated in *Miranda*. Here, although Quarles was in police custody and therefore should have been given the *Miranda* warnings, concern for public safety prevailed. In this case, said the Court, the gun was concealed somewhere in the supermarket and therefore posed more than one danger to the public. The Court hinted, however, that the "public safety" exception needs to be interpreted narrowly and added that police officers can and will distinguish almost instinctively between questions necessary to secure their own safety or the safety of the public and questions designed solely to elicit testimony evidence from a suspect. Whether the police will be able to do this remains to be seen.

9.6 Granting Immunity

One exception can be made to the privilege against self-incrimination. That is the granting of immunity from prosecution. Defendants, and witnesses, can be compelled to testify to information that might incriminate them if the government grants them immunity from prosecution. Two types of immunity exist: **use immunity** and **transactional immunity**. In use immunity, the government is prevented from using the testimony of the defendant or witness against him or her in the trial of the matter. If the evidence comes to the government from a different source, however, the defendant or witness can still be prosecuted for the crime. Alternatively, in transactional immunity, the defendant or witness is granted immunity from prosecution on the entire transaction no matter how the government gets the evidence. According to the Supreme Court, the only type of immunity that is required to meet constitutional guidelines is use immunity.

Kastigar v. United States, 406 U.S. 441 (1972)

Facts The petitioners were subpoenaed to appear before a U.S. grand jury to give testimony. The government anticipated that they would assert their Fifth Amendment privilege against self-incrimination and refuse to testify. The government obtained an order from the district court directing the petitioners to answer questions and produce evidence before the grand jury under a grant of immunity. The scope of immunity was based on the federal witness immunity statute, which stated that "the witness may not refuse to comply with the order on the basis of his privilege against self-incrimination; but no testimony or other information compelled under the order (or any information directly or indirectly derived from such testimony or other information) may be used against the witness in any criminal case, except a prosecution for perjury, giving a false statement, or otherwise failing to comply with the order." (18 U.S.C. § 6002)

The petitioners opposed the court order, arguing that the scope of immunity granted was insufficient and that they should be afforded full transactional immunity from any prosecution. Based on their assertion, they appeared before the grand jury, but refused to answer any questions on the grounds that the Fifth Amendment protected them from making statements that might incriminate them. They were found in contempt of court.

Issue The issue in the case was whether petitioners could be compelled to answer questions that might incriminate them once they had been granted immunity from the use of the testimony and the evidence directly derived from the testimony, or whether they should have been granted immunity from prosecution the entire offense to which the compelled testimony related.

Supreme Court Decision A grant of use immunity is sufficient to require the petitioners to testify. The proper form of immunity in such cases is "use and derivative use" immunity.

Reason "The statute's explicit proscription of the use in any criminal case of 'testimony or other information compelled under the order (or any information directly or indirectly derived from such testimony or other information)' is consonant with Fifth Amendment standards. We hold that such immunity from use and derivative use is coextensive with the scope of the privilege against self-incrimination, and therefore is sufficient to compel testimony over a claim of the privilege.. . .Transactional immunity, which accords full immunity from prosecution for the offense to which the compelled testimony relates, affords the witness considerably broader protection than does the Fifth Amendment privilege.. . .There can be no justification in reason or policy for holding that the Constitution requires an amnesty grant where, acting pursuant to statute and accompanying safeguards, testimony is compelled in exchange for immunity from use and derivative use when no such amnesty is required where the government, acting without colorable right, coerces a defendant into incriminating himself."

Case Significance Prior to Kastigar, granting of immunity was governed by *Counselman v. Hitchcock*, 142 U.S. 547 (1892), which provided for full "transactional" immunity in cases of compelled statements. "Transactional" immunity provides full protection from prosecution for the offense under investigation. In *Kastigar*, however, the Supreme Court overturned *Counselman*. Instead of providing full immunity from the transaction, the Court determined that the grant of immunity only applies to the use of the statements themselves and to any evidence gained as a result of the protected statements. This is known as "use and derivative use" immunity, in which "use" is the use of the protected statements, and "derivative use" pertains to any evidence gained as a result of the protected statements. This case limited Fifth Amendment protections because the person in question can still be prosecuted for the offense under investigation, as long as the prosecution relies solely on evidence other than the protected statements and their fruits. Some states continue to provide transactional immunity before one can be compelled to testify in a criminal trial, but the Supreme Court only calls for use immunity.

Although this case dealt with testimony at the grand jury, often police, in the course of investigating an incident, determine that the testimony from a suspect that leads to other defendants is more important than gaining a conviction of the particular suspect. In those situations, the suspect may be granted immunity in return for testimony that leads to the arrest and conviction of other participants in the crime. Based on Kastigar, the only type of immunity that would be necessary would be use immunity. At trial, what is known as a "Kastigar hearing" may be required for the prosecution to prove that the evidence used in the case was provided completely independent of any protected statements, or their fruits, obtained from the defendant at the investigation stage.

9.7 Summary

This chapter examines the particular instances in which the Fifth Amendment protects citizens from compelled verbal testimony against themselves. This protection applies when they are involved in a custodial interrogation by law enforcement officers. Specifically, the determination of custodial interrogation hinges upon whether the defendant is voluntarily present before law enforcement, is a defendant in the incident, is free to leave at any time, and is being ask specific questions about the crime. Defendants can waive their Fifth Amendment protections and agree to answer questions if the waiver is freely and voluntarily made. Such a waiver must occur after the defendant has been read his or her *Miranda* warnings. If the defendant asks for a lawyer, or asserts his or her Fifth Amendment rights, all questioning must cease until the defendant has had a chance to consult with an attorney. The only exception to that rule is if the defendant re-initiates the conversation of his or her own volition without any prompting from law enforcement. In limited circumstances, defendants can be compelled to testify against themselves if they are granted use immunity from prosecution, and their statements, or any evidence stemming directly from their statements, cannot be used against them.

Further Reading

Arizona v. Roberson, 468 U.S. 675 (1988).
Berghuis v. Thompkins, 560 U.S. ___ (2010) (No. 08-1470).
Berkemer v. McCarty, 468 U.S. 420 (1984).
Berkemer v. McCarty, 468 U.S. 420 (1984).
Counselman v. Hitchcock, 142 U.S. 547 (1892).
Davis v. United States, 512 U.S. 452 (1994).
Edwards v. Arizona, 451 U.S. 477 (1981).
Fellers v. United States, 540 U.S 519 (2004).
Illinois v. Perkins, 496 U.S. 292 (1990).
Kastigar v. United States, 406 U.S. 441 (1972).

Maryland v. Shatzer, 559 U.S. ___ (2010) (No. 08-680).
Michigan v. Harvey, 494 U.S. 344 (1990).
Michigan v. Jackson, 475 U.S. 625 (1986).
Miranda v. Arizona, 384 U.S. 436 (1966).
New York v. Quarles, 467 U.S. 649 (1984).
North Carolina v. Butler, 441 U.S. 369 (1979).
Patterson v. Illinois, 487 U.S. 285 (1988).
Solem v. Helm, 465 U.S. 277 (1983).

10

MISCELLANEOUS PROCEEDINGS: JUVENILE JUSTICE, MISDEMEANOR TRIALS, DAMAGE SUITS AGAINST POLICE, AND PRISONER RIGHTS

CHAPTER OUTLINE

KEY TERMS

Confrontation of witnesses
Felony
Indigent
Jury trial
Lineup
Misdemeanor
Photographic arrays
Showup
Speedy trial

LEARNING OBJECTIVES

- Understand the basic rights included in the Sixth Amendment.
- Identify when the Sixth Amendment rights attach.
- Understand when an attorney is required to be present at identification procedures.
- Understand the right to counsel at a criminal trial.

In all criminal prosecutions, the accused shall enjoy the right to a speedy and public trial, by an impartial jury of the State and district wherein the crime shall have been committed, which district shall have been previously ascertained by law, and to be informed of the nature and cause of the accusation; to be confronted with the witnesses against him; to have compulsory process for obtaining witnesses in his favor, and to have the Assistance of Counsel for his defence.

—Sixth Amendment

10.1 Introduction

The Sixth Amendment contains basic trial rights of the accused. These rights include a speedy and public trial by a jury. Additionally, the accused has the right to be informed of the accusations against him or her, to confront witnesses at the trial, to compel witnesses to testify on his behalf, and to have counsel for all critical stages of the trial process. These rights will be addressed individually in this chapter. The right to counsel, however, will be the element focused on the most.

The right to counsel in criminal prosecutions is guaranteed by the Sixth Amendment, which states that "in all criminal prosecutions, the accused shall enjoy the right...to have the Assistance of Counsel for his defense." Although generally associated with the trial, the right to counsel has been interpreted to apply to "every critical stage" of the criminal proceeding. Some encounters with the police are considered a critical stage of an investigation and therefore require the presence of a lawyer if the evidence obtained is to be admissible in court. Generally, these "critical stages" include any interaction with the defendant after formal charges have been made in court. These rights are most often an issue in any **lineup**, **showup**, or custodial interrogation that occurs after formal charges have been initiated against the defendant. As such, identification procedures will be addressed in this chapter as they relate to the right to counsel.

In a lineup, a victim or a witness to a crime is shown several possible suspects at the police station for identification. In a showup, only one suspect is shown to the witness or victim. This usually takes place at the scene of the crime and immediately following the arrest of the suspect. In photographic identification, the police show photographs of possible suspects to the victim or witnesses. While defendants have constitutional rights during these encounters, which specific rights they have depend upon what phase of the trial process is in effect. If the identification procedures occur prior to the defendant being formally charged, as part of the evidence gathering procedure, the Fifth Amendment covers the procedures, and because they do not involve testimonial evidence no attorney is required to be present. Although the Fifth Amendment, through the reading of *Miranda* rights, contains language about the right to counsel, that right is guaranteed for the sake of protecting the freedom from self-incrimination and should not be confused with the basic trial right to have an attorney present which is a Sixth Amendment right. If, however, the identification procedure occurs after the defendant has been formally charged, then the Sixth Amendment trial rights have attached and an attorney is required to be present. In all circumstances of identification procedures, defendants have a due process right that the procedure not be unduly suggestive, resulting in identification that inevitably violates a suspect's constitutional rights.

Once the case proceeds to trial, the defendant is entitled to be represented by an attorney during the trial. If the defendant cannot afford an attorney, the state is constitutionally bound to provide counsel for the defendant. Cases have established that the defendant is entitled to counsel in any criminal trial that could involve a sentence of confinement, regardless of whether the offense is labeled a **felony** or a **misdemeanor**. Additionally, the right to an attorney extends through the first appeal. The Court has determined that in any appeal beyond the first appeal the defendant is not guaranteed the right to counsel.

Finally, the Sixth Amendment guarantees the other trial rights such as a speedy trial, a jury, and the confrontation clause. Each of these issues will be addressed in this chapter.

10.2 Identification Procedures

The first area in which criminal defendants may be entitled to Sixth Amendment rights is at identification procedures that occur after indictment. The Supreme Court has rejected the claim that identification procedures "compel" defendants to be witnesses against themselves in violation of the Fifth Amendment (see Chapter 9). Because identification procedures are not oral testimony, they fall into the physical evidence category instead of the compelled oral testimony category, and defendants can be forced to comply with orders of law enforcement.

Lineups are identification procedures in which the defendant is placed in with a group of similar individuals and put before the victim or witness to see if the defendant can be picked out. For lineups to be considered "fair," the International Association of Chiefs of Police recommends that they have the following components:

1. Five to six participants
2. Same race, ethnicity, and skin color
3. Similar in age, height, weight, hair color, and body build
4. Similar clothing

The way lineups are conducted is also important to reducing the risk of picking the wrong person. Lineups need to be free from the power of suggestion. Officers should tell the witness that the offender may or may not be in the lineup. Officers conducting the lineup should not know who the suspect is, and they should ask the witness to give details about why he or she picked a particular person from the lineup to substantiate the selection. Because the power of suggestion is so great in the lineup procedure, if the accused has been formally charged lineups are considered to be critical stages in the proceedings and an attorney must be present. See the case of *United States v. Wade*, 388 U.S. 218 (1967).

United States v. Wade, 388 U.S. 218 (1967)

Facts A man with a small piece of tape on each side of his face entered a bank, pointed a pistol at a cashier and the vice president of the bank, and forced them to fill a pillow case with the bank's money. The man then drove away with an accomplice. An indictment was returned against Wade and others involved in the robbery. Wade was arrested and counsel was appointed. Fifteen days later, without notice to his counsel, Wade was placed in a lineup to be viewed by the bank personnel. Both employees identified Wade as the robber, but in court they admitted seeing Wade in the custody of officials prior to the lineup. At trial, the bank personnel re-identified Wade as the robber and the prior lineup identifications were admitted as evidence. Wade was convicted of bank robbery.

Issue Should the courtroom identification of an accused be excluded as evidence because the accused was exhibited to the witness before trial at a post-indictment lineup conducted for identification purposes and without notice to and in the absence of the accused's appointed lawyer? YES

Supreme Court Decision A police lineup or other "face-to-face" confrontation after the accused has been formally charged with a crime is considered a "critical stage of the proceedings"; therefore, the accused has the right to have counsel present. The absence of counsel during such proceedings renders the evidence obtained inadmissible.

Reason "Since it appears that there is grave potential for prejudice, intentional or not, in the pretrial lineup, which may not be capable of reconstruction at trial, and since presence of counsel itself can often avert prejudice and assure a meaningful confrontation at trial, there can be little doubt that for Wade the post-indictment lineup was a critical stage of the prosecution at which he was 'as much entitled to such aid [of counsel]. . .as at the trial itself.' Thus, both Wade and his counsel should have been notified of the impending lineup, and counsel's presence should have been requisite to conduct of the lineup, absent an 'intelligent waiver.'"

Case Significance The Wade case settled the issue of whether an accused has a right to counsel after the filing of a formal charge. The standard used by the Court was whether identification was part of the "critical stage of the proceedings."

The decision in *Wade* offered some guidance to law enforcement in lineup procedures. If the defendant has been formally charged, an attorney must be present. The Court, however, did not say exactly what was meant by the phrase "critical stage of the proceeding." Thus, lower courts did not know exactly where to draw the line. In a subsequent case, *Kirby v. Illinois*, 406 U.S. 682 (1972), the Court said that any pretrial identification prior to the filing of a formal charge was not part of a "critical stage of the proceedings," and no counsel was required.

Kirby v. Illinois, 406 U.S. 682 (1972)

Facts A man reported that two men robbed him of a wallet containing traveler's checks and a Social Security card. The following day, police officers stopped Kirby and a companion. When asked for identification, Kirby produced a wallet that contained three traveler's checks and the Social Security card bearing the name of the robbery victim. The officers took Kirby and his companion to the police station. Only after arriving at the police station and checking police records did the arresting officers learn of the robbery. The victim was then brought to the police station. Immediately upon entering the room in the police station where Kirby and his companion were seated, the man positively identified them as the men who had robbed him. No lawyer was present in the room, and neither Kirby nor his companion asked for legal assistance, nor were they advised by the police of any right to the presence of counsel. Kirby was convicted of robbery.

Issue Is a suspect entitled to the presence and advice of a lawyer during an identification procedure conducted before filing of formal charges? NO

Supreme Court Decision There is no right to counsel at police lineups or identification procedures prior to the time the suspect is formally charged with the crime.

Reason "The initiation of judicial criminal proceedings is far from mere formalism. It is the starting point of our whole adversarial system of criminal justice. For it is only then that the government has committed itself to prosecute, and only then that the adverse positions of government and defendant have solidified. It is then that a defendant finds himself faced with the prosecutorial forces of organized society, and immersed in the intricacies of substantive and procedural criminal law. It is this point, therefore, that marks the commencement of the 'criminal prosecutions' to which alone the explicit guarantees of the Sixth Amendment are applicable."

Case Significance Kirby was decided five years after *United States v. Wade.* It clarified an issue that was not directly resolved in Wade: whether the ruling in Wade applied to cases in which the lineup or pretrial identification takes place prior to the filing of a formal charge. The court answered this question in the negative, saying that what happened in Kirby was a matter of routine police investigation and hence not considered a "critical stage of the proceedings." The Court reasoned that a post-indictment lineup is a "critical stage" whereas a pre-indictment lineup is not.

These two cases now provide guidelines for law enforcement about what is required to protect the rights of the accused during the lineup procedures. Officers must first determine whether this is a pre-trial lineup or a post-indictment lineup. If the lineup is pre-trial, no attorney is necessary. If it is post-indictment, an attorney is required to be present during the lineup. In any event, the lineup must be conducted in a way that is not unduly suggestive. See, for example, *Foster v. California*, 394 U.S. 440 (1969).

Foster v. California, 394 U.S. 440 (1969)

Facts The day after a robbery, one of the robbers, Foster, surrendered to the police and implicated the other two people involved. Foster was placed in a lineup with two other men and was viewed by the only witness to the robbery. Foster was wearing a jacket similar to the one worn by the robber and was several inches taller than either of the two men. The witness could not positively identify Foster as the robber and asked to speak with him. Foster was brought into an office alone and was seated at a table with the witness, but still the witness could not positively identify Foster as the robber. A week to ten days later, the witness viewed a second lineup of Foster and four completely different men. This time the witness positively identified Foster as the robber. The witness testified to the identification of Foster in the lineups and repeated the identification in court. Foster was convicted of robbery.

Issue Do lineups conducted by the police that may bias a witness' identification of a suspect violate his or her constitutional rights? YES

Supreme Court Decision Lineups that are so suggestive as to make the resulting identifications virtually inevitable violate a suspect's constitutional right to due process.

Reason "This case presents a compelling example of unfair lineup procedures. In the first lineup arranged by the police, petitioner stood out from the other two men by the contrast of his height and by the fact that he was wearing a leather jacket similar to that worn by the robber. When this did not lead to positive identification, the police permitted a one-to-one confrontation between petitioner and the witness.. . .Even after this the witness' identification of petitioner was tentative. So some days later another lineup was arranged. Petitioner was the only person in this lineup who had also participated in the first lineup.. . .This finally produced a definitive identification.. . .The suggestive elements in this identification procedure made it all but inevitable that [the witness] would identify petitioner whether or not he was in fact 'the man.' In effect, the police repeatedly said to the witness, 'This is the man.' This procedure so undermined the reliability of the eyewitness identification as to violate due process."

Case Significance This case tells the police how not to conduct a lineup. Lineups are important to the accused as well as to the police and, therefore, must be conducted properly. Any lineup that practically identifies the suspect for the witness is unfair to the suspect and violates due process. The procedure followed by the police in this case practically ensured the suspect's identification by the witness. Lineups must be fair to the suspect; otherwise, the due process rights of the suspect are violated. A fair lineup is one that guarantees no bias against the suspect.

Two other types of identification procedures include showups and **photographic arrays**. Showups are identifications of a single person, which is substantially more suggestive than including multiple people in a lineup. Nonetheless, the court is likely to admit them in the following situations:

1. Witnesses accidentally run into suspect, such as in courthouse corridors
2. Emergencies, such as when witnesses are hospitalized
3. Suspects are loose, such as when police cruise crime scenes with witnesses

The Supreme Court has affirmed the use of showup identifications, despite the strong empirical evidence of their unreliability. The Court applies the totality of the circumstances test to determine if the showup is unduly suggestive. The determination of whether the accused is entitled to counsel at the showup again depends upon whether he or she has been formally charged with the offense.

The final form of witness identification is photographic arrays. The fewer number of pictures in the array, the less reliable the identification is because the suggestive nature of the process grows. The Court, however, has approved photographic arrays largely because they can be reproduced for the jury and the jury can determine the extent to which they are unduly suggestive. See the case of *Manson v. Brathwaite*, 432 U.S. 98 (1977).

Based on the above cases, determining whether counsel must be present and whether the identification procedure is

Manson v. Brathwaite, 432 U.S. 98 (1977)

Facts Glover (an undercover police officer) and an informant (Brown) went to an apartment building to buy narcotics from a known drug dealer (it was later determined that the officer and informant did not make the drug purchase from the intended person). As they stood at the door, the area was illuminated by natural light from a window in the hallway. Glover knocked on the door, and a man opened the door 12 to 18 inches. Brown identified himself, and Glover asked for "two things" of narcotics and then gave the man $20. The man closed the door and later returned and gave Glover two glassine bags. While the door was open, Glover stood within two feet of the man and observed his face. At headquarters, immediately after the sale, Glover described the seller to two other officers; however, at that time, Glover did not know the identity of the seller. He described the seller as "a colored man, approximately five feet eleven inches tall, dark complexion, black hair, short Afro style, and having high cheekbones, and of heavy build. He was wearing at the time blue pants and a plaid shirt." One of the officers suspected who the seller was, obtained a picture of Brathwaite from the Records Division, and left it in Glover's office. Glover identified the person as the man who sold him narcotics two days before. Brathwaite was arrested in the same apartment building where the narcotics sale had occurred. Brathwaite was charged with possession and sale of heroin. At his trial, the photograph from which Glover had identified Brathwaite was admitted into evidence. Although Glover had not seen Brathwaite in eight months, "there [was] no doubt whatsoever" in his mind that the person shown in the picture was Brathwaite. Glover also made a positive in-court identification of Brathwaite. Brathwaite testified that, on the day of the alleged sale, he had been ill at his apartment and at no time on that particular day had he been at the place of the drug deal. His wife, after Brathwaite had refreshed her memory, also testified that he was home all day. Brathwaite was found guilty of possession and sale of heroin.

Issue Should pretrial identification evidence obtained by a police examination of a single photograph be excluded as evidence under the due process clause if it was thought to be suggestive and unnecessary, regardless of whether it was reliable? NO

Supreme Court Decision "The admission of testimony concerning a suggestive and unnecessary identification procedure does not violate due process so long as the identification possesses sufficient aspects of reliability."

Reason Using a previous case, *Stovall v. Denno*, the Supreme Court concluded that reliability is the "linchpin in determining the admissibility of identification testimony." The factors for the court to consider for reliability were stated in *Neil v. Biggers*: (1) the opportunity for the witness to view the criminal at the time of the crime, (2) the witness' degree of attention, (3) the accuracy of any prior description of the criminal, (4) the level of certainty demonstrated at the identification procedure, and (5) the time between the crime and the identification procedure. The Court then took the facts of the case and applied the five-factor analysis. Glover had a substantial opportunity to view Brathwaite as he stood within two feet of Brathwaite for two to three minutes while the man twice stood with the door open. Also, there was natural light entering a window in the hallway aiding the view. Furthermore, Glover was not a casual observer, and, being of the same race as respondent, it was unlikely he would perceive only general features. Glover then provided a very detailed description of respondent to the other officer immediately after the sale and identified him from a picture two days later. Glover was also very positive in his identification of Brathwaite as he testified that there was no question whatsoever. The time between the crime and the identification procedure was very short, as Glover gave his description to the officer immediately after the crime and positively identified Brathwaite only two days later by the photograph. The Court concluded: "These indicators of

Glover's ability to make an accurate identification are hardly outweighed by the corrupting effect of the challenged identification itself."

Case Significance The Supreme Court concluded that the five factors set forth in Biggers should be used to test the reliability of the identification. The opportunity to view asks whether the officer was at a distance adequate enough to examine the suspect and whether the officer had a sufficient amount of time to examine him or her, while also considering the environmental factors, such as daylight. The degree of attention refers to the amount of attention the officer placed on examining the suspect. This could be revealed in the accuracy of the description: Did the officer provide a very detailed description of the suspect, such as Glover's, or an undetailed description? The witness' level of certainty describes how certain the officer was of his identification of the suspect after the alleged incident or crime occurred. Finally, the time between the crime and the confrontation or identification of the suspect is important because long periods of time between the crime and identification produce a greater likelihood of the officer forgetting the exact details that he first saw in the suspect, thus making the officer's identification less reliable.

unduly suggestive depends on each individual case. The Court has stated that identifications that occur after an accused has been formally charged are critical stages in the proceeding and must have counsel present. Whether or not counsel is required, identifications must comply with due process of law and not be unduly suggestive.

10.3 Interrogations after Formal Charges Have Been Filed

Defendants also have a right to counsel when they are being interrogated after they have been indicted but before trial. This right looks a lot like the Fifth Amendment rights contained in the *Miranda* warnings. In a Fifth Amendment situation, however, when the defendant has not been charged, courts have held that an undercover police officer can be placed in the cell with the defendant and engage in conversation about the offense without violating the Fifth Amendment rights included in the *Miranda* warning.[a] The Court reasoned that the Fifth Amendment privilege is not implicated when a suspect is not aware he is speaking to law enforcement and then gives incriminating statements. The Court determined that the suspect was motivated only by his desire to impress his fellow inmates, had no reason to think that the agent had

[a] *Illinois v. Perkins*, 496 U.S. 292 (1990).

legal authority to force the suspect to give testimony, and showed no signs of being intimidated. In the case of *Illinois v. Perkins*, 496 U.S. 292 (1990), no Sixth Amendment right to counsel concerns were applicable because the defendant had not been charged. An earlier decision reached a different result because the defendant had already been indicted. See *United States v. Henry*, 447 U.S. 264 (1980).

United States v. Henry, 447 U.S. 264 (1980)

Facts Henry was indicted for armed robbery and incarcerated. While in jail, government agents contacted an informant who was a cellmate of Henry and instructed him to be alert to any statements made by Henry, but not to initiate any conversations regarding the robbery. After the informant had been released from jail, he was contacted by the agents and paid for information he provided them concerning incriminating statements Henry made to him in reference to the robbery. There was no indication that the informant would have been paid had he not provided such information. Henry was convicted of robbery, based partly on the testimony of the informant.

Issue Is a defendant denied the right to counsel under the Sixth Amendment if the government uses a paid informant to create a situation likely to induce incriminating statements? YES

Supreme Court Decision The government violates a defendant's Sixth Amendment right to counsel by intentionally creating a situation likely to elicit incriminating statements.

Reason "The question here is whether under the facts of this case a Government agent 'deliberately elicited' incriminating statements from Henry.. . .Three factors are important. First, Nichols [the informant] was acting under instructions as a paid informant for the Government; second, Nichols was ostensibly no more than a fellow inmate of Henry; and third, Henry was in custody under indictment at the time he was engaged in conversation with Nichols.. . .The Government argues that federal agents instructed Nichols not to question Henry about the robbery. Yet, according to his own testimony, Nichols was not a passive listener; rather, he had 'some conversations with Mr. Henry' while he was in jail and Henry's incriminatory statements were 'the product of this conversation.'"

Case Significance This is a Sixth Amendment right to counsel case rather than a Fifth Amendment privilege against self-incrimination case. The evidence obtained was excluded because the government violated the suspect's right to a lawyer. The Court said that, here, the government created a situation likely to induce the suspect to make incriminating statements without the assistance of counsel. The Court said that incriminating statements were "deliberately elicited" by the informant, which the police cannot do in the absence of a lawyer. Great weight was given by the Court to the fact that the informant was acting under government instruction and that Henry was in custody under indictment at the time the incriminating statements were made.

The cases of *Illinois v. Perkins* and *United States v. Henry* seem almost indistinguishable at first glance. In both situations, government officials went into the cell with an inmate and obtained information that was later used against the inmate without the inmate's knowledge. In one of the cases, however, the Fifth Amendment analysis led to the conclusion that no violation had occurred, where in the other case, the Sixth Amendment analysis led to the conclusion that a violation had occurred. These cases illustrate the importance of understanding where the defendant is in the trial process at any given point to understand what Constitutional provision is guiding government actions.

10.4 Right to an Attorney at Trial

While arguments occur about what constitutes a critical stage of the trial process, no argument exists that the accused is entitled to have counsel at the actual trial. A difference exists, however, between the right to counsel and actually having counsel present. Courts have always recognized criminal defendants' Sixth Amendment right to retained counsel, but they did not recognize the right to appointed counsel until well into the 1900 s. **Indigent** defendants had to rely of those attorneys who were willing to act pro bono. Courts were not obligated to provide counsel for defendants when they could not pay. In the first cases establishing rights to counsel, defendants were only entitled to free attorneys in the most serious of cases. See, for example, *Powell v. Alabama,* 287 U.S. 45 (1932).

Powell v. Alabama, 287 U.S. 45 (1932)

Capsule The trial in state court of nine youths for a capital offense without a defense attorney violated their right to due process.

Facts Nine black youths were charged with the rape of two white girls while on a train in Alabama. All were illiterate. The atmosphere in the town was such that the boys had to be held in a different town under military guard during the proceedings. The judge appointed "all members of the bar" to assist the boys during the proceedings; however, they were not represented by any attorney by name until the day of the trial. Each of the trials lasted only a day and resulted in a conviction. The youths were given the death penalty.

Issue Were the defendants in this case denied their constitutional rights to counsel and due process? YES

Supreme Court Decision "In a capital case, where the defendant is unable to employ counsel, and is incapable adequately of making his own defense because of ignorance, feeblemindedness, illiteracy, or the like, it is the duty of the court, whether requested or not, to assign counsel for him as a necessary requisite of due process of law; and that duty is not discharged by an assignment at such a time or under such circumstances as to preclude the giving of effective aid in the preparation and trial of the case."

Reason "Even the intelligent and educated layman has small and sometimes no skill in the science of the law. Left without aid of counsel, he may be put on trial without proper charge, and convicted upon incompetent evidence irrelevant to the issue or otherwise against him. Without counsel, though he may not be guilty, he faces the danger of conviction because he does not know how to establish his innocence."

Case Significance The Sixth Amendment to the Constitution provides that "in all criminal prosecutions, the accused shall enjoy the right. . .to have the assistance of counsel for his defense." This case provides the often-quoted reason (penned by Justice Sutherland) for this constitutional provision. Without a lawyer, an accused may be convicted, not because he or she is guilty but because "he does not know how to establish his innocence." The right to counsel is a basic and fundamental right under the Constitution and must be respected by the police. Note that, in this case, the Court used the due process clause of the Fourteenth Amendment rather than the Sixth Amendment right to counsel to overturn the convictions. This is because, in 1932, when the case was decided, the provisions of the Bill of Rights had not yet been extended to state proceedings. Were this case to be decided today, the Sixth Amendment right to counsel provision would have been used.

In *Powell v. Alabama,* 287 U.S. 45 (1932), the Supreme Court held that the trial in state court for a capital offense without a defense attorney violated the right to due process. This case determined that, for a capitol offense, defendants must be represented by an attorney, but it did not go so far as to establish the requirement that an attorney be provided in all felony cases. That decision was reached in *Gideon v. Wainwright,* 372 U.S. 335 (1963).

Gideon v. Wainwright, 372 U.S. 335 (1963)

Facts Gideon was charged in a Florida state court with breaking and entering a poolroom with intent to commit a misdemeanor, an act classified as a felony offense under Florida law. Appearing in court without funds and without a lawyer, Gideon asked the court to appoint a lawyer for him. The court refused, saying that under Florida law the only time the court could appoint a lawyer to represent an accused was when the crime charged was a capital offense. Gideon conducted his own defense and was convicted.

Issue Does the Constitution require appointment of counsel for an indigent person who is charged in a state court with a felony offense? YES

Supreme Court Decision The Sixth Amendment requires that a person charged with a felony offense in a state court be appointed counsel if he or she cannot afford it.

Reason "The right of one charged with crime to counsel may not be deemed fundamental and essential to fair trials in some countries, but it is in ours. From the very beginning, our state and national constitutions and laws have laid great emphasis on procedural and substantive safeguards designed to assure fair trials before impartial tribunals in which every defendant stands equal before the law. This noble ideal cannot be realized if the poor man charged with a crime has to face his accusers without a lawyer to assist him."

Case Significance This case mandates that when an indigent person is charged with a felony in a state court counsel must be provided. This settled a controversy among lower courts, which had inconsistent rulings on the type of offense an indigent had to be charged with in order to be entitled to a lawyer. An earlier decision (*Betts v. Brady,* 316 U.S. 455 [1942]),which held that the requirement that counsel be provided to all indigent defendants in federal felony trials, did not extend to the states. This was overruled in the *Gideon* case when the Supreme Court held that the rule applied to criminal proceedings in state courts as well.

Since 1963, counsel must be appointed for indigent defendants in both federal and state courts when the defendant was accused of a felony. The holding in *Gideon* only required the appointment of counsel for indigents in felony cases. This was later extended to misdemeanor cases in *Argersinger v. Hamlin,* 407 U.S. 25 (1972). Today, any defendant who could face time in a secure facility, jail or prison, is entitled to have counsel appointed, at the expense of the state during the trial.

10.5 Speedy Trial

The concept of a **speedy trial** has been around for centuries, dating back to the *Magna Carta* in 1215. The right to a speedy trial balances several interests. For the accused, it prevents prolonged detention before trial, reduces the anxiety and uncertainty surrounding the prosecution, and guards against weakening the defense's case through the loss of witnesses and other evidence. The speedy trial provision also serves the interest of reaching the correct result. Lengthy delays leads to lost evidence and lost witnesses, or at least impaired memory, for the defense and prosecution equally. Issues related to speedy trial provisions, however, are not as straightforward as the guarantee may seem at first glance.

The Supreme Court has determined that the speedy trial clock does not start to run until the suspect has been formally charged with a crime. The time between when the crime occurred and when the defendant is arrested is not governed by the speedy trial provision but by the concept of statute of limitations. Some crimes have shorter statutes of limitations and some crimes have no statutes of limitations. Thus, when long delays have occurred between the commission of the crime and bringing formal charges against someone accused of the crime, the proper motion by the defendant is that prosecution is barred by the statute of limitations. Once the defendant has been charged, the time between charging and the actual trial gives rise to the claim of speedy trial violations.

The right to a speedy trial prohibits only undue delays. The Supreme Court has determined that the trial process must be flexible. It adopted a balancing test to decide whether delays prejudice the defendant's case. Four elements go into the balance:

1. The length of the delay
2. The reason for the delay
3. The defendant's assertion of his or her right to a speedy trial
4. The prejudice the delay caused the defendants case

The Court has declined to set a specific term, such as 18 months, as a bright line for violating the speedy trial provision. Some states, however, have set time limits for bringing cases to trial. These limits vary widely from state to state. The Federal Speedy Trial Act provides definite time periods in federal court. The government has to initiate prosecution within 30 days after arrest, 60 days if there is no grand jury in session; arraign defendants within 10 days after filing indictments or information; and bring defendants to trial within 60 days following arraignments. According to the act, the following delays do not count in computing days:

1. Delays needed to determine the defendant's competency to stand trial
2. Delays due to other trials of the defendant
3. Delays due to hearings on pretrial motions
4. Delays because of interlocutory appeals—provisional appeals that interrupt the proceedings, such as an appeal from a ruling on a pretrial motion

Furthermore, if defendants are not confined prior to trial, have been the one requesting the delay, or have not asserted the right to a speedy trial, it is unlikely that the court will find violations of the speedy trial clause.

10.6 Trial by Jury

Defendants are constitutionally entitled to a **jury trial** before a jury of their peers. This right was determined to be a fundamental right in *Duncan v. Louisiana,* 391 U.S. 145 (1968), where a defendant was convicted and sentenced for a misdemeanor without a jury trial.

Duncan v. Louisiana, 391 U.S. 145 (1968)

Facts In 1966, the appellant was driving his car when he saw his two younger black cousins on the side of the road with four white boys. The appellant's cousins had recently transferred to another school with reported racial problems. The appellant stopped the car and got out to approach the six boys. A discussion ensued, and the appellant and his cousins decided to get back into the car and leave. Prior to getting into the car, a white boy testified that the appellant slapped his elbow. The appellant stated that he merely touched the boy on the elbow. The appellant was charged with simple battery and requested a trial by jury. His request was denied. The trial judge concluded that the elements of simple battery were proven by the state and found the appellant guilty of the crime. The appellant sought review in the Louisiana Supreme Court, claiming the state's denial of trial by jury was a violation of the Constitution. The Supreme Court of Louisiana denied review.

Issue Does a state law granting a jury trial only in cases where the penalty is capital punishment or imprisonment at hard labor violate the Constitution? YES

Supreme Court Decision

Reason The Constitution was violated when appellant's demand for jury trial was refused. Trial by jury in criminal cases is fundamental to the American scheme of justice because it works to prevent governmental oppression.

Case Significance The right to a trial by jury in serious criminal cases works as a defense against arbitrary law enforcement and qualifies for protection under the due process clause of the Fourteenth Amendment of the Constitution. There has been debate over whether laymen can determine the facts in civil and criminal proceedings. Critics express a concern that juries are incapable of properly understanding evidence or determining issues of fact; however, juries do understand the evidence and come to sound conclusions in most cases presented to them. We are not suggesting that every criminal trial held before a judge is unfair or that a defendant may never be treated fairly by a judge. The purpose of a right to jury trial is to reduce the possibility of judicial or prosecutorial unfairness.

After *Duncan v. Louisiana*, all defendants in state criminal trials were constitutionally entitled to a trial by jury. Defendants can waive that right, but they are entitled to it. For some time, the 12-member jury was regarded as essential to the right to a jury trial. In *Williams v. Florida*, 399 U.S. 78 (1970), the Court retreated from that position, stating that we do not know the intent of the framers of the Constitution, the number 12 is based on superstition, and that history does not give good reasons to stick to the number 12 in today's world. Thus, the Court determined that the Sixth Amendment demands only enough jurors to achieve the goals of a jury trial: to find the truth and allow for community participation in criminal justice decision making. Still, there remains a preference for 12-member juries in most felony cases. The Court has allowed juries of six to pass constitutional scrutiny, but not five.[b] Although jury verdicts are not required to be unanimous in all cases, the Supreme Court has not answered the question of how many votes short of unanimity are required to satisfy the Sixth Amendment, but appears to be somewhere around a 2/3 majority, at least for non capital cases. In 1979, however, the U.S. Supreme Court determined that in juries composed of 6 members, the verdict must be unanimous. *Bush v. Louisiana*, 441 U.S. 130 (1979).

To comply with the jury requirement of the Sixth Amendment, juries must represent a fair cross section of the community. Furthermore, the equal protection clause of the Fourteenth Amendment prohibits the systematic exclusion of members of a defendant's racial, gender, ethnic, or religious group from the jury. Juries must be randomly selected from a cross-section of the community in the district or division where the court convenes, and no citizen shall be excluded from service based on race, color, religion, sex, national origin, or economic status.

Finally, jury trials must also be public. Public trials protect public access and allow the public to attend the proceedings, as well as the defendants' rights to attend their own trials. The right to a public trial extends to every stage of the trial, including jury selection, communication between judge and jury, jury instructions, and in-chamber conversations between judge and jurors. Some limitations to the public trial are put in place to protect the sanctity of the trial process and to protect the integrity of certain victims. For example, in cases of child sexual abuse cases, steps may be taken to protect the child victim from being re-traumatized. Also, in cases of particularly dangerous defendants, courts can require the defendant to appear under guard to protect the public, witnesses, and court officials from harm. As a general rule, however, defendants have a right both to be present and to be presented in a way that does not prejudice their case.

10.7 Summary

This chapter covers basic trial rights of a defendant. Trial rights generally apply after formal charges have been placed on the defendant. These rights can extend to circumstances outside of the actual trial process, however, such as lineups, showups, and photographic arrays. Additionally, if police question a

[b] *Ballow v. Georgia*, 435 U.S. 223 (1978).

defendant after he has been indicted, a violation of the Sixth Amendment may require that the testimony be excluded from trial.

Defendants are entitled to be represented by counsel at all critical stages of the proceedings, especially at trials. Representation is guaranteed for any criminal case which could result in confinement, regardless of whether it is considered a misdemeanor or felony. Further, if the defendant cannot afford an attorney, the state must provide one for him or her through the trial and the first appeal.

Defendants are entitled to a speedy trial before a jury of their peers. Jury trials are guaranteed in any criminal case in which the defendant could be sentenced to confinement regardless of whether the case is considered a misdemeanor or a felony. Juries must represent a broad cross-section of the community and should not be comprised on the basis of race, religion, ethnicity, or any other unique characteristic.

Further Reading

Argersinger v. Hamlin, 407 U.S. 25 (1972).
Ballow v. Georgia, 435 U.S. 223 (1978).
Betts v. Brady, 316 U.S. 455 (1942).
Bush v. Louisiana, 441 U.S. 130 (1979).
Duncan v. Louisiana, 391 U.S. 145 (1968).
Foster v. California, 394 U.S. 440 (1969).
Gideon v. Wainwright, 372 U.S. 335 (1963).
Illinois v. Perkins, 496 U.S. 292 (1990).
Kirby v. Illinois, 406 U.S. 682 (1972).
Manson v. Brathwait, 432 U.S. 98 (1977).
Powell v. Alabama, 287 U.S. 45 (1932).
United States v. Henry, 447 U.S. 264 (1980).
United States v. Wade, 388 U.S. 218 (1967).
Williams v. Florida, 399 U.S. 78 (1970).

11

THE ADVERSARY SYSTEM

CHAPTER OUTLINE

KEY TERMS

Adversary system
Advocates
Bench trial
Defense attorney
Jurist
Prosecutor

LEARNING OBJECTIVES

- Identify the key players in the adversary system of justice.
- Understand the difference between adversary system and accusatory system.
- Understand the role of each of the key players in the adversary system.
- Identify effective assistance of counsel.

Decency, security and liberty alike demand that government officials shall be subjected to the same rules of conduct that are commands to the citizen. In a government of laws, existence of the government will be imperiled if it fails to observe the law scrupulously. Our government is the potent, the omnipresent teacher. For good or for ill, it teaches the whole people by its example.

Mr. Justice Brandeis[a]

[a]*Olmstead v. United States*, 277 U.S. 438, 485, 48S. Ct. 564, 72L. Ed. 944 (1928) (dissenting opinion).

We know that a trial based on false or suppressed evidence is not trial at all. False or suppressed evidence can neither convict nor condemn.

United States ex rel., Hough v. Maroney[b]

11.1 Introduction

Our adversarial system of justice, which is based on the concept of a fair trial before a jury of one's peers and which is governed by written rules of law, is the successor to many other types of dispute resolutions that have been tried and failed. Most of the past attempts at resolving disputes have involved personal violence and less than fair processes. Many of them did not involve the benefit of trained legal counsel, nor did they involve a fair trial. Often the accused was subjected to some sort of "ordeal" or battle ([1]Abram, 1963). If he passed he was considered not guilty, but often he died in the ordeal or battle itself. The most common penalty for an accused, prior to our current system of justice, was death. One of the fundamental arguments in favor of resolving disputes in the courtroom is that no better method of resolving controversies has been found. Our system is an adversary system, which means that the accused and the state are represented by counsel. Further, our system affords the accused the benefit of the doubt, as he or she is innocent until proved guilty. Other systems of justice are acquisitory instead of adversary. The accused must prove his or her innocence before the trier of fact. In many other systems, the jury is not composed of ordinary citizens nor is the accused represented by counsel.

Another uniqueness of our system is that citizens are guaranteed a fair and impartial trial before a jury of their peers. Public trials that involve juries, by their nature, are unpredictable, and many times cases do not result in convictions. Occasionally, officers experience frustration over the length of the trial or the outcome of the trial. Officers may work on a case for one or two years only to have the jury return a not guilty verdict. Officers may sit in court day after day waiting to testify, or the judge may determine that critical evidence must be suppressed because officers' actions violated a constitutional protection. Such frustrations can cause one to call the entire

[b]247F. Supp. 767, 779 (W.D. Pa. 1965).

system into question. We should remember, however, the many types of dispute resolutions that have existed in our history and have failed.

Nine hundred years ago in England, a landowner unjustly deprived of his property had five days to round up an army and retake his property by storm. If the landowner failed, his land became the lawful property of the usurper. As late as the 1600s in the United States, those accused of crimes were sometimes thrown, with hands and feet bound, into tanks of water. If they floated, they were judged guilty and hanged. If they sank, they were declared innocent and, of course, drowned. These types of resolutions are far removed from the sense of liberty and ordered justice we currently enjoy. Today these methods for allegedly discovering the truth or bringing one to justice shock our conscience and seem barbaric. The application of the U.S. Constitution to the trial process has created the foundation of justice that we most think of today. The principles that have been discussed in this book provide the basis for calling us a civilized society and underscore our concepts of ordered liberty.

11.2 Responsibility of Advocates

The American court is based on an adversary process that is unique compared to other courts throughout the world. A perceptive commentator observed: "The adversarial component of the litigation process is the cornerstone of the American justice system. Ideally, if two equally matched attorneys zealously and competently represent their clients within the bounds of the ethical rules and the law, the correct result will ultimately be reached" ([4]Brown, 2001). Under our law, the success of the trial system depends upon both sides being represented by contentious opposing **advocates**. The principle that leads to spirited give-and-take in criminal prosecutions is one upon which our American theory of trial is based—that of an **adversary**, or contentious, **system** of justice.

This system is based on the assumption that the truth of any controversy will come out best when each side (the defendant as well as the state) vigorously presents its evidence and presses the theory of law supporting its case. Thus, the defense lawyer only does his or her duty to the client and the legal system when he or she conducts the client's cause with devotion, zeal, and professionalism. For practical purposes, the defense attorney in a criminal case represents the constitutional interest of the defendant. Only rights that we are prepared to give up for ourselves should we be willing to sacrifice for others. Thus, in any case, we must always ask if allowing state actions to further infringe on citizens rights is going further than we are prepared to go ourselves.

11.3 Role of the Defense Attorney

Ethical rules prohibit an attorney from knowingly using perjured testimony or offering evidence the attorney knows to be false. Perjured testimony is testimony that is false and is given under oath in a trial. If the perjury is discovered, the person giving it can be subjected to sanctions. Likewise, if an attorney knowingly allows a client to offered perjured testimony, the attorney can be subjected to sanctions for suborning perjury. Although a lawyer is bound by an ethical code to preserve the confidences and secrets of his or her client, the attorney is likewise bound professionally and ethically to respect our system of justice. If the defense attorney knows, or has reason to know, that the testimony a client will offer is false, the attorney should not call the client as a witness.

Additionally, while the **defense attorney** has the duty to advise the client, it is the client who decides what plea to enter. If the client pleads guilty, the attorney begins a process of negotiating the best possible sentence the client can get. If, however, the client pleads "not guilty," defense counsel has the responsibility to vigorously pursue the defense through trial of the case.

One observer has commented that attorneys representing defendants differ from other members of the profession and the general public—not because of any professional or moral superiority but because they play a unique and essential institutional role in our criminal justice system: "They serve as the necessary advocates of defendants' rights. By fulfilling that role, they vindicate limits the Constitution imposes upon government power, and assure that the adversary justice system functions correctly. Recognition of defense counsel's dual roles suggests that Sixth Amendment theory should do more than simply guarantee the right of individual defendants to a lawyer. It should also protect the ability of attorneys, individually and collectively, to provide that representation" ([7]Cloud, 1987).

Commentators have urged that, of all the rights that an accused person has, the right to representation by a trained lawyer is the most important: "Only the adversarial system can effectuate the search for the truth. The alternative is a nonadversarial society whereby one being accused is the equivalent of one being convicted. If criminal defense lawyers do not 'put the government to its proof whenever necessary or whenever the client requires it, then we are close to those totalitarian states where accusation equals guilt [and] the criminal defense lawyers are but an adjunct prosecutor expected to make the client confess and aid in his or her rehabilitation.' Hence, if criminal defendants are not represented, the foundation of the judicial system is eroded" (Jones, 1998).

11.4 Effective Assistance of Counsel

Implicit in the Sixth Amendment right to counsel is that counsel provide effective representation. This right means more than simply assigning a lawyer to a criminal defendant. The lawyer must fulfill the role of trained legal counsel in representing the accused. Although no checklist of determining effectiveness has been identified by the courts, at the very least counsel's conduct must comply with basic norms and procedures identified by the American Bar Association. Whether an attorney's representation of an accused crosses the threshold of constitutionally ineffective assistance of counsel depends on a two-part inquiry, as the Supreme Court explained in *Strickland v. Washington*, 466 U.S. 668 (1984). First, counsel's representation must fall below the basic standard of care required of an attorney. This analysis includes identifying whether counsel fulfilled his or her duty of loyalty to the defendant. Counsel has a duty to avoid conflicts of interest and to advocate the defendant's cause. Furthermore, counsel is required to consult with the defendant on important decisions and to keep the defendant informed of important developments in the case. Counsel is required in criminal cases because the Court has determined that special legal knowledge is required to ensure that the adversarial process arrives at a reliable conclusion. Thus, counsel is expected to use that specialized knowledge in preparing the defense of the case. In reviewing effectiveness of counsel, however, courts must give great deference to counsel's representation and not second guess counsel's decisions based on the negative outcome of the case. The court deciding an actual ineffectiveness claim must judge the reasonableness of counsel's challenged conduct on the facts of the particular case, as viewed as of the time of counsel's conduct, not viewed retrospectively based on the result of the case.

The second, and most important, consideration for an ineffective assistance of counsel claim is whether the error on the part of counsel had an adverse impact on the outcome of the case. The purpose of the Sixth Amendment guarantee of counsel is to ensure that a defendant has the assistance necessary to justify reliance on the outcome of the proceeding. Accordingly, any deficiencies in counsel's performance must be prejudicial to the defense to constitute ineffective assistance of counsel.

11.5 Role of the Prosecutor

The most famous and frequently quoted statement on the role of the **prosecutor** appears in *Berger v. United States*, 295 U.S. 78 (1935):

> *The United States Attorney is the representative not of an ordinary party to a controversy, but of a sovereignty whose obligation to govern impartially is as compelling as its obligation to govern at all; and whose interest, therefore, in a criminal prosecution is not that it shall win a case, but that justice shall be done. As such, he is in a peculiar and very definite sense the servant of the law, the twofold aim of which is that guilt shall not escape or innocence suffer. He may prosecute with earnestness and vigor—indeed, he should do so. But, while he may strike hard blows, he is not at liberty to strike foul ones. It is as much his duty to refrain from improper methods calculated to produce a wrongful conviction as it is to use every legitimate means to bring about a just one.*

Just as a witness has a responsibility to the truth and to correct the record, points detailed in the next section of the text, so does the prosecutor. When knowledge comes to a prosecutor that perjurious testimony has been used on behalf of the state, the prosecutor has a duty to correct it. In addition, the prosecutor is charged with the responsibility of turning over to the defense attorney any exculpatory evidence that might be discovered during the investigation. Failure to disclose such evidence is grounds for sanctions against the prosecutor.

The ultimate goal of the criminal prosecution, to seek the truth, can never be ignored. The prosecutor has a role to play in that as well. Overzealous prosecution for personal or political gain or selective prosecution based on some bias has no place in the American system of justice. The end can never justify the means.

11.6 Responsibility of Police Officers

Police officers are singularly important persons in the adversary process. Frequently, they are the chief witnesses for the government, and much of the zeal of the defense is spent on them. How a police officer reacts to this pressure in court will determine to a large extent whether the integrity of the legal process will be maintained. It is helpful to keep this in mind and to resist in the heat of battle any temptation to win by foul means. When the officer is in court, he or she should never refrain from correcting his or her testimony when an honest error has been made. The matter should be brought to the attention of the court as soon as the mistake is realized, for it is improper to leave inaccurate testimony standing in the record. Although the law enforcement officer is naturally interested in successful prosecutions, he or she must also guard against showing a specific interest in gaining a conviction. Respect is lost when a jury perceives a tenacious desire on an officer's part to achieve conviction at any cost. Telling the truth is of paramount importance. If testimony is shaded to help the prosecution, it will likely rebound to the detriment of the government, either in the trial itself or later in habeas corpus. "Fairness in our system, and the appearance of fairness, is essential if the system is to win the respect and cooperation of all citizens, without which crime cannot be controlled" ([5]Campbell et al., 1969).

The government wins in a criminal case only when justice is done. This means that both the police and the prosecutor have a particular responsibility to make certain that fair tactics and truthful evidence prevail in criminal trials. The following statement is as true today as when it was initially made in 1935: "It is as much his [the prosecutor's] duty to refrain from improper methods calculated to produce a wrongful conviction as it is to use every legitimate means to bring about a just one" (*Berger v. United States*, 295 U.S. 78 [1935]).

11.7 Responsibility of Judges

Whether the judge is accepting a guilty plea, presiding at a jury trial, or hearing a case without a jury, impartiality is essential. Particularly sensitive are cases in which the judge decides the case without a jury, conducting a **bench trial** in which the court sits as the sole trier of both the facts and the law:

> *When sitting as a trier of facts, a judge, like a jury, must be careful to exclude all considerations except those arising from the*

evidence before him. Anything less, even if it has no part in the ultimate decision, leaves the unsuccessful litigant convinced he has not had fair treatment. It is almost as important to avoid this appearance of unfairness as it is to avoid unfairness itself. Hall v. State, 325 N.W. 2d 752 (Iowa, 1982)

The judge faces a difficult task. If the trial judge wields her power arbitrarily in favor of the prosecution, the defendant and his or her family will think the defendant "got railroaded." At the other extreme, partiality in favor of a defendant will be scrutinized, and judicial handling of criminal cases has sometimes engendered public resentment when a prosecution was dismissed or a sentence was viewed as "soft." In such sensitive times, it is critical that trial judges handling criminal cases do so with deftness and with fairness to both sides in the process. In meting out justice, the judge must display "cold neutrality," in the words of Edmund Burke. In his classic definition of a good judge, Socrates cited the need for the **jurist** to hear courteously, consider soberly, and decide impartially. These principles were reviewed in a case involving actions by a trial judge when a defendant was tried on charges flowing from a drug deal that had fatal consequences. The defendant believed a person named Rowe owed her money for drugs she had supplied to Rowe. The defendant enlisted Arnold, Walton, and Turnipseed to assist in recovering the debt. When one of them said he intended to kill Rowe, the defendant replied: "I didn't tell y'all to kill nobody. [I] told you to go over there and whip his ass and take my money and take my dope."

While the defendant's threesome was searching Rowe's house, a friend of Rowe entered Rowe's home. Arnold shot him in the chest and killed him. The defendant was charged with conspiracy to commit armed robbery and felony murder. She was given a new trial because of the actions of the trial judge. A description of the judge's conduct is detailed in the state supreme court opinion and is outlined hereafter.

During jury selection, the defense attorney rose from his chair, presumably to address the judge. "According to a witness who was in the courtroom, however, before counsel could speak, the trial judge spoke in a loud, harsh and condemning voice, telling counsel to 'sit down and shut up'" (*Johnson v. State*, 278 Ga. 344 [2004]). The state supreme court, which reversed the defendant's conviction, spotted another error that the appellate justices deemed to be a glaring one. When the defense attorney objected to a question asked by the prosecutor, the judge warned the defense lawyer not to "interrupt the [State's witness examination] again" by raising objections. "Conversely, while defense counsel was cross-examining a different witness, the judge interposed his own objection to the questions being posed, even though the prosecutor had raised no objection on behalf of the State."

Finally, after a number of such incidents, the defense attorney asked the judge to remove himself from the bench because the judge had assisted the prosecutor in making the State's case before the jury. The trial judge responded by denying the defense motion, then warned the defense counsel that, if he sought again to bring discredit upon the court, the court would cite him for contempt. In view of this record, the state supreme court had grave doubts about whether the defendant was convicted in a fair trial. The reviewing court stated:

> *We are mindful of the extraordinary pressures attending a criminal trial of this magnitude. On the one hand, defense counsel is obligated to vigorously defend his client against all charges brought by the State. Likewise, prosecutors must effectively present the State's case to the jury. At the same time, the trial judge is charged with ensuring that the rules of evidence and procedure are followed, and that the proceedings are both orderly and fair. When these several interests come together in the courtroom during trial, we believe that occasional, brief disagreements between the bench and bar are to be expected.*
>
> *The instances discussed above, however, represent more than mere friction between zealous counsel and a diligent jurist. The judge's conduct, as discussed above, created the impression that he harbored an inclination to be biased against [the defendant] and partial toward the prosecution.... Because the trial judge's impartiality was questionable, it was error for him to deny appellant's motion for recusal. Because we cannot say it is likely that the incidents discussed above had no impact on the jury's disposition of this matter, we must reverse the judgments of conviction.*
>
> *Other authorities point out that a judge should not sneer at a witness's testimony nor laugh derisively at a lawyer's question. A trial judge should not "telegraph to a jury, by purposeful exclamations, gestures or facial expressions, his approval or disapproval, belief or disbelief, in the testimony of witnesses or arguments of counsel." Above all else, the trial court should not exhibit a hostile attitude toward any party in any case before the bench.* Long v. Broadlawns Medical Center, *656 N.W. 2d 71 (Iowa, 2002)*

11.8 Need for Support and Reform of System

Enforcement of the law, like the laws themselves, requires public assistance and cooperation. In addition to his or her attitude toward the trial process as previously noted, the relationship of the law officer to the court system as a whole is important. The court system needs our support, as well as our responsible criticism. The latter assists in catalyzing needed revisions and reforms. Those working in the criminal justice system are in an excellent position to provide both. Bill of Rights provisions, sometimes vigorously enforced by the courts to the detriment of the police, do indeed make it more difficult to secure convictions, but this is one of the prices we pay for living in a free society. Another need is that of society to provide adequate resources to assure efficient and responsible administration of the criminal laws. A task force report to the National Violence Commission has suggested that the public could assist the police in a much more meaningful way. The report suggests that we could greatly assist the police if we provided funding for additional crime laboratories, adequate prosecutorial staffs, and additional correctional treatment.

11.9 Summary

This chapter provides a summary of the role of the court system and the key players in that system. The judge, the prosecutor, the defense attorney, and the police each have critical roles to play in the administration of justice. The rules of criminal procedure are designed to ensure that the results of criminal trials are final and that fairness accompanies the court process from beginning to end. The Amendments to the U.S. Constitution provide basic protections to citizens in their interactions with government, and the jury provides an additional barrier between the state and the rights of its citizens. Although the adversarial jury system of the United States is not without its flaws and shortcomings, it is the successor to many failed attempts at resolving conflicts that arise in society. The system can, and should be, supported and improved through commitment of both human and monetary resources.

References

[1] Abram. The challenge of the courtroom: reflections on the adversary system. *University of Chicago Law School Record* 1963;11(1):4.

[2] Barrett E. The adversary system and the ethics of advocacy. *Notre Dame Lawyer* 1962;37(4):479.
[3] Barrett E. Are all laws technicalities? *Juris Doctor.* November 1974;16.
[4] Brown L. Ending illegitimate advocacy: reinvigorating Rule 11 through enhancement of the ethical duty to report. *Ohio State Law Journal* 2001; 62(5):1555, 1616.
[5] Campbell JS, Sahid JR, Stang DP. Law and Order Reconsidered: *Report of the Task Force on Law and Law Enforcement.* Washington, D.C.: National Commission on the Causes and Prevention of Violence; 1969.
[6] Carlson R. Competency and professionalism in modern litigation: the role of law schools. *Georgia Law Review* 1989;23(3):689.
[7] Cloud M. Forfeiting defense attorneys fees: applying an institutional role theory to define individual constitutional rights. *Wisconsin Law Review* 1987; 1:8–15.

Further reading

Berger v. United States, 295 U.S. 78 (1935).
Hall v. State, 325N.W.2d 752 (Iowa 1982); see *State v. Glanton,* 231 N.W.2d 31 (Iowa 1975). Iowa Supreme Court Justice David Harris provides an excellent profile of what constitutes an impartial jurist in this court opinion, drawing upon historical thinkers such as Sir Francis Bacon.
Hough v. Maroney, 247 F. Supp. 767, 779 (W.D. Pa. 1965).
Johnson v. State, 278 Ga. 344 (2004).
Jones, S (1998). A lawyer's ethical duty to represent the unpopular client, *Chapman Law Review,* 1(1), 105–107, quoting from Hall, J.W. (1996). *Professional Responsibility of the Criminal Lawyer,* 2nd ed., Clark Boardman Callaghan, New York, § 9:12.
Long v. Broadlawns Medical Center, 656 N.W. 2d 71 (Iowa, 2002).
Strickland v. Washington, 466 U.S. 668 (1984).

APPENDIX TO CHAPTER 1: GRAND JURY PROCEDURE

As noted in Section 4.2, a prosecutor is not bound by the magistrate's decision to bind over the accused. Under the law of most jurisdictions the case may be pursued or, if deemed non-meritorious, abandoned. As a general proposition the district attorney has the power to dismiss a case prior to indictment. "Whether to prosecute and what charge to bring before a grand jury are decisions that generally rest in the prosecutor's discretion."[a] In taking a case to the grand jury, the prosecutor's exercise of discretion to prosecute should not harmfully discriminate against any person.[b] The magistrate's decision does not bind the grand jury. If there has been a preliminary hearing and the magistrate dismissed the case, the prosecution can be reinstituted. On the other hand, a magistrate's decision at preliminary hearing that is adverse to the accused does not control the grand jury. "It [the grand jury] may refuse to indict even though the magistrate found probable cause."[c]

Justice Harlan, in his dissenting opinion in *Hurtado v. California,*[d] stressed the value of the grand jury as a mechanism for weeding out false or spiteful claims:

> *In the secrecy of the investigations by grand juries, the weak and helpless—proscribed, perhaps, because of their race, or pursued by an unreasoning public clamor—have found, and will continue to find, security against official oppression, the cruelty of mobs, the machinations of falsehood, and the malevolence of private persons who would use the machinery of the law to bring ruin upon their personal enemies.*

Grand jury proceedings are cloaked with secrecy, as a general rule, to protect the accused if the bill of indictment is not found to be a **true bill**.[e] The grand jury is conducting a screening of

[a] *Slater v. State*, 185 Ga. App. 889, 366 S.E.2d 240 (1988).
[b] Selective prosecution claims, see *Wayte v. United States*, 470 U.S. 598 (1985).
[c] Kamisar, Y., LaFave, W.R., Israel, J.H., and King, N.J. (2002). *Modern Criminal Procedure*, 10th ed., West, Eagen, MN, Ch. 1, Section 3.
[d] 110 U.S. 516, 554-555, 4 S. Ct. 111, 28 L. Ed. 232 (1884).
[e] Federal Rules of Criminal Procedure, Rule 6. On the right of the defendant to discover anything about grand jury testimony, see Section 6.3.

the evidence in a case, not a trial. Generally those present are attorneys for the government (prosecutors), witnesses under examination, a court reporter, and the jurors. The accused does not have a right to present evidence or a right to counsel at this proceeding. Statutes or court rules prevent the disclosure of evidence taken before the grand jury. As in the preliminary hearing, hearsay evidence is admissible, and police officers who investigated the case may be the major witnesses.[f]

In federal court, a grand jury may consist of 16 to 23 jurors, a pattern not dissimilar from that found in several states. A specified majority is generally required to indict a defendant—in federal procedure, 12 jurors. Usually no people other than the jurors may be present while the grand jury is deliberating or voting. If the evidence convinces the jurors that a crime has been committed and there is probable cause to believe the defendant committed it, an indictment (true bill) is found and returned against the defendant, constituting the formal accusation. If no probable cause is found, a "no bill" results.

In drawing names for and constructing the grand jury, court officials must take care that various population segments are not discriminated against. Proper selection of the grand jury panel requires that no large and identifiable segment of the community be excluded from jury service. Defense attorneys regularly make motions to dismiss an indictment if an indictment approved by a grand jury was not drawn from a fair cross-section of the community.

Finding racial discrimination in the makeup of a grand jury that indicted the defendant more than 24 years earlier, the Supreme Court unsettled the defendant's conviction in *Vasquez v. Hillery*.[g] "[E]ven if a grand jury's determination of probable cause is confirmed in hindsight of a conviction on the indicted offense, that confirmation in no way suggests that the discrimination did not impermissibly infect the framing of the indictment and, consequently, the nature or very existence of the proceedings to come."

The indictment in *Vasquez* was defective because of discrimination on the basis of race in the selection of members of a grand jury. When a defendant is indicted, other pretrial attacks may be made by the defense in an effort to have the indictment

[f]*Costello v. United States*, 350 U.S. 359, 76 S. Ct. 406, 100 L. Ed. 397 (1956). A few states reject Costello's hearsay holding.

[g]474 U.S. 254 (1986). On the issue of whether a nonminority defendant can complain about racial exclusion of blacks as grand jury foremen, see *Campbell v. Louisiana*, 118 S. Ct. 1419 (1998) (white defendant has standing to raise equal protection objection to discrimination against black persons).

dismissed. The following kinds of questions may be raised. When the grand jury considered probable cause, were any unauthorized people present in the grand jury room?[h] While hearsay may be used, did the prosecutor misrepresent its character to the grand jurors by failing to inform them that the evidence was hearsay? Were there other instances of prosecutorial misconduct, such as failing to safeguard grand jury secrecy?

A Supreme Court opinion addressed the last of these questions. May a judge dismiss an indictment for prosecutorial misconduct in a grand jury investigation? The issue was raised when a defendant complained that a prosecutor improperly argued with an expert witness in a tax fraud investigation after the witness gave testimony adverse to the government. This occurred in the presence of some grand jurors. In addition, it was claimed that the prosecutor violated the secrecy provisions of grand jury rules—provisions that cloak the investigations and deliberations of grand juries with privacy—by publicly identifying the targets and the subject matter of the grand jury investigation. The key question, in the view of the Supreme Court, was whether any misconduct by the prosecutor substantially influenced the grand jury's decision to indict. Here, the conclusion was that the totality of the circumstances did not lead to a conclusion that the grand jury's independence was infringed. There was no justification for dismissing the indictment against the defendant on the basis of prosecutorial misconduct, absent a finding that the defendant was prejudiced by such misconduct.[i]

Must the prosecutor present to the grand jury any significant evidence known to the prosecution that is helpful to the defendant, along with the customary presentation of prosecution proof and witnesses? Is it misconduct to fail to do so? Will the charge be dismissed if the prosecutor refuses to tell the grand jury about proof that favors a defendant, and the prosecutor's conduct is later found out? A court rule in one federal circuit required prosecutors to present "substantial **exculpatory evidence**" to the grand jury. The Supreme Court struck down this rule. Justice Scalia wrote for the court: "Imposing upon the prosecutor a legal obligation to present exculpatory evidence in his possession would be incompatible with the [grand jury] system." The Court's holding came in the face of a passage in the *Manual for*

[h] *United States v. Mechanik,* 106 S. Ct. 938 (1986).

[i] *Bank of Nova Scotia v. United States,* 108 S. Ct. 2369 (1988). A similar result obtained when defendant complained of public disclosure by the government of grand jury matters in another case, *Midland Asphalt Corp. v. United States,* 109 S. Ct. 1494 (1989).

United States Attorneys, which provided that when a prosecutor is personally aware of substantial evidence that directly negates the guilt of a subject under investigation, the prosecutor must "disclose such evidence to the grand jury before seeking an indictment against such person."[j]

While the rule of grand jury secrecy extends to attorneys, clerks, and grand jurors, witnesses are not included. Can a judge enter a special "gag" order on witnesses? What if a state passes a law prohibiting disclosure of testimony to the press or otherwise by a grand jury witness? Such an effort by one state was unsuccessful in *Butterworth v. Smith*,[k] at least after the grand jury's term had ended. The case established a new First Amendment principle. Although state and federal grand juries have traditionally been carried on in secret in order to encourage witnesses to come forward and to permit thorough investigations, Florida's law was overbroad. The state's interest in secrecy was not sufficiently compelling to warrant punishing witnesses with criminal sanctions when they reveal the contents of their own grand jury testimony. The Court stated:

> *We also take note of the fact that neither the drafters of the Federal Rules of Criminal Procedure, nor the drafters of similar rules in the majority of the States, found it necessary to impose an obligation of secrecy on grand jury witnesses with respect to their own testimony to protect reputational interests or any of the other interests asserted by Florida. Federal Rule of Criminal Procedure 6(e)(2), governing grand jury secrecy, expressly prohibits certain individuals other than witnesses from disclosing "matters occurring before the grand jury," and provides that "[n]o obligation of secrecy may be imposed on any person except in accordance with this rule." The pertinent Advisory Committee Notes on Rule 6(e)(2), 18 U.S.C. App., p. 726, expressly exempt witnesses from the obligation of secrecy, stating that, "The seal of secrecy on witnesses seems an unnecessary hardship and may lead to injustice if a witness is not permitted to make a disclosure to counsel or to an associate."*

Florida's law took a different direction from the above and prohibited a witness from ever disclosing testimony given before a grand jury, even after the grand jury's term had ended. By so doing it unconstitutionally violated First Amendment rights.

In the grand jury inquiry of President Clinton involving Monica Lewinsky, a number of witnesses went before

[j] *United States v. Williams*, 112 S. Ct. 1735, 118 L. Ed. 2d 352 (1992).
[k] 110 S. Ct. 1376 (1990).

microphones in front of the federal courthouse in Washington, D.C., immediately following their grand jury appearance. They summarized what they had just told the grand jury.

In addition to the screening function of the grand jury in ordinary criminal cases, it sometimes operates as an investigative agency. Especially prominent in cases of civic corruption or misconduct by public officers, the grand jury may independently subpoena witnesses to advance its investigative aims. The general discussion of the indictment process to this point has assumed the usual situation of the suspect's arrest, followed by eventual presentation of the case to a grand jury, but the grand jury can also look into criminal conduct prior to the arrest of any suspect, and frequently this pattern is followed in illegal drug cases.[l] The inquisitorial power of the grand jury may operate to develop evidence against civic corruption, organized crime, or a broad array of criminal activity.

In recent years there has been substantial litigation over the rights of witnesses to withhold evidence from grand juries. Newsgatherers have fought court battles to protect their sources of information. Where the source's information exposes criminal activity in the community, the newspaper reporter has no federal constitutional privilege to withhold the information and may be required to identify the source.[m] However, in many jurisdictions there are state "shield" laws that supply a privilege for news sources, allowing reporters to keep confidential the names of those who supply information.

The witness who is called before a grand jury may be a member of a criminal gang that is under investigation. Thus, the witness may be suspected of participation in criminal activity. Is such a witness entitled to refuse to answer grand jury questions? The self-incrimination privilege is available to witnesses before the grand jury, and if a witness is asked a question that would show that the witness himself was engaged in criminal activity, the witness could refuse to answer on Fifth Amendment grounds. One way for the grand jury to cut off the witness's right to withhold evidence is to grant him or her immunity.[n] With the

[l]*Id.* at 466, citing *United States v. Thompson*, 251 U.S. 407, 40 S. Ct. 289, 64 L. Ed. 333 (1920).

[m]*Branzburg v. Hayes*, 408 U.S. 665, 92 S. Ct. 2646, 33 L. Ed. 2d 626 (1972). The above text refers to the absence of a federally guaranteed news privilege; a number of states do provide such privileges to reporters as a matter of state policy.

[n]What a witness says may not be later used to prosecute that witness, under an immunity grant, nor may leads from the immunized testimony be used to supply evidence against the accused. See *Kastigar v. United States*, 406 U.S. 441, 92 S. Ct. 1653, 32 L. Ed. 2d 212 (1972).

approval of a judge, the prosecutor may secure an order protecting the witness from having his or her words used against him or her by granting the witness **immunity from prosecution**. Once this is granted, the witness must answer or be held in contempt. This immunity device is sometimes employed when a lesser member of a criminal gang appears as a witness and evidence against one of the higher-ups is sought by the grand jury.

While the Fifth Amendment may be asserted by a grand jury witness to block questions, at least before immunity is granted, objections by the witness based on the Fourth Amendment are treated differently.

Sometimes a witness declines to answer grand jury questions because the information that gave rise to the question was gained from an illegal entry and search of the witness's home or business. In a loan-sharking case from Ohio, a witness raised just such an objection to grand jury questions. The Supreme Court denied any right of the witness to refuse to cooperate. The Court reasoned that to allow a witness to invoke the exclusionary rule in cases like this would "unduly interfere with the effective. . .discharge of the grand jury's duties."[o]

The grand jury witness appears before the jury unaccompanied by counsel; however, sometimes a lawyer is retained to advise the witness and comes to the courthouse. For example, the federal grand jury investigating the Iran–Contra matter in June 1990 called Oliver North as a witness. "North repeatedly left the secret proceedings during nearly three hours of testimony to confer with his attorneys in a courthouse hallway."[p]

Subpoenas for information and records are frequently issued by grand juries as they investigate and seek evidence necessary to resolve the question of whether to indict.[q] A **subpoena** is an order directing the recipient to supply documents or to appear and testify. If a corporation is under investigation, a bookkeeper or company officer may be ordered to bring forward corporate

[o]*United States v. Calandra*, 414 U.S. 338, 94 S. Ct. 613, 38 L. Ed. 2d 561 (1974) (exclusionary rule does not operate in grand jury proceedings). But see *Gelbard v. United States*, 408 U.S. 41, 92 S. Ct. 2357, 33 L. Ed. 2d 179 (1972), where the government intrusion was not a physical one but consisted of electronic surveillance.

[p]Atlanta Constitution, June 3, 1990. Oliver North was convicted of some of the charges brought against him, but ultimately defeated them on appeal. *United States v. North*, 920 F.2d 940 (D.C. Cir. 1990).

[q]In *United States v. Dionisio*, 410 U.S. 1, 93 S. Ct. 764, 35 L. Ed. 2d 67 (1973), the Supreme Court upheld grand jury subpoenas directing 20 persons to submit to voice recordings in order to match them with recordings of unknown voices obtained by court-approved wiretaps. 108 S. Ct. 64 (1988).

books and records reflecting financial dealings. While purely personal records may be withheld by the individual under the Fifth Amendment privilege against self-incrimination, the cloak of privilege does not extend to company documents. In *Braswell v. United States*,[r] a federal grand jury issued a subpoena to Braswell requiring him to produce the books and records of a company of which he was the sole shareholder. Braswell moved to quash the subpoena, arguing that the act of producing the records would violate his constitutional rights. The Supreme Court responded: "[P]etitioner has operated his business through the corporate form, and we have long recognized that for purposes of the Fifth Amendment, corporations and other collective entities are treated differently from individuals... [T]he Court developed the **collective entity rule**, which declares simply that corporate records are not private and therefore are not protected by the Fifth Amendment."

Information gathering by grand juries formed the focus of another Supreme Court decision. In *Doe v. United States*,[s] the target of a grand jury investigation was ordered to produce records of transactions in accounts at three named banks in the Cayman Islands and Bermuda. The District Court found the defendant in contempt of court when he refused to comply with demands for cooperation, and the judge ordered him to be confined until he did so. The grand jury's investigation of suspected fraudulent manipulation of oil cargoes and receipt of unreported income awaited Supreme Court resolution of the constitutional question. The Court decided that a court order compelling disclosure of foreign bank records did not violate the individual's Fifth Amendment privilege against self-incrimination. The decision concluded that there was "no question that the foreign banks cannot invoke the Fifth Amendment in declining to produce the documents; the privilege does not extend to such artificial entities.. . .[As to the target of the grand jury's investigation, constitutional rights are involved when the Government's demand for information is a request for testimonial information; it is only] the attempt to force him 'to disclose the contents of his own mind' that implicates the self-incrimination clause."[t] Because the request here did not involve forced production

[r]108 S. Ct. 64 (1988).

[s]108 S. Ct. 2341 (1988).

[t]108 S. Ct. at 2348. Cases cited by the Court involved forced production of physical evidence, including handwriting exemplars, blood samples, and voice exemplars, as well as requiring an accused to wear particular clothing for identification. These examples were condoned by the Court; none involved intrusions upon the contents of the mind of the accused.

of a communication—written or oral words disclosing guilty knowledge or admissions of criminality by the accused—the self-incrimination clause was not violated by the District Court, and the contempt order against the defendant was affirmed.

Grand Jury Indictments

How does an indictment read? Sample grand jury indictments used in federal courts are instructive as to the form of this charging vehicle:

Indictment for Murder in the First Degree of Federal Officer

In the United States District Court for the ____________________ District of ____________________, ____________________ Division.

UNITED STATES OF AMERICA
v.
JOHN DOE
No. ____________________
(18 U.S.C. §§ 1111, 1114)

The grand jury charges:

On or about the _______ day of ____________, 20 ______, in the ________________ ________________ District of ______________, John Doe with premeditation and by means of shooting murdered John Roe, who was then an officer of the Federal Bureau of Investigation of the Department of Justice engaged in the performance of his official duties.

A True Bill.

______________________,
Foreperson.

______________________,
United States Attorney.

(As amended Dec. 27, 1948, eff. Oct. 20, 1949.)

Indictment for Mail Fraud

In the United States District Court for the ______________________, District of ______________________, ______________________, Division.

UNITED STATES OF AMERICA
v.
JOHN DOE ET AL.
No. ______________________,
(18 U.S.C. § 1341)

The grand jury charges:

1. Prior to the _____ day of _______, 20___, and continuing to the _____ day of _______, 20 _____,[1] the defendants John Doe, Richard Roe, John Stiles, and Richard Miles devised and intended to devise a scheme and artifice to defraud purchasers of stock of XY Company, a California corporation, and to obtain money and property by means of the following false and fraudulent pretenses, representations and promises, well knowing at the time that the pretenses, representations and promises would be false when made: That the XY Company owned a mine at or near San Bernardino, California; that the mine was in actual operation; that gold ore was being obtained at the mine and sold at a profit; that the current earnings of the company would be sufficient to pay dividends on its stock at the rate of six percent per annum.

2. On the _____ day of_______, 20 ____, in the _____________ District of ______________, the defendants for the purpose of executing the aforesaid scheme and artifice and attempting to do so, caused to be placed in an authorized depository for mail matter a letter addressed to Mrs. Mary Brown, 110 Main Street, Stockton, California, to be sent or delivered by the Post Office Establishment of the United States.

Second Count
1. The Grand Jury realleges all of the allegations of the first count of this indictment, except those contained in the last paragraph thereof.
2. On the ______ day of ______, 20___, in the ____________ District of __________________, the defendants, for the purpose of executing the aforesaid scheme and artifice and attempting to do so, caused to be placed in an authorized depository for mail matter a letter addressed to Mr. John J. Jones, 220 First Street, Batavia, New York, to be sent or delivered by the Post Office Establishment of the United States.
A True Bill.

__________________,
Foreperson.

__________________,
United States Attorney.

[1]Insert last mailing date alleged. (As amended Dec. 27, 1948, eff. Oct. 20, 1949. Forms are made available to United States Attorneys by the Department of Justice. Official forms are no longer appended to the Federal Rules of Criminal Procedure, Rule 58 abrogated.)

Bill of Information

States that permit prosecution upon information sometimes specify the specific form of this charging vehicle in the state code. An example appears in Rule 30, Iowa Rules of Criminal Procedure (1998):

Trial Information

IN THE IOWA DISTRICT COURT FOR ______________ COUNTY
THE STATE OF IOWA TRIAL INFORMATION
vs.
______________, Defendant No. ______________

COMES NOW _________ as Prosecuting Attorney of __________ County, Iowa, and in the name and by the Authority of the State of Iowa accuses ____________ of the crime of _________ committed as follows: The said ____________ on or about the _____ day of _____, 20 _____, in the County of ________ and State of Iowa did unlawfully and willfully ____ in violation of ______ of The Iowa Criminal Code.

A TRUE INFORMATION

____
Prosecuting Attorney

On ______ I find that the evidence contained in the within Trial Information and minutes of evidence, if unexplained would ________ warrant a conviction by the trial jury and being satisfied from the showing made herein that this case should ______ be prosecuted by Trial Information the same is __________ approved.

Defendant is released on:
1. personal recognizance ______________
2. appearance bond $______________
a. unsecured ______________
b. secured _______
3. other (specify) ______________________________________

____
Judge of the _______ Judicial
District of the State of Iowa

(Court file stamp)
Form 8 (back side)

This Trial Information, together with the minutes of evidence relating thereto, is duly filed in the District Court of Iowa for ______ County this _____ day of ______, 20____.

____

Clerk of the District Court of Iowa for _______ County

By:___________________________

District Clerk

Names of Witnesses

____

____

____

APPENDIX TO CHAPTER 2: MOTION TO SUPPRESS

At the suppression hearing, it is essential that the defendant establish "standing" to object to the seizure of evidence—that is, to show that his personal privacy was somehow invaded and his Fourth Amendment rights thereby violated. This is established when the defendant demonstrates that he was the "victim of a search and seizure, one against whom the search was directed, as distinguished from one who claims prejudice only through the use of evidence gathered as a consequence of a search and seizure directed at someone else." Only a defendant whose rights were violated when police obtained the evidence can demand suppression.[a]

To carry this burden, the defendant sometimes takes the stand at the suppression hearing. By so doing, he or she does not waive the right to refuse to testify at later trial on the merits, nor can a transcript of his or her hearing testimony be used against him or her at a subsequent trial.[b] In addition, where the defendant has taken the stand to testify to a narrow point, such as denying possession of a contraband item, the prosecutor cannot expand the suppression hearing to explore every avenue in the case. As stated in Rule 104 of the Federal Rules of Evidence, "The accused does not, by testifying upon a preliminary matter, subject himself to cross-examination as to other issues in the case."

When the defendant objects that evidence was illegally seized, the burden of showing that the challenged evidence was the product of an illegal search and seizure normally devolves upon the challenging party (the defendant) at the suppression hearing. However, there is one major exception to this rule, that

[a]Klotter, J.C., Kanovitz, J.R., and Kanovitz, M.I. (2005). *Constitutional Law*, 10th ed., Matthew Bender, New Providence, NJ, § 4.17. In a premises search, anyone legitimately on the premises where a search occurs may challenge its legality by way of a motion to suppress, when the person has a reasonable expectation of privacy and the fruits are proposed to be used against him or her. Automobile searches, see *Rakas v. Illinois*, 439 U.S. 128 (1978). Business office searches, see *Mancusi v. DeForte*, 392 U.S. 364, 88 S. Ct. 2120, 20 L. Ed. 2d 1154 (1968). Other cases on standing, see *Minnesota v. Olson*, 495 U.S. 91, 110 S. Ct. 1684, 109 L. Ed. 2d 85 (1990) (overnight guest).

[b]*Simmons v. United States*, 390 U.S. 377, 88 S. Ct. 967, 19 L. Ed. 2d 1247 (1968).

being where the government searched without a warrant but claims the search was validated by a consent. "[I]t has the burden of proving by clear and convincing evidence that the consent was voluntary and free from duress and coercion."[c] Where the challenged evidence is not a seized physical item but a confession, upon whom does the responsibility of carrying the burden of proof fall? Most jurisdictions place the burden on the prosecution in responding to a motion to suppress a confession. While some states hold that the government must carry this burden of proof beyond a reasonable doubt, the Supreme Court has authorized a less stringent standard. Thus, the prosecution must prove at least by a preponderance of the evidence that the confession was voluntary.[d] In lineup cases, once it is shown that the lineup was held during a critical stage in the proceedings, the prosecution is generally assumed to carry the burden of establishing that the defendant intelligently waived his right to counsel at lineup.

Form of Motion to Suppress

Today, countless texts address exclusionary rules in the criminal law field. While their coverage of constitutional rules may be adequate, very little attention is given to providing the reader with a glimpse of the courtroom motion used to invoke the **exclusionary rule**. This text will visually treat the subject of the method of raising objections to government evidence and will show the motion by which attorneys move the court to exclude constitutionally tainted proof.

The constitutional cases and rules governing exclusion of physical evidence illegally seized from an accused have been discussed in Section 2.2. As indicated previously in Chapter 2, a motion to suppress is the procedural vehicle to object to such evidence. When the property sought to be suppressed is not a physical item, such as a weapon seized from the accused, but rather consists of an oral admission made to police, what method of challenge may be employed? Again the motion

[c]*State v. Shephard*, 124 N.W.2d 712 (Iowa 1963). See also *Bumper v. North Carolina*, 391 U.S. 543, 88 S. Ct. 1788, 20 L. Ed. 2d 797 (1968); *Florida v. Royer*, 460 U.S. 491, 103 S. Ct. 1319 (1983).

[d]*Lego v. Twomey*, 404 U.S. 477 (1972). Preponderance of the evidence has been variously defined as 51% of the evidence, or 50.1% of the persuasiveness of the proof, or by the greater weight of the evidence but not so great as proof beyond a reasonable doubt.

to suppress evidence is a popular vehicle for raising objection to confessions or admissions.[e] In some criminal cases, a **motion in limine**[f] has been employed, and this may be another procedural method that is used to block the government from using a confession at trial.

It is helpful for the reader to see a motion to suppress at this point, and an illustrative motion to suppress physical evidence in federal court is reproduced here.

Motion to Suppress Evidence[g]

Attorneys for ___________
In the United States District Court in and for the Southern District of California Southern Division
United States of America,
Plaintiff,
v.

_______________________ No.________
_______________________ Motion to Suppress Evidence
____

Defendants.

Come now defendants __________ and _________, jointly and severally, by and through their counsel, and, pursuant to the provisions of Rule 12 of the Federal Rules of Criminal Procedure, hereby moves the Court for an Order to suppress for use in evidence the contraband upon which the indictment in the above-entitled cause is predicated, to-wit, approximately 20 pounds of marijuana, together with all other items of physical evidence obtained by persons who investigated the offenses charged against the moving defendants.

This Motion is based on the instant Motion, the Notice of Motion attached hereto, the affidavit attached hereto, the records and files in the above-entitled cause, and any and all other matters which may be presented prior to or at the time of the hearing of said Motion.

____
By__________
Attorney for Defendant

____
Attorney for Defendant

Points and Authorities in Support of Motion to Suppress

Attorney for defendants ___________
In the United States District Court in and for the Southern District of California Southern Division
United States of America,
Plaintiff,
v.

_______________________ No.________
_______________________ Points and Authorities in Support
_______________________ of Motion to Suppress

[e]Much of the remainder of this section of the text is adapted from Ladd, M. and Carlson, R.L. (1972). *Cases and Materials on Evidence,* Callaghan, Chicago, IL, § 6.9.

[f]"A 'motion in limine' is a term used to describe a written motion that is usually made before or after the beginning of a jury trial for a protective order against prejudicial questions and statements." *Burrus v. Silhavy,* 155 Ind. App. 558, 293 N. E.2d 794, at 796 (1973).

[g]Federal Defender's Program of San Diego (1967). *Handbook on Criminal Procedure in the United States District Court,* West, Eagen, MN, §§ 6.32, 6.34. Reprinted by permission of copyright owner. New cases and rule numbers added to original by author of this text.

Defendants.

I.

". . . Those lawfully within the country, entitled to use public highways, have a right to free passage without interruption or search unless there is known to a competent official authorized to search, probable cause for believing that their vehicles are carrying contraband or illegal merchandise."

Carroll v. United States, 267 U.S. 132, 154, 45 S. Ct. 280, 285, 69 L. Ed. 543, 39 A.L.R. 790 (1925), certiorari denied 282 U.S. 873, 51 S. Ct. 78, 75 L. Ed. 771 (1930).

"But after entry has been completed, a search and seizure can be made only on a showing of probable cause."

Cervantes v. United States, 263 F.2d 800, 830 (9th Cir. 1959).

See also: *Plazola v. United States*, 291 F2d 56 (9th Cir. 1961), and *Jones v. United States*, 326 F2d 124 (9th Cir, 1964), certiorari denied 377 U.S. 956, 84 S. Ct. 1635, 12 L. Ed. 2d 499 (1964).

II.

"The word automobile is not a talisman in whose presence the Fourth Amendment fades away and disappears."

Coolidge v. New Hampshire, 403 U.S. 433 (1971).

The defendant has standing to raise this motion in that he was the owner and operator of the vehicle which was searched in the instant case. In order to complain that a search and seizure was illegal and resulted in contraband, marijuana or narcotics being seized, the moving party need not be placed in the dilemma of asserting an interest in the contraband in order to complain of the search and seizure.

Jones v. United States, 362 U.S. 257, 80 S. Ct. 725; 4 L. Ed. 2d 697; 78 A.L.R.2d 233 (1960).

Respectfully submitted:

____

By __________

Attorney for defendant __________

By __________

Attorney for defendant __________

Hearsay Evidence Inadmissible in Criminal Trials

The classic definition of **hearsay** is a "statement made out of court and offered in court to prove the truth of the facts asserted in the statement." When the prosecutor asks a question that calls for hearsay, the police officer will be barred from answering it if defense counsel makes proper and timely objection. An illustration will help further define the important concept of hearsay. Suppose Jones is a police officer who is investigating an automobile accident. On the day after the accident he talks to W, a witness who personally observed the collision between cars driven by D and X. X was killed in the crash. In the trial of D for vehicular homicide, Jones is on the witness stand. The prosecutor asks him if he interviewed witnesses who were at the accident scene, and Jones replies that he did. The prosecutor then asks Jones to relate any conversations that occurred with such witnesses. Jones is about to answer that he talked to W, that W reported seeing the accident, and that W saw D traveling at a high rate of speed prior to the collision. Jones is interrupted by defense counsel's objection that the question calls for hearsay. If W is in the jurisdiction, he should be subpoenaed into court to testify himself.

It makes good sense when trying to find out about something to make inquiry of the person who has personally perceived the matter. The courts in establishing the hearsay rule are simply fulfilling a demand that people would generally make in obtaining information about a fact from the person who had actual knowledge. The truth about a matter in dispute can be discovered from those who know about it, rather than have another testify as to what the man who knew had said. In this respect, the hearsay rule is like the best evidence rule, which requires the production of the original, if available.[h]

Section 6.14. Exceptions to the Hearsay Rule

While most hearsay evidence is inadmissible in criminal trials, certain types of hearsay, because of their special reliability, are admissible. The classes of hearsay evidence that are admissible are categorized as exceptions to the hearsay rule. Some of the exceptions most commonly encountered in criminal cases are briefly outlined.

Confessions and Admissions

Whether oral or written, this class of hearsay is admissible where constitutional guidelines were observed in taking the statements. Confessions are powerful proof against a defendant and may be introduced early in the prosecutor's case-in-chief. Often the method of introduction is to have the detective who interrogated the defendant read the defendant's words to the jury. In this manner confessions may be employed to show the defendant's guilt during the prosecutor's case. Also, during the defense presentation of evidence, a confession may be used to impeach the accused if he or she takes the stand to testify and the live testimony is contradicted by the prior written statement.

Dying Declarations

This is another example of an out-of-court statement made by a witness that is introduced in court through testimony of a

[h]Ladd, M. and Carlson, R.L. (1972). *Cases and Materials on Evidence*, Callaghan, Chicago, IL, pp. 803-804.

different person. A man dies, but before he expires he whispers to a police officer that, "D killed me." When D is tried for murder, the officer is entitled to take the stand and relate what the man whispered. The reasons are twofold: (1) the deceased is no longer available, and a special necessity to allow hearsay proof as to his pre-death declaration arises; and (2) special reliability is provided by the fact that the man realized he was near death when he spoke. The law has long assumed that a deathbed statement will be truthful, in almost all cases, and that a person will not go to his death with a lie on his lips. In most states, certain matters must coalesce in order to render the dying declaration admissible: (1) the declarant must be conscious of his impending death; (2) the declarant must be shown to have had an opportunity to know the facts, and the statement sought to be admitted must be a declaration of fact, not opinion; and (3) the statement is admissible only in criminal homicide cases dealing with the death of the deceased who made the declaration. Evidence rules for federal trials alter this pattern in federal courts. Under the Federal Rules of Evidence, dying declarations are admissible in prosecutions for homicide or in civil actions.

Reported Testimony

Suppose Smith is tried for murder. On the testimony of X, an eyewitness to the homicide, he is convicted; however, Smith appeals his case, wins on the appeal, and the case is remanded to the trial court for retrial.[i] Fourteen months elapse between the time of the first trial and the retrial, the delay being attributable to the time-consuming task of preparing, briefing, and arguing the case through the appellate courts. In the interim X, who was an elderly man at the time of the first trial, dies. Several questions now arise. Can X's testimony be presented in some form at the retrial? Would his earlier testimony be hearsay in the second trial? What about the right of the accused to confront the witness against him? One commentator responds to these questions:[j]

> *The admission of former testimony in a subsequent proceeding is conditioned upon (1) an inability to obtain the witness;*

[i]When a prisoner successfully appeals because improper evidence was used against him, see Section 9.6 of this text on the state's right to retry him on the same charge.

[j]Note, *The Use of Prior Recorded Testimony and the Right of Confrontation,* 54 Iowa L. Rev. 360 (1968). If there was adequate opportunity for prior cross-examination and the witness is unavailable for trial, the constitutional right to confrontation appears satisfied. A similar question is confronted when the prosecution decides to use a transcript of the preliminary hearing to place in evidence the testimony of a state witness who appeared there but has since become unavailable.

> *(2) an opportunity to cross-examine the witness in the former trial; (3) an identity or substantial identity of issues in the two proceedings; and (4) substantial identity of parties. The opportunity for cross-examination is considered to be the most essential element because the credibility of the witness can be tested through direct confrontation.*

In *Ohio v. Roberts*,[k] the trial judge permitted the prosecutor to prove the state's case by reading into the trial record a witness's preliminary hearing testimony. The witness had been called by the defense at the preliminary hearing to testify, in effect, as a hostile witness. After the preliminary hearing, the witness apparently left the area and could not be located by the prosecutor for trial. The Supreme Court ruled that the defendant's confrontation rights were not denied by the prosecutor's use of the earlier testimony; the defense had the opportunity to interrogate the witness at the preliminary hearing.

Preliminary hearing testimony should be sharply distinguished from a grand jury transcript. It is to be remembered that a grand jury is not an adversary proceeding. The defense is not present and is unable to cross-examine government witnesses. Grand jury testimony may not be substituted for live testimony of a trial witness.

When the trial judge rules that the prior recorded testimony is admissible matter in the second trial, the evidence is usually presented by the official court reporter reading to the jury his notes of the questions put to the witness at the first trial, and the answers given by the witness. If these notes have been put into typed form (transcript) before the second trial, the prosecutor may authenticate the transcript by the testimony of the court reporter and then introduce the typewritten document into evidence.

Official Statements

Official records that a public official has a duty to maintain are admissible. Thus, reports of the county medical examiner as to the time and cause of death, weather reports maintained by the U.S. Weather Bureau, and recorded deeds or mortgages come into evidence under this exception to the hearsay rule. So also may the physician's report on blood-alcohol content in a drunk-driving case, although the presence of the physician to

[k]448 U.S. 56 (1980).

authenticate the report and to be cross-examined will probably be required.

Miscellaneous Exceptions

There are several other hearsay problems that may arise in a criminal case, including the admissibility of statements of co-conspirators in a conspiracy trial,[l] **res gestae statements**,[m] declarations against interest, especially by persons who declare themselves guilty of a crime charged against another,[n] flight by the accused, and business records. Suppose that immediately after a murder the chief suspect flees the jurisdiction and is eventually returned from another state by extradition or an unlawful flight warrant. From an evidentiary standpoint, the known facts that establish his flight can be described to the jury upon his trial for murder. Like a confession, flight is receivable as evidence of guilt.

Business and hospital records of facts that are routinely made and kept and that are relied on in the daily work of the institution are admissible.[o] Statements made to doctors and nurses when a person is being treated medically can be reported in a later court case by that doctor or nurse. This is the medical examination exception to the hearsay rule.

Accomplice confessions or incriminating statements are frequently offered into evidence against a defendant. Suppose A and D are jointly suspected of pulling a robbery, and A is picked up. A tells police he knows all about the robbery. D did it,

[l]Declarations of one co-conspirator are admissible against another if they were made while the conspiracy was pending and in furtherance of its objectives. Ladd and Carlson, *supra* note 90, at 895-899.

[m]*Res gestae* is a term decried by evidence commentators but employed by most courts. Courts commonly classify excited utterances of people who saw a crime under the res gestae exception to the hearsay rule and render these statements admissible. An excited utterance, admissible as an exception to the hearsay rule, is defined in Rule 803(2), Federal Rules of Evidence: "A statement relating to a startling event or condition made while the defendant was under the stress of excitement caused by the event or condition."

[n]Chambers was charged with murder. McDonald had stated to friends that he, McDonald, had done the killing Chambers was charged with. The Mississippi courts would not allow Chambers to prove this at trial, but the Supreme Court disagreed. The Court cited the declaration against interest exception to the hearsay rule, and authorized the admission of McDonald's statements. Declarations against interest constitute "an exception founded on the assumption that a person is unlikely to fabricate a statement against his own interest" unless it be true. *Chambers v. Mississippi*, 410 U.S. 284, 93 S. Ct. 1038, 35 L. Ed. 2d 297 (1973).

[o]See Rule 803(6) of the Federal Rules of Evidence (business records exception to hearsay rule).

A says, and A helped to fence the objects that D stole. At the trial of State versus D, the prosecutor may seek to have Officer X read the accomplice's signed statement into the record against D. Will the judge permit this? "No" is the answer supplied by the Supreme Court. In *Crawford v. Washington*,[p] decided in 2004, such hearsay statements are inadmissible unless the accomplice is cross-examined at trial. A must testify as a witness, and in his absence his statement is worthless. Testimonial statements such as the one from the accomplice in this illustration, statements that a declarant would reasonably expect to be used against a defendant at trial, must be exposed to the defendant's cross-examination. The right to confront adverse witnesses that is contained in the Sixth Amendment to the U.S. Constitution demands nothing less.

[p]124 S. Ct. 1354 (2004).

APPENDIX TO CHAPTER 3: RULE 4 OF THE FEDERAL RULES OF CRIMINAL PROCEDURE: ARREST WARRANT OR SUMMONS ON A COMPLAINT

(a) FORM.

(1) *Warrant.* A warrant must:

(A) contain the defendant's name or, if it is unknown, a name or description by which the defendant can be identified with reasonable certainty;

(B) describe the offense charged in the complaint;

(C) command that the defendant be arrested and brought without unnecessary delay before a magistrate judge or, if none is reasonably available, before a state or local judicial officer; and

(D) be signed by a judge.

(2) *Summons.* A summons must be in the same form as a warrant except that it must require the defendant to appear before a magistrate judge at a stated time and place.

(b) EXECUTION OR SERVICE, AND RETURN.

(A) A summons is served on an individual defendant:

(i) by delivering a copy to the defendant personally; or

(ii) by leaving a copy at the defendant's residence or usual place of abode with a person of suitable age and discretion residing at that location and by mailing a copy to the defendant's last known address.

(B) A summons is served on an organization by delivering a copy to an officer, to a managing or general agent, or to another agent appointed or legally authorized to receive service of process. A copy must also be mailed to the organization's last known address within the district or to its principal place of business elsewhere in the United States.

APPENDIX TO CHAPTER 4: RULE 41 OF THE FEDERAL RULES OF CRIMINAL PROCEDURE: SEARCH AND SEIZURE

(a) Authority to Issue a Warrant. At the request of a federal law enforcement officer or an attorney for the government:

(1) a magistrate judge with authority in the district—or if none is reasonably available, a judge of a state court of record in the district—has authority to issue a warrant to search for and seize a person or property located within the district; and

(2) a magistrate judge with authority in the district has authority to issue a warrant for a person or property outside the district if the person or property is located within the district when the warrant is issued but might move or be moved outside the district before the warrant is executed; and

(3) a magistrate judge—in an investigation of domestic terrorism or international terrorism (as defined in 18 U.S.C. § 2331)—having authority in any district in which activities related to the terrorism may have occurred, may issue a warrant for a person or property within or outside that district.

(b) Persons or Property Subject to Search and Seizure. A warrant may be issued for any of the following:

(1) evidence of a crime;

(2) contraband, fruits of crime, or other items illegally possessed;

(3) property designed for use, intended for use, or used in committing a crime; or

(4) a person to be arrested or a person who is unlawfully restrained.

(c) Obtaining a Warrant.

(1) *In General.* After receiving an affidavit or other information, a magistrate judge or a judge of a state court of record must issue the warrant if there is probable cause to search for and seize a person or property under Rule 41(c).

(2) *Requesting a Warrant in the Presence of a Judge.*

(A) *Warrant on an Affidavit.* When a federal law enforcement officer or an attorney for the government presents an affidavit in support of a warrant, the judge may require the affiant to appear personally and may examine under oath the affiant and any witness the affiant produces.

(B) *Warrant on Sworn Testimony.* The judge may wholly or partially dispense with a written affidavit and base a warrant on sworn testimony if doing so is reasonable under the circumstances.

(C) *Recording Testimony.* Testimony taken in support of a warrant must be recorded by a court reporter or by a suitable recording device, and the judge must file the transcript or recording with the clerk, along with any affidavit.

(3) *Requesting a Warrant by Telephonic or Other Means.*

(A) *In General.* A magistrate judge may issue a warrant based on information communicated by telephone or other appropriate means, including facsimile transmission.

(B) *Recording Testimony.* Upon learning that an applicant is requesting a warrant, a magistrate judge must:

(i) place under oath the applicant and any person on whose testimony the application is based; and

(ii) make a verbatim record of the conversation with a suitable recording device, if available, or by a court reporter, or in writing.

(C) *Certifying Testimony.* The magistrate judge must have any recording or court reporter's notes transcribed, certify the transcription's accuracy, and file a copy of the record and the transcription with the clerk. Any written verbatim record must be signed by the magistrate judge and filed with the clerk.

(D) *Suppression Limited.* Absent a finding of bad faith, evidence obtained from a warrant issued under Rule 41(d)(3)(A) is not subject to suppression on the ground that issuing the warrant in that manner was unreasonable under the circumstances.

(d) ISSUING THE WARRANT.

(1) *In General.* The magistrate judge or a judge of a state court of record must issue the warrant to an officer authorized to execute it.

(2) *Contents of the Warrant.* The warrant must identify the person or property to be searched, identify any person or property to be seized, and designate the magistrate judge to whom it must be returned. The warrant must command the officer to:

(A) execute the warrant within a specified time no longer than 10 days;

(B) execute the warrant during the daytime, unless the judge for good cause expressly authorizes execution at another time; and

(C) return the warrant to the magistrate judge designated in the warrant.

(e) EXECUTING AND RETURNING THE WARRANT.

(1) Warrant to Search for and Seize a Person or Property.

(A) *Noting the Time.* The officer executing the warrant must enter on its face the exact date and time it is executed.

(B) *Inventory.* An officer present during the execution of the warrant must prepare and verify an inventory of any property seized. The officer must do so in the presence of another officer and the person from whom, or from whose premises, the property was taken. If either one is not present, the officer must prepare and verify the inventory in the presence of at least one other credible person.

(C) *Receipt.* The officer executing the warrant must give a copy of the warrant and a receipt for the property taken to the person from whom, or from whose premises, the property was taken or leave a copy of the warrant and receipt at the place where the officer took the property.

(D) *Return.* The officer executing the warrant must promptly return it—together with a copy of the inventory—to the magistrate judge designated on the warrant. The judge must, on request, give a copy of the inventory to the person from whom, or from whose premises, the property was taken and to the applicant for the warrant.

APPENDIX TO CHAPTER 9: THE FIFTH AMENDMENT DOUBLE JEOPARDY CLAUSE: APPLICATION TO STATES

After years of controversy over the point, the U.S. Supreme Court ruled in *Benton v. Maryland* in 1969 that the double jeopardy provision of the U.S. Constitution applied to the states.[a] In extending the federal guarantee, the Supreme Court cited the fundamental character of double jeopardy protection to the American scheme of justice. The decision that accomplished this result overruled the earlier landmark case of *Palko v. Connecticut*,[b] in which the Court in 1937 had refused to make the federal double jeopardy provision applicable in state trials. In *Benton,* the defendant had been originally charged with both burglary and larceny. Upon trial by jury he was acquitted of the larceny but convicted of the burglary. He appealed the burglary conviction to the Maryland Court of Appeals and won, and the case was remanded to the trial court for a new trial. The defendant argued to the trial court that he had run the gauntlet of trial on the larceny charge, had been acquitted, and was thus immune from reprosecution for that offense. The trial judge disagreed, and the defendant was charged again with both burglary and larceny. This time he was convicted of both offenses. Upon review, the Supreme Court ruled the larceny conviction could not stand:

> *The fundamental nature of the guarantee against double jeopardy can hardly be obtained. Its origins can be traced to Greek and Roman times, and it became established in the common law of England long before this Nation's independence. See* Bartkus v. Illinois, *359 U.S. 121, 151-155, 79 S. Ct. 676, 697,*

[a]*Benton v. Maryland,* 395 U.S. 784, 89 S. Ct. 2056, 23 L. Ed. 2d 707 (1969). *Benton* was followed by *Price v. Georgia,* 398 U.S. 323, 90 S. Ct. 1757, 26 L. Ed. 2d 300 (1970). The Supreme Court held it unconstitutional for a state to retry a defendant for an offense that was rejected in the first trial, the jury having convicted the defendant of the lesser of two offenses upon the first trial of the case. Retrial could only be had of the lesser offense, the conviction that the defendant had appealed.

[b]302 U.S. 319, 58 S. Ct. 149, 82 L. Ed. 288 (1937).

> *3 L. Ed. 2d. 684 (1959) (Black, J. dissenting). As with many other elements of the common law, it was carried into the jurisprudence of this Country through the medium of Blackstone, who codified the doctrine in his Commentaries. "[T]he plea of* autrefois acquit, *or a former acquittal," he wrote, "is grounded on this universal maxim of the common law of England, that no man is to be brought into jeopardy of his life more than once for the same offense." Today, every State incorporates some form of the prohibition in its constitution or common law. As this Court put it in* Green v. United States, *355 U.S. 184, 187-188, 78 S. Ct. 221, 223, 2 L. Ed. 2d 199 (1957), "The underlying idea, one that is deeply ingrained in at least the Anglo-American system of jurisprudence, is that the State with all its resources and power should not be allowed to make repeated attempts to convict an individual for an alleged offense, thereby subjecting him to embarrassment, expense and ordeal and compelling him to live in a continuing state of anxiety and insecurity, as well as enhancing the possibility that even though innocent he may be found guilty." This underlying notion has from the very beginning been part of our constitutional tradition. Like the right to trial by jury, it is clearly "fundamental to the American scheme of justice." The validity of petitioner's larceny conviction must be judged not by the watered-down standards enunciated in Palko, but under this Court's interpretations of the Fifth Amendment double jeopardy provision.*

While virtually every state has its own statutory or constitutional provision on double jeopardy,[c] the federal clause is considerably more stringent than many of the state prohibitions. For example, some states provide that jeopardy attaches to bar retrial of a person only upon that person's conviction or acquittal of a particular charge. Suppose a criminal trial begins, and the prosecutor declares midway through the government's case that he or she has discovered that a key prosecution witness has left on vacation and is absent from the state. In these circumstances, the prosecutor might request that a mistrial be declared by the trial judge, the prosecutor's intent being to begin trial anew upon this witness's return. Older cases in some jurisdictions have held that the defendant might be put on trial again because the first case had been terminated prior to conviction or acquittal, and jeopardy had not yet attached. However, in a federal court a contrary result would almost certainly prevail because of the federal view that jeopardy attaches

[c]For example, O.C.G.A. § 16-1-6 (2004) (Georgia).

in a jury case once the jurors have been empaneled and sworn.[d] Because of the 1969 application of the federal jeopardy clause to the states, the more stringent federal standard concerning the time when jeopardy attaches controls state trials also.[e]

The double jeopardy clause prevents both double jeopardy prosecutions as well as double punishments for the same crime. The protection against multiple punishments prohibits the government from punishing a person twice for the same offense.

The Supreme Court has found no double punishments in connection with a number of modern sanctions against lawbreakers. First, there was the question of forfeiting a defendant's property after he had suffered a criminal court conviction. Civil forfeiture laws are designed to strip defendants of proceeds of crime, such as money obtained from drug trafficking. Property purchased by crime profits may be confiscated under laws requiring disgorgement of the fruits of illegal conduct. Is it double jeopardy to both punish a defendant for a criminal offense and forfeit his property for that same offense in a separate civil proceeding? No, said the Supreme Court in *United States v. Ursery.*[f] Vehicles used in criminal enterprises may also be forfeited. The theory is that when an owner of property uses it to commit crimes, the owner can be held accountable for the misuse of the property. As Justice Kennedy points out in *Ursery,* the same rationale enables forfeiture of currency used to facilitate a criminal offense. Forfeiture punishes an owner by taking property involved in a crime, and it often happens that the owner is also the wrongdoer charged with a criminal offense.

In other sorts of situations the court also found no impermissible double punishment. After a sexual offender completes his or her prison term, he or she can be confined further in a civil commitment under sexual predator laws. Such a commitment does not violate double jeopardy rules,[g] nor does a law that requires authorities to tell communities the whereabouts of a convicted sexual offender when one moves into the neighborhood. Sexual offenders in New Jersey and New York complained that the notification provisions punished them a second time

[d]*Serfass v. United States,* 420 U.S. 377, 95 S. Ct. 1055, 43 L. Ed. 2d 265 (1975). In a nonjury trial jeopardy attaches when the court begins to hear evidence. For a review of state rules on when jeopardy attaches, see Annotation, *When Does Jeopardy Attach in a Nonjury Trial?,* 49 A.L.R.3D 1039 (1973).

[e]*State v. Moriwake,* 647 P.2d 705 (Haw. 1982).

[f]116 S. Ct. 2135 (1996) (civil forfeiture does not constitute punishment for double jeopardy purposes).

[g]*Selig v. Yount,* 531 U.S. 250 (2001); *Kansas v. Hendricks,* 117 S. Ct. 2072 (1997).

by holding them up to public humiliation after they had served their criminal sentences. The Supreme Court disagreed.

Section 9.6. Retrial of the Accused: When Permitted

Where two separate criminal convictions are involved, even if they come under two distinct statutory provisions, double jeopardy bars double convictions unless each statutory provision requires proof of a fact that the other does not. Where the underlying conduct for which defendant is punished is exactly the same under both statutes, one of the convictions must be vacated.[h] In so holding, the Supreme Court reaffirmed the long-standing *Blockburger* test, which ordains that two statutes on a related topic define different offenses only if "each provision requires proof of a fact which the other does not."[i]

Occasionally unforeseen circumstances arise during a trial, making its completion impossible. A case involving this problem reached the Supreme Court, raising the question of whether jeopardy attaches when this occurs. In *United States v. Jorn,*[j] the defendant was charged with willfully assisting taxpayers to prepare fraudulent income tax returns in violation of the United States Code. He came to trial before a jury in the U.S. District Court for the District of Utah. After the jury was selected and sworn, the first government witness testified. This was an Internal Revenue Service official. Thereafter, the first of a series of individual taxpayers whom the defendant allegedly assisted in preparing false returns took the stand on behalf of the prosecution. After this witness was sworn, counsel for the accused interjected that each of the taxpayer witnesses should be warned as to his or her constitutional rights. Following this request, the trial judge addressed the witness on the stand and informed him of his right to consult counsel before testifying and of his right to remain silent. The witness, referring to himself and his wife, responded to the judge that "our returns have information in them that we know is wrong, and we have admitted this, and I would admit it farther in this court."

The judge dismissed the witness ("I am not going to let you admit it any further in this court.") and instructed him to step down. The trial judge then asked the Assistant U.S. Attorney

[h] *Rutledge v. United States,* 116 S. Ct. 1241 (1996).
[i] *Blockburger v. United States,* 284 U.S. 299 (1932).
[j] 400 U.S. 470, 91 S. Ct. 547, 27 L. Ed. 2d 543 (1971).

whether the taxpayer witnesses had been given warnings as to their constitutional rights. Subsequent to the ensuing dialogue on this question, the court indicated doubt that the taxpayers had been appropriately warned by the government, dismissed the jury, vacated the case, and then called the taxpayer witnesses before him and advised them to consult counsel before deciding to testify. When the case was scheduled for a new trial thereafter, the defendant moved to dismiss on the ground of double jeopardy. The defendant's motion was granted, and the government's case against the defendant was dismissed by the trial judge. The government prosecuted an appeal to the Supreme Court, which affirmed the dismissal.

A critical question involved in the case centers on the ability of the government to put to trial an accused person who has already been tried on a prior occasion, but which trial was aborted before completion. Certain federal cases determining whether the accused must undergo a second trial in such circumstances have fallen into distinct patterns. If the first trial was interrupted and terminated before completion because of some omission by the government, the defendant was entitled to his or her freedom. If the second trial was necessitated by some activity of the accused, he or she could be retried. An example of the latter situation occurs when the defendant pleads that a mistrial be declared because his or her star witness, yet to testify in the case, has become seriously ill. Suppose the judge stops the proceedings and declares a mistrial? Retrial may be later initiated without legal difficulty upon recovery of this witness.

Retrial is also permitted when a convicted person attacks his conviction on appeal or in habeas corpus and wins, perhaps because the trial jury was improperly selected or because of an erroneous trial court ruling on a point of evidence. In such situations, the accused may be prosecuted again, under the general rule, and the Supreme Court has so held.[k] A similar rule holds that reprosecution may be had where the trial judge deems it necessary to expel the defendant's attorney for misconduct during the opening statement and a mistrial is thereafter declared upon defendant's motion. When circumstances develop that are not attributable to prosecutorial or judicial overreaching, a motion by the defendant for mistrial is ordinarily assumed to remove any barrier to reprosecution.[l]

[k] *United States v. Tateo*, 377 U.S. 463, 84 S. Ct. 1587, 12 L. Ed. 2d 448 (1964).
[l] *United States v. Dinitz*, 424 U.S. 600, 96 S. Ct. 1075, 47 L. Ed. 2d 267 (1976).

Assume that after a case is fully tried and given to the jury to decide, they deadlock and cannot agree on a verdict. Has jeopardy attached in such a case? When the first trial ends in a hung jury, retrial is permitted.[m]

As is apparent, a number of circumstances can cause the first trial of a defendant to end without a verdict. Equally apparent is the conclusion that many of these unresolved or prematurely terminated cases may be retried.[n] Retrial is permissible after a conviction is reversed on appeal.[o] Some court decisions emphasize that reprosecution is not barred unless the appellate reversal was based on a finding that the evidence did not authorize a verdict—insufficiency of the evidence is a key. Where, for example, the ground for reversal was the trial court's instructional error, defendant's objection to retrial (which objection was contained in a **motion in autrefois convict** and plea of former jeopardy) was denied.[p] Incorrect receipt or rejection of evidence, incorrect instructions, or other trial error that is not grounded in insufficiency of the evidence may result in reversal of defendant's original conviction but does not bar readjudication of guilt in a proceeding free from error.[q]

Conversely, where the prosecution fails to prove an essential element of an offense in achieving a conviction and the case is reversed on appeal, retrial is prohibited. "Unless the evidence at the first trial is sufficient to authorize the verdict of guilty, a second prosecution is barred."[r] A similar result obtains if, at the close of the prosecution's case-in-chief at a bench trial, the trial court dismisses or grants a directed verdict because the evidence is legally insufficient to sustain a guilty verdict.[s]

Other decisions have spelled out additional details of the double jeopardy rule. In *Breed v. Jones*,[t] Justice Burger announced the rule that a prisoner who is tried first as a juvenile in a full adjudication proceeding cannot be retried for the same offense as an adult. The Supreme Court has also adjudicated the right of

[m]*United States v. Perez*, 22 U.S. (9 Wheat.) 579 (1824); *Walters v. State*, 503 S. W.2d 895 (Ark. 1974).

[n]*Illinois v. Somerville*, 410 U.S. 458, 93 S. Ct. 1066, 35 L. Ed. 2d 425 (1973). The Somerville approach was followed in *United States v. Sanford*, 429 U.S. 14, 97 S. Ct. 20, 50 L. Ed. 2d 17 (1976).

[o]*Montana v. Hall*, 107 S. Ct. 1825 (1987).

[p]*Price v. State*, 370 S.E.2d 6 (Ga. App. 1988).

[q]*Lockhart v. Nelson*, 109 S. Ct. 285 (1988).

[r]*Holcomb v. Peachtree City*, 370 S.E.2d 23 (Ga. App. 1988). See *Hudson v. Louisiana*, 450 U.S. 40 (1981) (retrial barred where conviction set aside because of insufficient evidence).

[s]*Smalis v. Pennsylvania*, 476 U.S. 140 (1986).

[t]421 U.S. 519, 95 S. Ct. 1779, 44 L. Ed. 2d 346 (1975). See § 10.4 *infra*.

the state to retry a defendant after the first trial was aborted in consequence of a prosecutor's improper question. In *Oregon v. Kennedy,*[u] the prosecutor asked a witness if he had ever done business with the defendant. When the witness replied that he had not, the prosecutor inquired: "Is that because he is a crook?" The defendant asked for a mistrial based on the prosecutor's remark, and the trial judge granted it. On retrial, the trial court rejected the defendant's double jeopardy objection. The Supreme Court upheld this approach.

When the defendant moves for a mistrial and the judge grants it, the defendant cannot complain when the case is retried. There is a narrow exception to this rule that occurs when a prosecutor behaves so badly that a defendant is virtually forced to ask for a mistrial. These are cases in which the prosecutor's bad acts "were done 'in order to goad the [defendant] into requesting a mistrial.'" The prosecutor's actions in *Oregon v. Kennedy* did not fall into this category. The Supreme Court could find no malicious intent on the part of the prosecutor to elicit a mistrial request from the defendant. In the absence of any finding that the prosecutor engaged in extreme bad faith misconduct, the court upheld Kennedy's theft conviction.

Section 9.7. Heavier Sentence upon Retrial

Absent extraordinary circumstances, it is held that the accused may be tried for a second time for the same offense as that for which he or she was originally convicted when his or her prior conviction has been set aside at defendant's own initiative.[v] A problem may arise when a defendant is reconvicted on the second trial, but this time the judge imposes a harsher sentence upon him or her. For example, suppose state law permits the sentencing judge to impose a fixed maximum term ranging from 10 years to life imprisonment in cases where a defendant is convicted of second-degree murder. The defendant is so convicted and is sentenced to 20 years by the trial judge. He appeals and wins, and the first conviction and sentence are vacated. Upon retrial, the defendant is again convicted of second-degree murder, but this time he is sentenced to life imprisonment.

Does this prisoner have grounds for a constitutional objection because of the new sentence? Probably so, under the

[u]456 U.S. 667 (1982).

[v]Klotter, J.C., Kanovitz, J.R., and Kanovitz, M.I. (2005). *Constitutional Law,* 10th ed., Matthew Bender, New Providence, NJ, p. 395.

Supreme Court decision in *North Carolina v. Pearce*.[W] On facts similar to those set forth in the example above, the Supreme Court ruled that more severe punishment could only be imposed by the judge at resentencing if based upon conduct occurring between the time of the first and second sentence. In cases in which there is no identifiable conduct during this period that justifies a harsher sentence, and fresh information has not surfaced that would justify the increased sentence, a more severe sentence is barred as unconstitutional. And, the trial judge who does increase upon a second conviction must explain his or her reasons at the time of imposing same, placing the factual data upon which the increased sentence is based in the trial court record.[X]

Later cases have expanded the material upon which an enhanced sentence may be based. Along with misconduct by the accused after the first trial, the sentencing judge in the second case can also consider new information that only became available to the court at or near the time of the second sentencing proceeding. This information might relate to much earlier conduct by the defendant. In the absence of objective information justifying it, an enhanced second sentence is presumed to be vindictive. The Supreme Court remarked:

> *As we explained in* Texas v. McCullough, *[475 U.S. at 138], "the evil the [*Pearce*] Court sought to prevent" was not the imposition of "enlarged sentences after a new trial" but "vindictiveness of a sentencing judge."* Ibid. *See also* Chaffin v. Stynchcombe, *412 U.S. 17, 25, 93 S. Ct. 1977, 1982, 36 L. Ed. 2d 714 (1973) (the* Pearce *presumption was not designed to prevent the imposition of an increased sentence on retrial "for some valid reason associated with the need for flexibility and discretion in the sentencing process," but was "premised on the apparent need to guard against vindictiveness in the resentencing process").*[y]

What about retrial of a capital case? Can a second trial end in the death penalty for a defendant after the first litigation resulted in a sentence of life imprisonment? An early case on the point, which applied *Pearce* principles, was the decision

[W]395 U.S. 711, 89 S. Ct. 2072, 23 L. Ed. 2d 656 (1969). The *Pearce* doctrine has removed the major obstacle that prevents a defendant who received a moderate sentence from appealing his first conviction.

[X]In Ashman, A. (1969). The prisoner's dilemma: harsher punishment upon retrial, *ABA Journal*, 55:928, the author states that "without question" *North Carolina v. Pearce* has removed most of the obstacles that deter a defendant from attacking his first conviction. See *United States v. Tucker*, 581 F.2d 602 (7th Cir. 1978).

[Y]*Alabama v. Smith*, 109 S. Ct. 2201 (1989).

of the Pennsylvania Supreme Court in *Commonwealth v. Littlejohn.*[z] In an opinion by Justice Roberts, that court ruled it improper for the Commonwealth to seek the death penalty on retrial in cases in which defendants had been found guilty of murder in the first degree and sentenced to life imprisonment on the first trial, then successfully attacked the conviction on appeal and won a new trial. Without such a rule, a defendant would face the dilemma of choosing between serving out a sentence imposed after trial in which error was committed or running the risk of the death penalty if he or she3 attacks it, a choice that would place an unconstitutional burden on the prisoner, in the view of the court.[aa]

When the Supreme Court addressed the *Littlejohn* problem, they decided it the same way. In *Bullington v. Missouri,*[bb] the prosecution was barred from seeking imposition of the death penalty upon retrial of Bullington for capital murder. Bullington was convicted of murder in his first trial, and the jury fixed his punishment at life imprisonment. After the trial, Bullington complained because of the improper makeup of the trial jury; his claim was deemed meritorious, and he won a new trial. As the case was readied for the second trial, an issue arose as to whether the state could seek the death penalty, or whether the most severe potential sentence was life imprisonment. The Supreme Court ruled that, whereas the first jury had rejected death, it could not be imposed in the second trial because of the double jeopardy clause. As will be seen, however, a different rule applies to noncapital crimes.

Even the *Bullington* rule has an important qualification for capital case defendants. In *Bullington,* the jury entered a life sentence against defendant Bullington. That decision controlled Bullington's retrial. The maximum sentence was limited to life. What if, instead of clearly deciding the issue, there was a hung jury as to the severity of the sentence when the murder jury was deliberating? A 2003 Supreme Court decision involved a hopelessly deadlocked jury. The trial judge discharged the jury without receiving a sentencing verdict from them. The court

[z]250 A.2d 811 (Pa. 1969).

[aa]The court likened such a choice to that faced by defendants charged under the Federal Kidnapping Act; if a defendant chose to be tried by a jury he was subject to the death penalty, but if he was tried by the court alone he was not exposed to capital punishment. In *United States v. Jackson,* 390 U.S. 570, 88 S. Ct. 1209, 20 L. Ed. 2d 138 (1968), the Supreme Court struck down this feature of the Federal Act, ruling that the invalidated provision unconstitutionally chilled the free exercise of a defendant's right to trial by jury.

[bb]101 S. Ct. 1853 (1981); accord, *Arizona v. Rumsey,* 467 U.S. 203 (1984).

entered a sentence of life imprisonment, as provided by law. On appeal, the defendant's first-degree murder conviction was reversed. The case was sent back to the trial court for a new trial. This time, a fresh jury fixed the punishment at death, after the defendant was convicted of murder again. The Supreme Court affirmed that decision, holding that double jeopardy does not preclude a second jury's consideration of the death penalty.[cc] The key was that the first jury had not decided on a punishment.

In the years since *North Carolina v. Pearce* was announced in 1969, the Supreme Court has answered several questions raised by the *Pearce* decision. For example, what about states where the jury fixes the sentence in noncapital felonies? What if the jury fixes a higher sentence when a defendant is tried a second time than that fixed by the original jury? There is authority that would allow a jury to fix a 20-year sentence on retrial of a robbery charge (where that is the maximum) in a case in which the defendant was originally convicted and sentenced to 10 years, appealed, and won a retrial. In *Chaffin v. Stynchcombe*,[dd] for example, the Supreme Court upheld a higher sentence imposed by a jury that had not been informed of the defendant's prior sentence.

In misdemeanor cases, defendants may typically appeal petty offense convictions, taking the case on appeal from a magistrate's court to a circuit or district court for **trial de novo**.[ee] The court of general trial jurisdiction (district, superior, or circuit court) could give a heavier sentence than that given by the magistrate.[ff] Why doesn't this rule disturb the *Pearce* principle? Some hairsplitting has been done by the Supreme Court. What the defendant is getting in these circumstances is a completely new misdemeanor trial, subject to a fresh view on the imposition of punishment. Further, although trial courts may increase the sentence following trial de novo and second conviction of the same misdemeanor, separate rules control prosecutors who attempt to file different, heavier charges. *Blackledge v. Perry*[gg] illustrates the point. There, a North Carolina defendant was convicted of a misdemeanor arising out of a fight in which the defendant had engaged. He decided to appeal his assault conviction and filed a notice of appeal to have his case heard de novo in the County Superior Court.

[cc]*Sattazahn v. Pennsylvania*, 537 U.S. 101 (2003).
[dd]412 U.S. 17, 93 S. Ct. 1977, 36 L. Ed. 2d 714 (1973).
[ee]Trial *de novo* means that a fresh determination of guilt or innocence will be made in the second trial, unaffected by the result in the first trial.
[ff]*Colten v. Kentucky*, 407 U.S. 104, 92 S. Ct. 1953, 32 L. Ed. 2d 584 (1972).
[gg]417 U.S. 21, 94 S. Ct. 2098, 40 L. Ed. 2d 628 (1974).

While the appeal was pending, the prosecutor obtained an indictment from the grand jury charging the defendant with a serious felony. This indictment for felonious assault covered the same conduct for which the defendant had been convicted in the preceding misdemeanor trial. The Supreme Court disallowed the new charge because it violated the *Pearce* doctrine: "A person convicted of an offense is entitled to pursue his statutory right to a trial de novo, without apprehension that the State will retaliate by substituting a more serious charge for the original one thus subjecting him to a significantly increased potential period of incarceration."[hh]

In summary, although the *Pearce* principle has been distinguished as inapplicable in a number of procedural settings arising since the decision was originally announced, its core philosophy remains. A prosecutor may not seek a higher penalty in retrial of a case simply to punish the accused for pursuing his constitutional rights.

Section 9.8. Different Victims or Sovereigns

Exploration of the full meaning of the double jeopardy concept has been a major focus of the Supreme Court since federal jeopardy protection was made applicable in state prosecutions. In *Ashe v. Swenson*,[ii] the Supreme Court analyzed **collateral estoppel**, the concept that provides that when a defendant has been adjudged not guilty under a particular set of facts, he or she may not be retried on the same facts in any future lawsuit between the same plaintiff and defendant. An armed robbery defendant was tried for participating in the robbery of one victim of a poker game stickup and found not guilty. Six weeks later he was brought to trial again, this time for the robbery of another participant in the same poker game. On the new trial he was convicted and sentenced to a 35-year term in the state penitentiary. This conviction was ultimately upset in the Supreme Court, which held that after the first jury had determined by its verdict that the petitioner was not one of the robbers (or at least there was reasonable doubt that he was), the state could not constitutionally haul him before a new jury to litigate that issue again. Collateral estoppel is embodied in the double jeopardy guarantee.[jj]

[hh]However, not all "upping" of charges will be deemed vindictive and improper. See *United States v. Goodwin*, 457 U.S. 368 (1982).

[ii]397 U.S. 436, 90 S. Ct. 1189, 25 L. Ed. 2d 469 (1970).

[jj]Following *Ashe*, see *Harris v. Washington*, 404 U.S. 55, 92 S. Ct. 183, 30 L. Ed. 2d 212 (1971).

In another important decision, the Supreme Court ruled that the double jeopardy clause prohibited a state from trying the defendant for grand larceny following his conviction under two city ordinances, the municipal ordinance violations being based upon the same acts that gave rise to the felony charge. The Supreme Court unanimously rejected the state's theory that state and municipal prosecutions are brought by separate sovereigns and that the defendant may thus be tried on separate charges arising from the same criminal activity. Unlike the rule applicable to successive federal–state trials over the same facts, the court pointed out that state and municipal courts are merely separate arms of the same sovereign, and the double jeopardy clause prohibits the state's felony trial when the city has already prosecuted on the same facts.[kk]

Separate charges filed by the city and state within the same jurisdiction are treated differently from state and federal prosecutions for the same conduct. Federal and state governments often exercise concurrent jurisdiction over criminal acts arising from a single transaction. Suppose a person robs a federally insured bank in a particular state. Prosecution of a defendant by the state for bank robbery after the defendant had been tried and acquitted of the same crime in federal court was approved in *Bartkus v. Illinois.*[ll]

Today, as a matter of policy, numerous states decline the *Bartkus* invitation to try a suspect who has been tried for the same transaction in federal court. Over half the states prohibit state prosecution following federal prosecution covering the same offense.[mm] Oklahoma is apparently not one of these. Terry Nichols was first tried and convicted in federal court for helping to bomb a federal building and was given a life sentence. Local prosecutors in the state of Oklahoma wanted to make him suffer the death penalty, so they brought state charges.

The case was a serious one. Terry Nichols was accused of collaborating with Timothy McVeigh in planning the blast that killed 168 people and injured more than 500 others. McVeigh was the one who actually carried out the bombing of the Murrah Federal Building in Oklahoma City. "Had [McVeigh] had his way, the death toll would have been much higher. It was

[kk]*Waller v. Florida*, 397 U.S. 387, 90 S. Ct. 1184, 25 L. Ed. 2d 435 (1970).

[ll]359 U.S. 121, 79 S. Ct. 676, 3 L. Ed. 2d 684 (1959). On successive state–federal prosecutions, see *Pope v. Thone*, 671 F.2d 298 (8th Cir. 1982); Annotation, 18A.L.R. Fed. 393 (1974).

[mm]Davies, S. (2003). Profiling terror, *Ohio State Journal of Criminal Law*, 1:45, 78.

purely and simply a fortuity not in any way creditable to him that more people were not killed when he detonated the bomb outside the Murrah Federal Building. When asked if he had any regrets, McVeigh replied that his only regret was that the building had not collapsed completely. Before the events of September 11, [2001], McVeigh's malicious and premeditated crime was frequently referred to as 'the deadliest act of terrorism ever committed on American soil.'"[nn] Nichols was convicted by Oklahoma jurors of helping McVeigh acquire components for the bomb, but they did not condemn him to death.

As noted, the Oklahoma pattern illustrated in the *Nichols* case runs counter to the general rule. States do not usually prosecute after a defendant has been sent to federal prison. The general rule also controls the reverse situation, in which federal authorities are asked to pursue charges after state officials have fully tried a defendant. Their usual answer to this request is "no." The federal pattern is explained in *State v. Rogers*.[oo]

United States v. Watts, 505 F.2d 951 (Cir. 1974), affirmed a federal conviction after a prior acquittal in Georgia. The Supreme Court vacated the conviction at the request of the Solicitor General. The conviction was not vacated because the conviction was barred by legal doctrine; instead, it was vacated because the conviction did not conform to Department of Justice policy of not prosecuting individuals previously tried in state court unless compelling reasons existed for such a prosecution. See *Watts v. United States*, 422 U.S. 1032, 45 L. Ed.2d 688, 95 S. Ct. 2648 (1975).

In *State v. Rogers*, a federal jury had found Rogers not guilty of charges similar to those brought subsequently by the State of New Mexico, and the state court dismissed the New Mexico prosecution for kidnapping.

The federal policy of declining to prosecute state prisoners who are involved in state trials is often referred to as the *Petite* policy.[pp] "The rationale for the *Petite* policy is to vindicate substantial federal interests through appropriate federal prosecutions, to protect persons charged with criminal conduct from the burdens associated with multiple prosecutions and punishments for substantially the same act(s) or transaction(s), to promote efficient utilization of Department resources, and

[nn]90 N.M. 673, 568 P.2d 199 (1977).

[oo]*Petite v. United States*, 361 U.S. 529 (1960) (*Petite* policy); *Rinaldi v. United States*, 434 U.S. 22 (1977).

[pp]Podgor, E. (2004). Department of Justice guidelines, *Cornell Journal of Law and Public Policy*, 13:167, 179.

to promote coordination and cooperation between federal and state prosecutors."[qq] Despite general policy, federal prosecutors occasionally proceed with federal criminal cases based on substantially the same conduct, after a state prosecution. Such federal litigation is limited to exceptional cases.

What are the "compelling reasons" that might prompt federal authorities to prosecute a state court defendant who has already run the gauntlet of a criminal trial in state court? Civil rights cases have sometimes prompted a successive federal prosecution. During the early morning hours of March 3, 1991, Rodney King led officers on a high-speed chase in California. He was on parole after serving a one-year sentence for armed robbery. After King was out of his car, he was struck several times by officers with batons. Some of the officers involved in the apprehension of King were charged with use of excessive force. The jury in the state trial acquitted all defendants except officer Powell; the jury hung on one of the assault charges against him.

Riots followed, and a federal grand jury returned an indictment against four officers for federal civil rights violations drawn from the incident. The federal trial jury found two of the defendant officers guilty and acquitted the other two.

Prosecution of the officers was not without its critics. The American Civil Liberties Union (ACLU) studied the issue and concluded that the officers had been twice put in jeopardy for the same offense. The organization was critical of the dual sovereignty doctrine, explained earlier in this section. A member of the ACLU National Board of Directors also observed that the prosecution was unprecedented. Sergeant Stacey Koon had been originally acquitted. Until this federal case, "[t]he Supreme Court has never held that reprosecution following an acquittal is permissible under the Double Jeopardy Clause."[rr]

It should be noted that historically the federal prosecution of state prisoners has been the exception, not the rule. Notwithstanding occasional exceptions, the states under our system have historically shouldered the primary responsibility for defining and prosecuting crime, especially street crime; however, that may be changing. There is a trend toward federalization of crime, and with the change an enhanced need

[qq]Herman, S. (1994). Double jeopardy all over again, *UCLA Law Review*, 41:609, 610. See further discussion in Levinson, L. (1994). The future of state and federal civil rights prosecutions: the lessons of the Rodney King trial, *UCLA Law Review*, 41:509, 532; Amar, A. and Marcus, J. (1995). Double jeopardy law after Rodney King, *Columbia Law Review*, 95:1.

[rr]Smith (1994). Closing in on crime bill, *Criminal Justice*, Summer, 38-40. The bill is captioned the Violent Crime Control and Law Enforcement Act of 1994.

arises to determine whether a defendant will be prosecuted in state or federal court, or both.

Several prosecutors, judges, and attorneys have sounded an alarm regarding this trend, visible in the federal crime bill of 1994. Juvenile offenders who possess a firearm during a crime of violence are now subject to federal jurisdiction. Carjackings that result in a homicide can now go to federal court. "Similar reprehensible offenses that result in death but traditionally have been prosecuted on the local level are also federalized, such as drive-by shootings, murder-for-hire, sexual exploitation of children, and torture. Other new federal crimes include disposal of firearms or receipt of firearms by persons who have committed domestic abuse, and committing a crime of violence against a spouse or intimate partner if the offender traveled across state lines to make contact with that person. The release of personal information on motor vehicle records by state motor vehicle department employees is subject to federal criminal fines and redress through civil action."[ss] The federal death penalty was extended to cover more than 60 additional crimes. One federal judge and his coauthor observed that while the U.S. Constitution originally mentioned only three federal crimes, "there are now over three thousand federal crimes and the list is growing."[tt]

What is wrong with having two sovereigns available to prosecute essentially the same criminal act, on a wholesale basis? Objections are raised on the following grounds. Violent street crime has always been dealt with by local prosecutors. Critics urge that too much power is being shifted into the hands of the central government and away from the states. There are concerns that, in a desperate effort to control the modern crime crisis, Congress's shift of responsibility will overload federal resources and raise a host of legal concerns. "Incentives to refer state cases to federal court include the expenses a state saves by transferring from the state to the federal government the cost of processing, trying, and imprisoning defendants. In some cases both state and federal governments may have to pay these expenses. As the Rodney King beating cases illustrated, criminal defendants may be prosecuted first in state court, then in federal court, for the same conduct made criminal by separate state and federal statutes. New double jeopardy problems

[ss]Carrigan, J.R. and Lee, J.B. (1994). Criminalizing the federal courts, *Trial*, 30(6):50-51.

[tt]*Id.* at 52. The 1994 crime bill added many new federal offenses and broadened existing ones, resulting in a total of more than 3000 federal crimes. See Beale, S.S. (1995). Too many and yet too few, *Hastings Law Journal*, 46:979.

probably will arise as a result of criminalizing the federal courts."[uu]

When the question does not involve federal and state governments seeking separate trials, but rather one state's attempt to try a defendant after trial in another state for the same offense, the case of *State v. Glover*[vv] holds that there may be successive prosecutions where the transaction violates the laws of both jurisdictions. As noted earlier, some crimes have multi-state aspects.[ww] The general rule holds that conviction or acquittal in one state is not a bar to prosecution in another state, in the absence of a statute.[76] The Supreme Court confirmed reprosecution by a different sovereign in *Heath v. Alabama*.[xx] The defendant, a resident of Alabama, met with two accomplices in Georgia, just over the border from the defendant's Alabama home. They conspired to kill the defendant's wife. The defendant led them to his home, then left the premises. The other two kidnapped the defendant's wife. A car with her body inside was later found on the side of a road in Troup County, Georgia. The cause of death was a gunshot wound to the head. Georgia and Alabama authorities pursued dual investigations. The grand jury of Troup County, Georgia, indicted the defendant for the offense of "malice" murder. Defendant pled guilty and was sentenced to life imprisonment. Thereafter, an Alabama grand jury returned an indictment for the capital offense of murder. Before trial, the defendant entered a plea of former jeopardy. The judge ruled that double jeopardy did not bar successive prosecutions by two different states for the same act. Upon trial, the Alabama jury convicted the defendant, and he was sentenced to death. The Supreme Court upheld the right of Alabama to try and sentence the defendant in its own way, observing: "To deny a State its power to enforce its criminal laws because another State has won the race to the courthouse 'would be a shocking and untoward deprivation of the historic right and obligation of the States to maintain peace and order within their confines.'"

[uu]500 S.W.2d 271 (Mo. App. 1973).

[vv]*See* note 8 *supra*.

[ww]Some states have statutes barring such prosecutions.

[xx]474 U.S. 82 (1985).

APPENDIX TO CHAPTER 10: PRETRIAL MOTIONS AND HEARINGS

Pretrial hearings commonly deal with one of four areas of criminal law and procedure: (1) discovery of evidence, (2) suppression of seized evidence, (3) suppression of a defendant's confession, or (4) suppression of lineup and eyewitness testimony.

Discovery of Evidence

Defense lawyers frequently make a motion asking the trial judge to require the prosecutor to turn over certain records or documents to help the defendant prepare for trial of the case. Examples of items that might be requested by the defense include statements given to the police or the prosecutor by government witnesses, reports of scientific tests made by the government (e.g., ballistics, fingerprints), or copies of photographs taken by the police photographer in a homicide case showing the position of the victim's body at the crime scene. On many occasions the prosecutor may not want the defendant to see and inspect certain of these items before the trial. When controversy exists about whether or not a defendant is entitled to see a specific item, the court must hold a hearing in advance of the trial to determine whether the government is correct in resisting the defendant's desire to inspect a particular item or document. At the hearing, the defendant is the moving or requesting party. As such, he or she has the burden of proving that the item he wants to inspect is material to the preparation of the defendant's case and that his request is reasonable.

Why do prosecutors resist requests to see several items in the government's possession? Certain arguments have been advanced, including: (1) fabrication of evidence to meet the government's proof might result if the defendant knows the details of the prosecutor's evidence in advance of trial, or (2) witness intimidation could increase if the defendant learns the identity of a witness and the substance of his or her testimony.

When the defendant is successful in securing information from the prosecutor in advance of the trial, this process is referred to as **pretrial discovery** of the government's case. In several respects, discovery by a criminal defendant is more limited than is the discovery process available to parties in personal injury or product liability cases. For example, under most state codes a criminal defendant cannot freely notice the government's witnesses for discovery **depositions**. On the other hand, at such depositions in civil cases, opposing witnesses are regularly required to name all other persons who might have observed the incident or occurrence under investigation. As noted, this sort of discovery is disallowed under numerous state codes in criminal cases. The contrast with civil practice is apparent.

Whether the defendant should be entitled to more liberal discovery than is allowed under current law in most states is a source of legal debate. Arguments on both sides of this issue are drawn from the writings of two prominent jurists. In the first, Chief Justice Vanderbilt of the New Jersey Supreme Court lodged several objections to pretrial discovery:[a]

> *In criminal proceedings long experience has taught the courts that often discovery will lead not to honest fact-finding, but on the contrary to perjury and the suppression of evidence. Thus the criminal who is aware of the whole case against him will often procure perjured testimony in order to set up a false defense.*
>
> *Another result of full discovery would be that the criminal defendant who is informed of the names of all of the State's witnesses may take steps to bribe or frighten them into giving perjured testimony or into absenting themselves so that they are unavailable to testify. Moreover, many witnesses, if they know that the defendant will have knowledge of their names prior to trial, will be reluctant to come forward with information during the investigation of the crime.*

A different view is provided by Justice William Brennan, Jr., of the U.S. Supreme Court:[b]

> *The argument that disclosure may lead to witness intimidation has proved a major obstacle to discovery of witness lists which would enable the defense to interview and investigate prosecution witnesses and which are a prerequisite to the taking of*

[a]*State v. Tune*, 98 A.2d 881, 884 (N.J. 1953).

[b]Brennan, Jr., W.J. (1990). The criminal prosecution: sporting event or quest for truth? a progress report, *Washington University Law Review*, 68(1):14.

> *depositions by the defense. It has also stood in the way of pretrial disclosure of witness statements. I do not deny that discovery may lead to the intimidation—or worse—of some witnesses in some cases, or that it may dissuade some witnesses from coming forward in the first place. We have all read of instances in which informants who have agreed to testify, in particular against organized crime, have been threatened or murdered, and the federal witness protection program is clearly a very costly and disruptive method of protecting witnesses who may be in danger. But the proper response to the intimidation problem cannot be to prevent discovery altogether; it is rather to regulate discovery in those cases in which it is thought that witness intimidation is a real possibility. It is idle to suggest that we cannot tailor discovery of witness lists and the like to particular cases. As one scholar has put it, "there is a considerable difference between a tax evasion or antitrust case and a case involving murder or organized crime, and between the ordinary indigent accused and the hardened professional criminal."*

The discovery debate continues. Assistant Attorney General Edward S.G. Dennis, Jr., responded to Justice Brennan's 1989 lecture and 1990 article: "Justice Brennan's arguments are, in our judgment, based on flawed assumptions. First, the assumption that reform is needed is incorrect. Federal criminal trials are fair now, a fact not disputed directly by advocates of broader discovery.. . .As long as human nature drives defendants to take desperate measures to escape criminal liability, broader discovery will only promote and facilitate defendants' attempts to subvert justice. This is what the majority in *Tune* so clearly understood in 1953, and human nature has not changed drastically in thirty-six years."[c]

The Supreme Court approved the validity of this Florida rule in *Williams v. Florida*,[d] emphasizing that, while Florida law gave the prosecutor alibi discovery rights, it also contained liberal discovery in favor of a defendant in criminal cases. Under the Court's view, in order for a state to maintain a notice-of-alibi requirement the prosecution must similarly be open to substantial discovery obligations.[e]

[c]Dennis, Jr., E.S.G. (1990). The discovery process in criminal prosecutions: toward fair trials and just verdicts, *Washington University Law Review*, 68(1):63-65.

[d]399 U.S. 78, 90 S. Ct. 1893, 26 L. Ed. 2d 446 (1970).

[e]The burden of proof on the defenses of alibi and insanity is discussed in § 6.25 of this chapter.

The Federal Rules of Criminal Procedure provide as follows in three subdivisions of Rule 12.1:

Rule 12.1 Notice of Alibi

(a) GOVERNMENT'S REQUEST FOR NOTICE AND DEFENDANT'S RESPONSE.

(1) *Government's Request.* An attorney for the government may request in writing that the defendant notify an attorney for the government of any intended alibi defense. The request must state the time, date, and place of the alleged offense.

(2) *Defendant's Response.* Within 10 days after the request, or at some other time the court sets, the defendant must serve written notice on an attorney for the government of any intended alibi defense. The defendant's notice must state:

- each specific place where the defendant claims to have been at the time of the alleged offense; and
- the name, address, and telephone number of each alibi witness on whom the defendant intends to rely.

(b) DISCLOSING GOVERNMENT WITNESSES.

(1) *Disclosure.* If the defendant serves a Rule 12.1(a)(2) notice, an attorney for the government must disclose in writing to the defendant or the defendant's attorney:

- the name, address, and telephone number of each witness the government intends to rely on to establish the defendant's presence at the scene of the alleged offense; and
- each government rebuttal witness to the defendant's alibi defense.

. . .

(c) FAILURE TO COMPLY. If a party fails to comply with this rule, the court may exclude the testimony of any undisclosed witness regarding the defendant's alibi. This rule does not limit the defendant's right to testify.

Motions to suppress government evidence are usually made before trial, and a pretrial hearing without the trial jury being present is the normal mode of litigation. In federal practice, Rule 12 provides that a motion to suppress must be made prior to trial. Frequently this motion is coupled with one for return of property. There is also a rule covering return of property:

Rule 41

. . .

(a) MOTION TO RETURN PROPERTY. A person aggrieved by an unlawful search and seizure of property or by the deprivation of property may move for the property's return. The motion must be filed in the district where the property was seized. The court must receive evidence on any factual issue necessary to decide the motion. If it grants the motion, the court must return the property to the movant, but may impose reasonable conditions to protect access to the property and its use in later proceedings.

Similar practice exists in numerous states as a result of court rule or judicial decision.

Securing Witnesses at Trial

Subpoenas are available to both sides in a criminal case to secure witnesses for trial, as well as documents that are not privileged or confidential, the latter under a **subpoena duces tecum**. The rules for federal courts illustrate the point:

Federal Criminal Procedure Rule 17. Subpoena

(a) CONTENT. A subpoena must state the court's name and the title of the proceeding, include the seal of the court, and command the witness to attend and testify at the time and place the subpoena specifies. The clerk must issue a blank subpoena—signed and sealed—to the party requesting it, and that party must fill in the blanks before the subpoena is served.

(b) DEFENDANT UNABLE TO PAY. Upon a defendant's ex parte application, the court must order that a subpoena be issued for a named witness if the defendant shows an inability to pay the witness's fees and the necessity of the witness's presence for an adequate defense. If the court orders a subpoena to be issued, the process costs and witness fees will be paid in the same manner as those paid for witnesses the government subpoenas.

(c) Producing Documents and Objects.

(1) *In General.* A subpoena may order the witness to produce any books, papers, documents, data, or other objects the subpoena designates. The court may direct the witness to produce the designated items in court before trial or before they are to be offered in evidence. When the items arrive, the court may permit the parties and their attorneys to inspect all or part of them.

(2) *Quashing or Modifying the Subpoena.* On motion made promptly, the court may quash or modify the subpoena if compliance would be unreasonable or oppressive.

. . .

(d) CONTEMPT. The court (other than a magistrate judge) may hold in contempt a witness who, without adequate excuse, disobeys a subpoena issued by a federal court in that district. A magistrate judge may hold in contempt a witness who, without adequate excuse, disobeys a subpoena issued by that magistrate judge as provided in 28 U.S.C. § 636(e).

How to Act When a Witness

- *Tell the truth!* Nothing else contained in this pamphlet is as important as this one admonition. If you try to color, shade, or change your testimony to help one side or the other, you are headed for trouble. Never become so anxious to help one of the parties that you permit yourself to take sides. No matter how skillful a lawyer is in cross-examination, he will never confuse or embarrass you if you stick to the truth.
- *Never lose your temper!* If you do, you are lost. If a witness becomes so prejudiced in favor of one side that he loses his temper when facts that are not favorable to his friend are elicited, he places himself at the mercy of the cross-examiner and makes himself worthless to the side he tries to favor. Judges and juries are not interested in prejudiced testimony; they are interested only in facts. Keep your temper and your service as a witness will be pleasant.
- *Don't be afraid of the lawyers!* If you give your information honestly, there is no question a lawyer can ask that will cause you any trouble. It is only when you "cross-examine yourself" that a lawyer can show up your testimony as false. The lawyers are only interested in obtaining the truth. They will be more courteous to you as the character of your testimony merits courtesy.
- *Speak clearly!* There is nothing as unpleasant to a court, jury, and lawyers as to have a witness who refuses to speak loudly enough to be heard. Such low tone of voice not only detracts from the value of your testimony but also tends to make the court and jury think that you are not certain of what you are saying. Everyone in the courtroom is entitled to know what you have to say. There are no secrets in court.
- *If you don't understand a question, ask that it be explained.* Many times a witness will not understand a question that has been asked but will nevertheless go right ahead and try to answer it. This is confusing to the court, jury, and lawyers.

It also extends the time a witness will be on the witness stand because the lawyers must go back and correct any misinformation given by a witness who does not understand the question. If you do not understand, feel free to say so and ask that the question be explained to you. It will save time and confusion.

- *Answer all questions directly!* Too often a witness will be so anxious to tell his story that he will want to get it all told when answering the first question. Listen to the question. If you can answer it with a "yes" or "no," do so. Never volunteer information the question does not ask for. What you volunteer may be damaging to the side with which you are friendly.
- *Stick to the facts!* The only thing that you will be permitted to testify to is what you personally know. Seldom is what someone else told you admissible in the case. What you KNOW is important; what you THINK is unimportant.
- *Don't be apprehensive!* There is no reason to fear being called as a witness. To begin with, the lawyers will always be courteous and the judge is there to ensure that you will be permitted to tell your story in accordance with the rules of evidence. If you are afraid when you give your testimony, your mind will not be clear and you will probably not be able to tell what you know as clearly as if you were completely composed.
- *If you don't know, admit it!* Some witnesses think they should have an answer to every question asked. No witness knows all the facts, but your lawyer may not know every detail of which you have knowledge. It is for this reason that he may ask you questions about things of which you have no knowledge. If this is true, tell him that you don't know. It is to your credit to be honest, rather than try to have an answer for everything that is asked you.
- *Don't try to memorize your story!* The administration of justice requires only that a witness tell his story to the best of his ability. No witness is expected to know every detail perfectly. For this reason, it is urged that you never try to memorize your story. There is no more certain way to cross yourself than to memorize your story. Before you go into court, discuss your testimony with the lawyer who calls you, if you wish. Sometimes it is essential that you do so. If you do and are asked about it on the witness stand, do not hesitate to admit it. There is nothing wrong with discussing your testimony with the lawyers.

- *Don't answer too quickly!* Most of the courts in which you will be called to testify as a witness will be what are known as "Courts of Record." This means merely that a record is made by a court reporter of everything that is said by everyone in the court room. In order to make this work easier, you should never answer a question until it is completely finished. Frequently, one of the lawyers will make an objection to a question. You should never try to answer before the objection is completed. Take your time and give the court reporter a chance to do his work and give the lawyers an opportunity to make their objections. Evidence must be legally admissible and the only way in which this can be assured is to permit the lawyers to object when they believe the testimony asked for is improper. Wait until you are called, tell what you know, in the way you know it, and you will have no trouble.

Extradition and Transfer of Custody for Trial

Interstate Extradition

The Uniform Criminal Extradition Act, adopted in the vast majority of states, provides that it is the duty of a state governor to deliver up a person from his or her state to another state when that person has fled the other state to avoid prosecution. Delivery of the fugitive to the executive authority of the state that desires custody of such person is appropriate when the defendant is charged with "treason, felony, or other crime."[f] Demand for **extradition** must be written and must be accompanied by a copy of an indictment, information warrant, or magistrate's affidavit, which charges the demanded person with a crime. If the defendant escaped from confinement in the demanding state, a copy of a judgment of conviction or any sentence imposed must accompany the demand.

When the governor of the state where the defendant is located decides the demand should be complied with, he or she signs a warrant of arrest directed to a peace officer for

[f]Under an expansive reading of the term "fugitive," modern extradition acts have done away with the requirement that, in order to be subject to extradition, every defendant must have fled from justice. Thus, David who lives in State B and conspired to commit an offense in State A might be extradited to State A for trial even though he never lived there and did not "flee from justice" in that state. See Uniform Criminal Extradition Act, 11 U.L.A. 6 (1974). (Governor of state may surrender the accused to another state where the crime was committed even though the accused was not in that state at the time of commission of crime.)

execution. After arrest of the named person on the fugitive warrant, such person is taken before a judge of a court of record who must inform him or her of the demand made for his or her surrender and of the crime charged in the demanding state. Advice as to legal rights (right to counsel, hearing) should be given at this time. When requested by the accused, a hearing will be set, with notice to the prosecuting officer of the county in which the arrest was made as well as the agent of the demanding state. This hearing is designed to inquire into whether the person is a fugitive subject to extradition. It is frequently waived by the accused.[g]

A Supreme Court opinion aptly summarized the philosophy of criminal extradition. In *Michigan v. Doran,*[h] the governor of Michigan decided to send Robert W. Doran to Arizona to face charges that he stole a truck. The governor ordered extradition. Doran resisted, petitioning in the Michigan courts for a writ of habeas corpus. He won a decision granting his freedom; however, the U.S. Supreme Court reversed the decision of the Michigan Supreme Court that had mandated Doran's release. The U.S. Supreme Court stated:

> *The Extradition Clause was intended to enable each state to bring offenders to trial as swiftly as possible in the state where the alleged offense was committed.... The purpose of the Clause was to preclude any state from becoming a sanctuary for fugitives from the justice of another state and thus "balkanize" the administration of criminal justice among the several states.*

Governors are required to cooperate with each other in surrendering prisoners. When the papers from the demanding state are in order and a proper identification of the defendant has been made, the governor of the asylum state (the place to which

[g]See Uniform Criminal Extradition Act, 11 U.L.A. 290 (1974). Many states have adopted reciprocal arrangements on detainers under the detainer compact, captioned the Interstate Agreement on Detainers, to expedite trial of prisoners held in custody in other jurisdictions. See also the Uniform Mandatory Disposition of Detainer Act, 11 U.L.A. 321 (1974). Interstate extradition has a constitutional base. The U.S. Constitution provides that "a person charged in any state with treason, felony, or other crime who shall flee from justice and be found in another state, shall on demand of the executive authority of the state from which he fled, be delivered up to be removed to the state having jurisdiction of the crime." Art. 4 § 2. To the effect that the word *crime* in this context includes a misdemeanor, rendering it an extraditable offense, see *Ex parte Reggel,* 114 U.S. 642, 5 S. Ct. 1148, 29 L. Ed. 250 (1885). For a list of the countries with which the United States has entered into treaties of extradition, see 18 U.S.C. § 3181. The federal extradition statute appears at 18 U.S.C. §§ 3181 to 3195.

[h]99 S. Ct. 530 (1978). In accord with *Doran,* see *Pacileo v. Walker,* 449 U.S. 86 (1980).

the defendant has fled) must comply. It is not only the governor whose actions are circumscribed, however. The *courts* of the asylum state may not pose unreasonable obstacles to the process by setting the defendant free. The *Doran* case explains:

> *[When the governor of the state where the person is found, the asylum state, grants extradition, such] grant of extradition is prima facie evidence that the constitutional and statutory requirements have been met. Cf.* Bassing v. Cady, *208 U.S. 386, 392, 28 S. Ct. 392, 393, 52 L. Ed. 540 (1908). Once the governor has granted extradition, a court considering release on habeas corpus can do no more than decide (a) whether the extradition documents on their face are in order; (b) whether the petitioner has been charged with a crime in the demanding state; (c) whether the petitioner is the person named in the request for extradition; and (d) whether the petitioner is a fugitive. These are historic facts readily verifiable.*

Neither the governor of the asylum state nor its courts have the power to interfere with and stymie transfer of a fugitive. The governor of the asylum state no longer has the discretion not to extradite.[i] It is no defense to extradition that the defendant claims that he fled the state where the crime occurred under duress. In *New Mexico ex rel. Ortiz v. Reed,*[j] the Supreme Court held that the state of New Mexico was required to return a fugitive to Ohio. Responding to the defendant's fear that he faced physical harm if sent to an Ohio prison, the Court held that "what may be expected to happen in the demanding state when the fugitive returns [is an issue] that must be tried in the Courts of that State, and not in those of the asylum State."

Notwithstanding the language of *Doran* that interstate extradition was intended to be a summary proceeding, many state laws have developed numerous ponderous steps in the process, once a fugitive refuses to waive extradition. This poses special difficulties for prosecutors in cities that border another state. For example, many communities are located along rivers that separate two states, and sprawling urban areas commonly spread across state boundaries. A thief can steal a car and by driving it to another part of the urban area or by crossing a river (and thereby removing himself to another state) successfully trigger the operation of substantial procedural steps required to secure extradition. With modern emphasis on reducing pretrial delays and making the delivery of justice more effective,

[i] *Puerto Rico v. Branstad,* 107zS. Ct. 2802 (1987).
[j] 118 S. Ct. 1860 (1998).

proposals to overhaul interstate extradition of fugitives have appeared. One such suggestion, an interstate extradition compact, would simplify the multiple procedural steps currently required in a simple extradition case. One of the features of the suggested compact allows extradition to be requested by the prosecutor of the city where the crime occurred and granted by the prosecutor where the fugitive is apprehended. In situations of interstate flight by criminals, the proposed compact eliminates the need to involve the governor of the demanding state and the surrendering state.[k]

In addition to extradition, a federal statute is designed to assist state prosecutions and deter those intending to flee jurisdictions in order to frustrate the administration of justice. The statute makes it a felony to travel in interstate commerce to avoid prosecution or the giving of testimony, and provides as follows:[l]

> *18 U.S.C. § 1073. Flight to avoid prosecution or giving testimony*
> *Whoever moves or travels in interstate or foreign commerce with intent either (1) to avoid prosecution, or custody or confinement after conviction, under the laws of the place from which he flees, for a crime, or an attempt to commit a crime, punishable by death or which is a felony under the laws of the place from which the fugitive flees, or (2) to avoid giving testimony in any criminal proceedings in such place in which the commission of an offense punishable by death or which is a felony under the laws of said State, is charged, or (3) to avoid service of, or contempt proceedings for alleged disobedience of, lawful process requiring attendance and the giving of testimony or the production of documentary evidence before an agency of a State empowered by the law of such State to conduct investigations of alleged criminal activities, shall be fined under this title or imprisoned not more than five years, or both.*
>
> ...
>
> *Violations of this section may be prosecuted only in the Federal judicial district in which the original crime was alleged to have been committed, or in which the person was held in custody or confinement, or in which an avoidance of service of process or a contempt referred to in clause (3) of the first paragraph of this section is alleged to have been committed, and only upon formal*

[k]Iowa Code ch. 818 (1998).

[l]18 U.S.C. § 1073. By a 1980 addition to this section, Congress expressly declared its intent that Section 1073 of Title 18, United States Code, apply to cases involving parental kidnapping and interstate or international flight to avoid prosecution under applicable state felony statutes.

approval in writing by the Attorney General, the Deputy Attorney General, the Associate Attorney General, or an Assistant Attorney General of the United States, which function of approving prosecutions may not be delegated.

The federal statute just cited provides for the transfer of witnesses from one jurisdiction to another. To further combat problems in producing witness testimony, most states have enacted reciprocal legislation patterned after the Uniform Act to Secure the Attendance of Witnesses from Without a State in Criminal Proceedings. These laws operate between and among participating states and provide legal machinery whereby the state in which the criminal proceeding is being held can obtain the testimony of an unwilling witness who is a nonresident or has fled the state. The Supreme Court upheld the power of a state to order a witness to appear in another state in *New York v. O'Neill.*[m] By holding such statutes constitutional, the Supreme Court furthered the administration of justice by enabling defendants as well as state prosecutors to obtain witnesses who might otherwise be difficult to reach.

International Extradition

What about securing the presence of a defendant in an American trial from a foreign country? How is this handled when, for example, a U.S. court wants to try a citizen of Colombia for conspiracy to commit drug crimes in an American jurisdiction? What about the converse of this situation? Can an American court send a U.S. citizen to a foreign nation for trial?

The last question arose in a dramatic case, the extradition of John Demjanjuk from northern Ohio to the State of Israel. Demjanjuk was a native of the Ukraine, one of the republics of the Soviet Union. After World War II he came to the United States and became a naturalized citizen in 1958. The district court found that Demjanjuk was conscripted into the Soviet Army in 1940 and was captured by the Germans in 1942. Although he steadfastly denied it, the district court further found that Demjanjuk became a guard for the Germans at the Treblinka concentration camp in Poland. Five Treblinka survivors and one former German guard identified him as the Ukrainian guard at the camp who was known as "Ivan the Terrible."

[m]359 U.S. 1, 79 S. Ct. 564, 3 L. Ed. 2d 585 (1959). The uniform act on witnesses has been widely adopted.

The State of Israel filed a request for extradition with the U. S. Department of State. Following a hearing in federal court in Ohio, the district court ordered Demjanjuk extradited for trial in Israel pursuant to a treaty of extradition between the United States and Israel. The treaty provided that each contracting party (the United States and Israel) would deliver people found in its territory for prosecution in the other country when they have been charged in the requesting country with crimes such as murder, manslaughter, or inflicting grievous bodily harm.

The U.S. Court of Appeals approved extradition. "It is a fundamental requirement for international extradition that the crime for which extradition is sought be one provided for by the treaty between the requesting and the requested nation." Because an offense is extraditable only if the acts charged are criminal by the laws of both countries, the court ruled: "Murder is a crime in every state of the United States. The fact that there is no separate offense of mass murder or murder of tens of thousands of Jews in this country is beside the point. The act of unlawfully killing one or more persons with the requisite malice is punishable as murder. That is the test. The acts charged are criminal both in Israel and throughout the United States, including Ohio."[n]

The principle of double criminality is the key to international extradition. It holds that an offense is not extraditable unless it constitutes a crime in the country where the defendant is found, as well as in the requesting country.[o] Hence, the emphasis on this point in the Demjanjuk litigation. Ultimately, the case against the defendant was dismissed. John Demjanjuk was released by Israel's Supreme Court upon a finding of reasonable doubt as to guilt.

International extradition requires a treaty with the cooperating country. The United States cannot extradite someone to another country in the absence of a valid treaty. The United States has extradition treaties with numerous countries, and there are currently a number of active extradition cases involving fugitives in the United States who are wanted by other countries who are in America as well as cases involving criminals wanted in the United States who are living abroad.[27]

[n]*Demjanjuk v. Petrovsky,* 776 F.2d 571, 580 (6th Cir. 1985). See Bernholz, S.A., Bernholz, M.J., and Herman, G.N. (1985). Problems of double criminality, *Trial* 21(1):58-63.

[o]For a list of countries with which the United States has extradition treaties, see 18 U.S.C. § 3181-3195.

APPENDIX TO CHAPTER 11: PLEA BARGAINING

Plea bargaining is a controversial feature of the American justice system. It is appropriate, having reviewed in this chapter the plea procedures in state and federal courts, to look at what has been called the "invisible process" behind guilty pleas. Under one view, plea bargaining is essential and (if properly implemented) even desirable. A competing view demands the end to this "dangerous and unwholesome feature of American justice." Because of the import of this debate, selections supporting each view are presented for review.

First, drawing together ideas that favor plea bargaining is the Federal Advisory Committee Note to Rule 11, Federal Rules of Criminal Procedure:

> *In* Santobello v. New York, *404 U.S. 257, 260, 92 S. Ct. 495, 498, 30 L. Ed. 2d 427 (1971), the court said: "The disposition of criminal charges by agreement between the prosecutor and the accused, sometimes loosely called 'plea bargaining,' is an essential component of the administration of justice. Properly administered, it is to be encouraged."*
>
> *Administratively, the criminal justice system has come to depend upon pleas of guilty and, hence, upon plea discussions. See, e.g., President's Commission on Law Enforcement and Administration of Justice, Task Report: The Courts 9 (1967); Note, Guilty Plea Bargaining: Compromises By Prosecutors To Secure Guilty Pleas, 112 U. Pa. L. Rev. 865 (1964).*
>
> . . .
>
> *Where the defendant by his plea aids in insuring prompt and certain application of correctional measures, the proper ends of the criminal justice system are furthered because swift and certain punishment serves the ends of both general deterrence and the rehabilitation of the individual defendant. Cf. Note, The Influence of the Defendant's Plea on Judicial Determination of Sentence, 66 Yale L.J. 204, 211 (1956). Where the defendant has acknowledged his guilt and shown a willingness to assume responsibility for his conduct, it has been thought proper to recognize this in sentencing. . . .A plea of guilty avoids the necessity of a public trial and may protect the innocent victim of a crime against the trauma of direct and cross-examination.*

The Federal Advisory Committee discussed some of the primary methods of plea bargaining, describing the concessions that may be given to induce a defendant to plead guilty:[a]

> *First, the charge may be reduced to a lesser or related offense. Second, the attorney for the government may promise to move for dismissal of other charges. Third, the attorney for the government may agree to recommend or not oppose the imposition of a particular sentence. Fourth, the attorneys for the government and the defense may agree that a given sentence is an appropriate disposition of the case.*

To provide for adequate judicial policing of plea agreements, the Federal Advisory Committee cited the need to bring plea agreements into the open:

> *Because the process has been abused, there needs to be judicial oversight of plea agreements. The only way to accomplish this is to require their disclosure.*

Under federal law, where an agreement is struck between the prosecutor and the defense attorney, it must be disclosed in open court, in most cases. Subdivision (e) referred to in the foregoing passage is a section of the Federal Rules of Criminal Procedure applicable to guilty pleas in federal cases. In order to bring plea agreements out into the open, the Federal Rules of Criminal Procedure were amended by adding the following provision to the guilty plea rule, Rule 11:

> ***Disclosing a Plea Agreement.*** *The parties must disclose the plea agreement in open court when the plea is offered, unless the court for good cause allows the parties to disclose the plea agreement* in camera.

In camera is defined as "in private" and often involves a proceeding in the judge's chambers, away from the public courtroom.

The Supreme Court has upheld the practice of plea bargaining as necessary and proper. The *Santobello* case has already been mentioned. In *Bordenkircher v. Hayes,*[b] the Court observed that plea bargaining is an important component of this country's criminal justice system. A plea may be induced by the prosecutor's promise that he or she will recommend a lenient sentence or drop charges; the fact that a defendant who asks for

[a]In the federal system, the flexibility to make a specific sentence recommendation has been affected by federal sentencing guidelines. State prosecutors remain generally able to plea bargain in this fashion, however.
[b]434 U.S. 357 (1978).

a trial risks more severe punishment does not render the process unconstitutional. A prosecutor should not be prohibited from persuading a defendant to plead guilty, in the opinion of the Court.

A different view of plea bargaining was taken by the National Advisory Commission on Criminal Justice Standards and Goals. While this commission favored opening plea agreements and making them matters of record as the Federal Rules of Criminal Procedure have done, the Commission urged the abolition of plea bargaining as an ultimate goal. In its report,[c] the Commission argued as follows:

> Danger to Society's Need for Protection—*Critics of plea bargaining have asserted that since the prosecutor must give up something in return for the defendant's agreement to plead guilty, the frequent result of plea bargaining is that defendants are not dealt with as severely as might otherwise be the case. Thus plea bargaining results in leniency that reduces the deterrent impact of the law.*

These opinions resulted in a recommendation by the National Commission on Criminal Justice Standards quite at odds with views previously advanced in this section. The comments of the Federal Rules Advisory Committee, as well as the view of former Chief Justice Warren Burger, who wrote the *Santobello* opinion cited in that selection, reveal a different appraisal of plea bargaining. The opposing National Commission report recommended the abolition of this process. Views similar to those contained in the Commission's recommendations prompted Alaska to abandon plea bargaining. In 1975, the Attorney General of Alaska forbade all prosecutors in that state to engage in plea negotiations, including abolition of the practice of reducing or dropping charges in exchange for a guilty plea. Three years later, an empirical study on the effects of the Alaska experiment concluded that although the rate of trials did increase substantially, the unmanageable onslaught that had been forecast did not materialize.[d]

The Alaska experience was evaluated again 15 years after the attorney general had originally banned plea bargaining.[e] It was concluded that during that time, the ban had caused a substantial decrease in sentence bargaining. The Alaska Judicial

[c] National Advisory Commission on Criminal Justice Standards and Goals, Courts, pp. 43-44 (1973).

[d] Rubenstein, M.L. and White, T.J. (1978). Plea bargaining: can Alaska live without it? *Judicature*, 62(6):266.

[e] Carns, T.W. and Kruse, J. (1991). *A Re-Evaluation of Alaska's Plea Bargaining Ban,* 8 *Alaska Law Review*, 8:27.

Council's Report found that, over the 15-year period, the percentage of convicted offenders sentenced to jail time increased, as did the length of sentence. On the other hand, while the Alaska approach seems to have virtually ended bargaining over sentences, it was apparently not effective in stanching bargaining over charges. The Alaska rules were modestly revised a few years after their inception to allow prosecutors some leeway to reduce and dismiss the charges they had originally filed in order to resolve cases.

In the federal system today, post-indictment plea bargaining seems to have been sharply reduced by the advent of the Federal Sentencing Guidelines. The history of these guidelines is traced in Sections 7.2(2) and 7.6(2) of this text. Under them, the prosecutor's discretion to drop charges has been limited by Justice Department standards. Charges are not to be bargained away or dismissed unless the prosecutor has a good-faith doubt about the prosecution's ability to readily prove a charge. One area of bargaining that remains is the ability of the prosecutor to recommend reduction of the sentence when the defendant substantially assists the government in the investigation or prosecution of another person. The court may make a downward adjustment in the sentence on motion by the government; the adjustment requires court approval and the request should be clearly presented to the court as part of the plea agreement so the judge can accept or reject it.

While the Federal Sentencing Guidelines had as an objective the elimination of significant, unwarranted disparity in sentences imposed by judges on similarly situated defendants, the rate of downward departures has been difficult to police. Without a government motion, a court cannot reduce a sentence. Accordingly, whether a defendant gets a break depends on the prosecutor. The process is largely secret, and the rate of downward departures based on substantial assistance varies dramatically from place to place. The goal of uniformity in sentencing across the country has not been completely achieved.[f]

Recently, however, Congress has imposed restrictions on judicial reduction of sentences. This effort to even out sentences around the country will be detailed in the next paragraphs of this section, as well as in Section 7.6(2).

The legislative effort to equalize sentencing concessions resulted in a national enactment in 2003. Reductions in federal sentences that depart from stated guidelines became a target

[f]Saris, P.B. (1997). Below the radar screens: have the sentencing guidelines eliminated disparity? One judge's perspective, *Suffolk University Law Review*, 30:1027.

for congressional critics of lenient sentencing. Some members of Congress were harshly critical of judges who too readily departed downward from established sentencing norms. In addition to reductions because a defendant helped to convict other parties, judges have adjusted sentences downward for a host of additional reasons. These included factors such as whether a defendant made monetary restitution to the victim or because the accused had local community ties and family responsibilities. Although these are valuable things to do, they do not warrant a dramatically lowered sentence, in the view of many lawmakers. Accordingly, Congress passed legislation in 2003 to prevent these latter considerations from being used to reduce sentences.

In addition, the Justice Department decided to gather data on federal judges who regularly sentence defendants to prison terms that are less than those called for by law. The U.S. Attorney General distributed a directive to federal prosecutors to report federal judges to the Department of Justice when a judge issues a sentence that falls below sentencing guidelines.

As is apparent, the foregoing steps make it more difficult for a prosecutor to offer a light sentence to a defendant in order to get him to plead guilty. Plea bargaining is restricted. In addition, to further impede generous plea deals, the Justice Department took direct action to cut down on the number of plea concessions by prosecutors. Plea bargaining in the federal system was discouraged in a directive from Attorney General John Ashcroft to all federal prosecutors. It provided: "It is the policy of the Department of Justice that, in all federal criminal cases, federal prosecutors *must charge and pursue* the most serious, readily provable offense or offenses that are supported by the facts of the case..." (emphasis added).[g]

[g]U.S. Department of Justice, Departmental Policy Concerning Criminal Offenses, Disposition of Charges, and Sentencing [memorandum], September 22, 2003.

GLOSSARY

abandoned property doctrine For purposes of seizure of evidence outside Fourth Amendment protection, an officer is permitted to pick up property dropped or abandoned by a suspect, examine it, and retain it as evidence if useful.

acquittal A finding of not guilty in a criminal trial.

adjudication The formal judgment, decree, or determination.

admission A defendant's statement that he or she committed the crime, or the defendant's declaration that he or she did an act that contributed to the offense.

adversary system A system of law whereby opposing parties contend against one another in front of an impartial deciding body.

advocate One who assists, defends, or pleads for another.

affirm (a case) To confirm; in appellate courts, to affirm a judgment, decree, or order is to confirm that it is valid and that it stands as correct.

"Allen" instruction Derived from *Allen v. United States*, 164 U.S. 492, 17 S. Ct. 154, 41 L. Ed. 528 (1896), where such an instruction was approved, it refers to an instruction given to jurors when they report an inability to agree on a verdict advising jurors to listen to each other's views with a willingness to be convinced by each other's arguments; also referred to as a "dynamite" or "hammer" instruction.

alternative sentencing Nontraditional sentences that allow for alternatives to conventional jail terms.

American Law Institute test Combining the *M'Naghten* and "irresistible impulse" tests for insanity, under this most commonly used test an accused person is not held criminally responsible if proven that as a result of mental disease or defect at the time of the offense the accused lacked the ability to appreciate the wrongfulness of the act or the ability to conduct himself or herself according to the law—it does not require a complete lack of knowledge of the wrongness of the criminal act, only the lack of capacity to understand right from wrong or to conform conduct to the law. *See also* M'Naghten rule and irresistible impulse test.

apparent authority When law enforcement officers rely on the consent of someone who has apparent authority over the subject of the search, the search is valid. Apparent authority is a subjective determination based on the facts and circumstances available to the officer.

appeal Resort to a higher (appellate) court for review of a trial court; in the federal system, an appeal can go to an intermediate appellate court and then to the Supreme Court.

arraignment Procedure where the accused is brought before the court to plead to the criminal charge in an indictment or information; in the federal system, the charge is read to the accused and he or she must plead "guilty," "not guilty," or, where permitted, "nolo contendere."

arrest To deprive a person of liberty by legal authority; taking a person into custody or detention to answer to criminal charges.

arrest warrant A written order based on a complaint commanding a law enforcement official to arrest a person and bring him or her before a magistrate.

authority to consent One has authority to consent to a search if that person is over 18, is the owner of the property, or has common use over the property.

automobile Any object that is easily movable is considered an automobile. This includes houseboats, motorcycles, and motor homes that are found on the roadway.

bail The surety or sureties put forth by a party to obtain release of a person under arrest by becoming responsible for the person's appearance at the time and place designated by the court. Cash bail bond is a sum of money designated by the court and posted by the defendant or another person to the court with the understanding that it will be forfeited if the defendant does not comply with court appearance instructions. Unsecured bail bond is a bail bond for which the defendant is liable upon failure to comply with court appearance instructions but which is not secured by deposit of funds.

bench trial A trial held before a judge without a jury.

bind over Whereby a court or magistrate requires a person to appear for trial; also refers to the act of a lower court transferring a case to higher court or grand jury after a finding of probable cause that the defendant committed the crime.

body scans Recent technology that uses x-rays to provide images in graphic anatomical detail for review by Transportation Security Administration (TSA) employees; they are required of all passengers boarding commercial airlines.

booking a suspect An administrative procedure by which an arrested person at the police station is put on the police "blotter," including information such as the person's name, crime for which arrested and other facts; may also include photographing and fingerprinting the suspect.

brief A written document that summarizes the legal arguments of a party; in criminal practice, both the prosecutor and the defense counsel usually file competing briefs when a defendant moves to dismiss the government's case.

burden of proof In the law of evidence, it is the burden of one party of proving a fact or facts in dispute.

capital punishment Punishment by death for capital crimes.

certiorari A writ issued by a superior court to an inferior court requiring the court to provide a certified record of a particular case so that the court who issued the writ can inspect the proceedings for irregularities.

charge To indict or formally accuse.

checkpoints Points set up for police to stop citizens without reasonable suspicion or probable cause; they serve a variety of legitimate government interests, such as vehicle safety checks, driver's license checks, weigh stations, game warden road checks, sobriety checks, and border stops.

citation An order form issued by the police or the court for a person to appear before a magistrate or judge at a specified time and date.

clear and convincing evidence Generally, this means proof to a high level of certainty, certainly more than a preponderance of the evidence but somewhat less than proof beyond a reasonable doubt.

confrontation of witnesses A right guaranteed by the Sixth Amendment as a part of the trial process. Those accused have the right to have witnesses appear in court to testify against them. Through this process, the accused may cross-examine the witness and get to the truth. Any testimonial evidence offered in court by someone other than the original declarant is hearsay and must fit within one of the exceptions before it will be admissible.

closing argument (final argument or summation) The final statements by the attorneys to the jury or court; each side summarizes the evidence they believe they have established and what they feel the other side has failed to establish; in federal criminal cases, the prosecution goes first, the defense replies, and then the prosecution is allowed to reply.

common law As opposed to law created by legislatures, common law is the law established over time by custom and usage; it begins with the ancient, unwritten law of England and includes statutory and case law of the American colonies.

complainant The person who instigates prosecution or applies to the courts for legal redress by filing a complaint (i.e., plaintiff).

complaint The original pleading that initiates an action; it is a written statement of the essential facts of the offense charged; in some jurisdictions, "complaint" is the equivalent of "information."

consent search A search made by police after the subject of the search has agreed to the search, or when the occupant of the premises lets police in to search the place.

constitutional law That body of law emanating directly from the U.S. Constitution. The Bill of Rights is included in this body of law. For the study of criminal procedure, the Fourth, Fifth, and Sixth Amendments are of particular concern.

contemporaneous searches Dealing with the timeliness of searches, this refers to the rule that a search must follow an arrest as soon as reasonably possible, the more immediate the better.

conviction The result of a criminal trial that ends with the defendant being found guilty as charged.

count Each separate and independent claim; a civil petition or a criminal indictment may contain several counts. "Count" and "charge," referring to allegations in an indictment or information, are synonymous.

critical stage The stages of a criminal case in which the right to counsel attaches; the defendant is entitled to have a lawyer represent him or her at all critical stages of the case, including preliminary hearing and trial.

cross-examination The examination of a witness by the opposing party that called him or her; generally, the scope of examination is limited to matters covered on direct examination.

curtilage An area outside of the home, but close enough to the home that the area continues to get the highest level of constitutional protection from unwarranted government intrusion. Typically, this includes the areas in which family would gather such as the back yard, the carport or garage, pool areas, and other spaces within close proximity to the home.

custodial interrogation The threshold determination of whether a suspect is entitled to the *Miranda* warning. If a suspect has been commanded to appear and answer questions of the police and is no longer free to leave, that person is likely in custody. If the person is being asked direct questions about a criminal event, an interrogation is occurring. In that instance, a suspect is entitled to an attorney to protect the Fifth Amendment right against self-incrimination.

custody The confinement or control of a thing or person; being "in custody" refers to restraint of liberty, and custodial interrogation of the accused takes place when the defendant is not free to leave the interrogation room.

deadly force Force likely or intended to cause death or great bodily harm.

defendant The person defending or denying criminal responsibility; the accused person or the party against whom relief or recovery is sought.

defense attorney The lawyer who represents the accused/defendant.

directed verdict *See* motion for judgment of acquittal.

direct examination (examination in chief) The first interrogation or examination of a witness by the person who called the witness to the stand.

discretionary review Form of appellate review that is not required but is a matter of choice; for example, the Supreme Court chooses its cases for review and is not required to review matters on appeal.

dismissal with prejudice An adjudication on the merits and final disposition, it bars the right to bring or maintain an action of the same claim or cause.

dismissal without prejudice Refers to a dismissal or finding that extinguishes a legal action but which allows the disappointed party to bring the action again at a later time.

disposition In criminal procedure, refers to the sentencing or other final finding in the case.

dissenting opinion Most commonly refers to the opinion provided by one or more judges of a court that expresses explicit disagreement with the decision handed down by the majority; a dissent may or may not be accompanied by a written opinion.

diversion Referring to alternative sentencing measures, it is a disposition of a criminal defendant where the court directs defendant to participate in some form of program or other alternative to traditional incarceration.

double jeopardy Refers to being subject to prosecution more than once for the same offense; the Fifth Amendment of the Constitution prohibits a second prosecution after a first trial for the same offense.

dual sovereignty Federal and state governments are each sovereign in their own right, so in some cases a person can be tried twice for the same act or acts because the crime violated both state and federal laws; thus, double jeopardy does not apply because it refers to more than one prosecution by the same sovereign jurisdiction for the same offense.

due process Due process is guaranteed by the Fifth and Fourteenth Amendments to the Constitution. At the basic level, due process means that defendants have the right to notice of the charges against them and the opportunity to be heard. More detailed meaning includes fairness and equity of dealing throughout the criminal trial process.

Durham test The irresistible impulse test of criminal responsibility resulting from *Durham v. United States*, 214 F.2d 862, 875 (C.A.D.C. 1954). Under the Durham test, to find a defendant not guilty by reason of insanity of mental irresponsibility the jury must find that the defendant was suffering from mental disease at the time of commission of the act and that there was a causal relation between the disease and the act.

evidence Any court materials or proof, such as witness testimony, documents, exhibits, physical items or objects, etc.

excessive force Any amount of force beyond what is necessary and justifiable, given the particulars of the events and the people involved.

exclusionary rule Under the exclusionary rule, any evidence that has been obtained in violation of the privileges guaranteed by the U.S. Constitution must be excluded at trial.

exculpatory evidence Evidence that clears or tends to clear the defendant.

exigent circumstances These emergency or emergency-like circumstances may provide permission by police to make warrantless entry or warrantless search and seizure because delay may pose a danger to persons or allow destruction of evidence.

false arrest An arrest without proper legal authority, resulting in unlawful restraint of a person's liberty.

false imprisonment Because an arrest restrains the liberty of a person, false arrest is also false imprisonment, whereby a person unlawfully loses his or her liberty.

felony Contrasted with misdemeanor, felony is a more serious offense, usually characterized as an offense that is punishable by death or imprisonment in a state prison (versus imprisonment in a local jail), or a crime for which the term of imprisonment is more than year.

"fruit of the poisonous tree" doctrine Evidence that is obtained from or is discovered as a result of an illegal search or is generally inadmissible against the defendant because it is tainted by being a product of a bad initial search.

good faith exception This exception to the exclusionary rule allows the admission into court of evidence obtained with error or mistake as long as the error or mistake was honest and reasonable.

grand jury A group of citizens, the number of which may vary by state, who are gathered to determine whether probable cause exists that a crime has been committed and whether an indictment (true bill) should be returned against the accused; its purpose is merely to determine if the case will go to trial and not to determine whether the accused is guilty; grand jury proceedings are not public proceedings.

guilty plea Formal admission of guilt in court by the defendant; it is only admissible if the defendant has been fully advised of his or her rights, understands those rights, and makes the plea voluntarily.

habeas corpus *See* writ of habeas corpus.

hearings Formal proceedings, usually public but less formal than a trial, with issues of fact or law; frequently describes any proceedings before magistrates sitting without a jury. Generally, the introduction and admissibility of evidence is less stringent in hearings than in trials.

hearsay evidence Testimony in court of a statement made out of court by someone other than the person testifying; it does not come from personal knowledge of the witness who is on the stand but from something the witness heard others say. Use of hearsay evidence is strictly limited.

hot pursuit Also known as fresh pursuit, refers to the right of law enforcement officials to chase a suspect and even cross jurisdictional lines (in jurisdictions that allow it) in pursuit of a felon in order to arrest the person for a crime committed in the first jurisdiction.

hung jury A jury divided in opinion and unable to come to a unanimous verdict after lengthy attempts. *See also* "Allen" instruction.

immunity from prosecution If granted by the prosecution, a witness may be protected from being prosecuted pursuant to his or her testimony. *Use immunity* prohibits the use of the witness's compelled testimony from being used in any subsequent criminal prosecution of the witness. When a witness testifies about a crime under the protection of *transactional immunity,* any later prosecution of the witness for that crime is prohibited after the person gives his or her immunized testimony.

in the officer's presence This phrase is one of the elements that can give rise to a valid arrest without a warrant. Officer's may arrest for offenses, both felony and misdemeanor, that occur within their presence. Courts have had more lenient interpretation of this provision in felony cases and have included circumstances that come to the attention of officers through any of their senses, not just sight.

incompetence Severe mental disability or impairment; lacking understanding or ability to make or communicate responsible decisions.

indictment An accusation in writing originating with a prosecutor and issued by a grand jury charging a person with a crime—referred to as a "true bill." Failure to indict is a "no bill." *See also* information.

independent source An exception to the exclusionary rule. If otherwise tainted evidence is discovered by a completely independent source, it will be allowed.

ineffective assistance of counsel A post-trial motion that asserts that the defendant's attorney was ineffective and therefore a new trial should be granted. The attorney's performance must fall below the normal standard of care, and the defendant must show that his or her case was prejudiced by the attorney's performance.

inevitable discovery An exception to the exclusionary rule. If the evidence would have been discovered anyway, even without the illegal action on the part of law enforcement, it may be admitted at trial. This is called the "inevitable discovery doctrine," which was discussed in *Nix v. Williams,* 467 U.S. 431 (1984).

information An accusation against a person for a crime, presented by a public officer such as a prosecutor (as opposed to an indictment, which is handed down by the grand jury); in many states, information may be used in place of a grand jury indictment to bring a person to trial.

inventory search An exception to the search warrant requirement, it is an inventory of all of the contents of a vehicle once it is removed to the impound yard that is in compliance with departmental policy. Justifications include to protect an owner's property while it is under police control; to ensure against claims of lost, stolen, or vandalized property; and to protect the police from danger.

investigative stops A stop based on reasonable suspicion instead of probable cause. In this stop situation, officers may only investigate a suspected illegality. The stop is limited both in scope and duration.

irresistible impulse test As used in an insanity defense, refers to an impulse on the part of the accused that he or she is incapable of resisting due to mental disease that affects the person's self-control and choice of actions; this test is broader than the M'Naghten test because, under the irresistible impulse test, the person may avoid responsibility even though he or she understood the nature of the act and its wrongness. *See also* American Law Institute test and M'Naghten rule.

issues of fact Arise when a fact is maintained by one party and denied by the other party; issues of fact are determined by the jury at the trial level.

issues of law Arises when matters of law in a case are in question; appeals courts review issues of law.

***Jackson v. Denno* hearing** A pretrial hearing addressing a defendant's *Miranda* or voluntariness objections to validity of a confession. The court will hear evidence to determine whether the trial jury will get to hear and see the confession.

Jencks Act A criminal defendant in federal court is entitled to access to government documents for assistance in cross-examination of witnesses in order to impeach for prior inconsistent statements. See *Jencks v. United States*, 353 U.S. 657, 77 S. Ct. 1007, 1 L. Ed. 2d 1103 (1957), leading to federal statute 18 U.S.C. § 3500.

jurisprudence The philosophy or science of law, ascertaining the principles on which legal rules are based.

jurist A person who is skilled in the law, often used to refer to a person who is officially qualified to decide legal matters, such as a magistrate, judge, or justice.

jury A specified number of men and women selected and sworn to determine matters of fact and decide the truth of the evidence presented to them.

jury instructions A direction given by the judge to the jury concerning the law of the case that informs the jury of the law applicable to the case and the rules or principles of law that the jurors are bound to accept and apply.

jury nullification Jury nullification occurs when the jury's verdict is at odds with the weight of the evidence presented at trial, particularly when jurors affirmatively decide not to follow the law; jurors who nullify have decided to substitute their own notion of law over that given by the court, although the Supreme Court rejects the practice of juries in effect declaring laws unconstitutional.

K-9 sniff This is an exception to the warrant requirement. Officers may have a trained police dog sniff a car, as well as containers, and if the dog alerts then officers have probable cause to search. Trained police dogs conducting the sniffs are not considered to be searching within the meaning of the Fourth Amendment.

"knock-and-announce" rule A rule requiring officers to let householders know that they are there to arrest or search; in specified cases, a peace officer, whether with a warrant or on probable cause without a warrant, may after announcement of authority and purpose break through a door to gain admittance to a dwelling.

lineup A police identification procedure by which the suspect in a crime is exhibited before the victim or witness. A number of individuals are lined up from whom the witness may then make an identification; the procedure must meet certain standards and be free of suggestion as to the suspect. *See also* showup.

M'Naghten rule A widely used and long-established test to be applied for the defense of insanity under which the accused is not criminally responsible if at the time of committing the act he or she suffered such a defect of reason or mental disease that he or she did not know the nature and quality of the act or did not understand that the act was wrong (*M'Naghten's Case*, 8 Eng. Rep. 718 [1843]). *See also* American Law Institute test and irresistible impulse test.

magistrate A public officer with judicial power.

***Miranda* warning** Prior to any custodial interrogation in which a person is deprived of his or her freedom in any significant way, the person must be warned that he or she: (1) has the right to remain silent; (2) that any statement made may be used as evidence against him or her; (3) that he or she has the right to an attorney; (4) that if he or she cannot afford an attorney, one will be appointed prior to any questions if so desired. Administration of these warnings or waiver of them must be demonstrated for any evidence obtained during interrogation to be admissible in court.

misdemeanor Contrasted with felony, misdemeanor is a less serious offense, generally punishable by fine or imprisonment in local jail as opposed to state penitentiary; certain states have various classes of misdemeanors.

motion An application to a court or judge to obtain a ruling or order.

motion to suppress A motion to bar evidence from the trial that has either been illegally obtained or that is viewed as irrelevant or prejudicial to the case.

negligence Failure to use the care that any reasonable and careful person would use, characterized by inadvertence, thoughtlessness, and inattention.

neutral and detached magistrate One of the requirements for a warrant to be valid is that it must be signed by a neutral and detached magistrate. To be considered neutral and detached, the magistrate must not have any interest in the outcome of the case, and the magistrate must be able to arrive at an independent judgment that probable cause is evident to believe that the item to be seized is located in the place to be searched.

"no-knock" statutes These quick-entry statutes enacted in some jurisdictions aim to prevent destruction of evidence and to increase officer safety by allowing unannounced forcible entry in some circumstances, under judicial authorization, with approval for action being given beforehand and included in the search warrant.

nolo contendere plea Literally, "I will not contest it." A plea in a criminal case that has a similar legal effect to pleading guilty except that the plea of nolo contendere cannot be used against the defendant in a civil action as an admission of guilt; this plea is only allowed with consent of the court.

non-routine borders searches A non-routine border search is more invasive than a routine border search and ranges from intensively checking everything in the vehicle to a full body search. Strip, body cavity, and other search techniques such as x-rays can be used in the process of preventing unlawful items from coming into the country so long as reasonable suspicion is involved. If the circumstances surrounding the search give rise to reasonable suspicion, officials can hold individuals as well as property for a longer period of time.

open fields An exception to the warrant requirement. Any area so removed from the curtilage of the home is considered an open field and is treated as public space for the Fourth Amendment. Officers may search the area without probable cause or a warrant.

opening statement Statement made by counsel at the start of a trial that outlines or summarizes the nature of the case and the anticipated proof; it is intended to advise the jury of the facts and issues involved and to give the jury a general picture of the case at trial.

opinion of the court The statement by a judge or court of the decision reached, outlining the law applied to the case and detailing the reasoning behind the judgment.

pardon An act from a governing power that mitigates the punishment instituted; at the state level, the power to pardon generally rests with the governor while the President of the United States has the power to pardon federal offenses.

particularity A component of the warrant requirement that must be met for a valid warrant. The warrant must particularly describe the person or thing to be seized and the places to be searched. The description must be detailed and contain enough information that a reasonable person would know what is covered under the warrant.

photographic array An array of photographs that include the defendant; it is used in lieu of a lineup. Suspects are not entitled to an attorney at the photographic array because the array can be reproduced for the jury if an allegation of violation of due process arises.

plain view doctrine During search and seizure situations, objects that are in plain view of the peace officer who has the right to be in that particular place are subject to seizure without a warrant and may be admitted into evidence.

plea The answer the defendant gives to the prosecutor's accusation.

plea bargaining The process in which the prosecutor and the defendant come to an agreement on the disposition of the case subject to court approval; it usually means that the defendant pleads guilty to a lesser charge or only one of several charges in return for a sentence that is lighter than that possible or likely for the more serious or numerous charges.

post-conviction remedy A procedure allowing a prisoner to challenge the constitutionality of his or her sentence, moving the court to vacate, set aside, or correct the original verdict or imposed sentence.

preliminary hearing (preliminary examination) A hearing by a judge to determine whether a person charged with a crime should be held for trial; in felony cases, it is prior to indictment and the state must prove evidence to establish probable cause that a crime has been committed by the defendant.

preponderance of evidence Evidence of greater weight or more convincing than the evidence that is offered in opposition to it; it shows that the fact it is meant to prove is more probable than not.

pretrial conference A conference called at the discretion of the court that brings opposing counsel together with the purpose of narrowing the issues to be tried, establishing guidelines for matters and evidence to be presented, and taking other steps to help disposition of the case.

pretrial discovery Opportunities available to both parties of a case prior to trial that aid in the gathering of information and evidence, including interrogatories, depositions, requests for admission of fact, etc., provided under rules of procedure and statutes.

preventive detention laws Confinement of a defendant while awaiting trial in order to protect others.

prima facie evidence Evidence that is sufficient to establish a fact and which, if not contradicted, will remain sufficient to sustain a judgment in favor of the issue it supports, until contradicted by other evidence.

probable cause A reasonable ground for belief in the existence of a fact; probable cause for an arrest occurs when a prudent person would reasonably conclude that a crime was committed and the defendant committed it.

probative value That which furnishes, establishes, or contributes a decision on disputed facts in a case. Evidence that has probative value helps to decide the case.

proof beyond a reasonable doubt Proof that is wholly consistent with the defendant's guilt and inconsistent with any other rational conclusion.

prosecution A proceeding initiated by the governing body before a judge or jury to determine the guilt or innocence of a person charged with a crime.

prosecutor The person acting on the part of the governing body who initiates and takes charge of a case and serves as the trial lawyer for the people.

public safety exception An exception to the *Miranda* rule. If officers determine that public safety is likely to be compromised, they can ask questions of a defendant without reading *Miranda* warnings and evidence resulting from that questioning will not be excluded.

real evidence Evidence provided by items themselves as opposed to descriptions of the evidence; in criminal cases, guns or knives or drugs are examples of real evidence, as opposed to oral testimony from human witnesses.

reasonable expectation of privacy The principle outlined by the Court in *United States v. Katz*,389 U.S. 347 (1967) which identifies that the Fourth Amendment is not specific to place but depends upon the expectation of the person. Whatsoever a person seeks to preserve as private, even in a public place, may be constitutionally protected if that expectation is one that society is prepared to recognize as reasonable.

reasonable suspicion A standard less than probable cause that allows a limited stop for investigatory purposes. When all of the facts and circumstances known to the officer would lead a reasonable officer to suspect that criminal activity has occurred or is about to occur, officers may briefly detain a suspect for investigation.

recidivist A repeat offender.

re-direct An examination of a witness by the direct examiner following the cross-examination.

regulated business Businesses that are regulated because of the type of business, such as outlets for alcohol and weapon sales. These businesses can be searched without warrants and without probable cause because of the nature of the business.

release on own recognizance When an accused person is released without monetary bail, usually because of strong ties to the community and there is every reason to believe that he or she will appear for trial.

remand (a case) When an appellate court sends a case back to the original court for the purpose of having it looked at again or for having some action taken.

restitution The act of making good or repaying for the act committed.

reverse (a case or judgment) To overturn the decision made.

right to counsel As guaranteed by the Sixth and Fourteenth Amendments to the U.S. Constitution as well as by court rule and statute, it is the right of a criminal defendant to be represented at critical stages of a case by his or her own lawyer or by a court-appointed attorney if he or she cannot afford to hire one.

roadblocks General stops by the police that are not based on reasonable suspicion or probable cause, but are part of a regulatory process such as apprehending fleeing felons and illegal aliens.

routine border searches Routine searches occur at the border and are minimally invasive. A routine search consists of checking documents, emptying pockets, and checking vehicles and cargo.

rules of evidence The rules of the court that govern the admissibility of evidence at trials and hearings, such as the Federal Rules of Evidence, the Uniform Rules of Evidence, and state rules of evidence.

screening A way of disposing of a case at some point prior to prosecution, such as when police or prosecutors dismiss a charge or an officer makes a decision not to formally charge a suspect.

search warrant An order, based on probable cause and issued by a magistrate or justice, that directs a law enforcement officer to search for and seize property or evidence that is being or has been used in connection with a crime.

searches incident to lawful arrest A law enforcement officer who has lawfully arrested a person has the right to search that person and the immediate area of the arrest for weapons.

showup A type of pretrial identification procedure in which a suspect is brought before a victim or witness to a crime; less formal than a lineup but serving the same purpose; the procedure must meet certain standards to be admissible in court. *See also* lineup.

speedy trial One of the rights identified within the Sixth Amendment that requires a case be brought to trial within a reasonable period of time.

statutory law The body of law created by the legislature in contrast to laws created by judicial opinions and administrative bodies.

stop-and-frisk The temporary seizure and patting down of a person who raises suspicion and appears to be armed; an officer is not required to have full probable cause that a person poses the threat of crime, but the stop cannot be based on hunch alone. The scope of the search is limited to that justified by the circumstances that led the officer to stop the person.

subpoena A command to appear at a certain time and place to give testimony about a particular matter.

summons A written instrument designed to give notification to a person of an action against him or her in court and the requirement to appear at a given date and time to answer the complaint.

suppression hearing A pretrial proceeding where the defendant attempts to block the admission of particular evidence from being introduced at trial because it has been illegally obtained or is irrelevant and/or prejudicial.

"totality of circumstances" test In *Illinois v. Gates*, the Supreme Court allowed that, even though one piece of evidence standing alone might not provide probable cause for a search, a collection of evidence corroborated by police follow-up can provide a totality of circumstances that substantiate a search warrant.

trial A judicial review and determination of issues between parties in a lawsuit; this review may be by the judge alone in a bench trial or by a jury in a jury trial.

transactional immunity The government is prevented from prosecuting a witness for the entire transaction about which he or she is compelled to testify, no matter how the evidence comes to the government.

"true bill" of indictment The endorsement made by a grand jury following a bill of indictment where they find that there is sufficient evidence to support a criminal charge.

use immunity The government is prevented from using the testimony of a witness against him or her in the trial of the matter, unless the evidence comes to the government from a different source.

verdict The formal decision or finding that resolves the case, either by jury or judge.

waiver Sometimes defendants waive, or voluntarily relinquish, certain of their constitutional or statutory rights; for example, defendants sometimes waive their right to a preliminary hearing. Defendants can also waive their right to silence during police interrogations and ta1lk with the officers about the crime under investigation.

TABLE OF CASES

INDEX

Note: Page numbers followed by *b* refer to boxes, respectively.